FRIEND v. FRIEND

ETHAN J. LEIB

FRIEND V. FRIEND

The Transformation of Friendship—and
What the Law Has to Do with It

OXFORD
UNIVERSITY PRESS

2011

OXFORD
UNIVERSITY PRESS

Oxford University Press, Inc., publishes works that further
Oxford University's objective of excellence
in research, scholarship, and education.

Oxford   New York
Auckland   Cape Town   Dar es Salaam   Hong Kong   Karachi
Kuala Lumpur   Madrid   Melbourne   Mexico City   Nairobi
New Delhi   Shanghai   Taipei   Toronto

With offices in
Argentina   Austria   Brazil   Chile   Czech Republic   France   Greece
Guatemala   Hungary   Italy   Japan   Poland   Portugal   Singapore
South Korea   Switzerland   Thailand   Turkey   Ukraine   Vietnam

Copyright © 2011 by Ethan J. Leib

Published by Oxford University Press, Inc.
198 Madison Avenue, New York, New York 10016

www.oup.com

Oxford is a registered trademark of Oxford University Press

Library of Congress Cataloging-in-Publication Data
Leib, Ethan J.
Friend v. friend : the transformation of friendship and what
the law has to do with it / Ethan J. Leib
p.   cm.
Includes bibliographical references and index.
ISBN-13: 978-0-19-973960-8 (hardcover : alk. paper)
ISBN-10: 0-19-973960-9 (alk. paper)
1. Friendship—Sociological aspects.   2. Sociological jurisprudence.
I. Title.   II. Title: Friend versus friend.
HM1161.L45 2011
302.3'40973—dc22   2010013440

Printed in the United States of America
on acid-free paper

FOR ZOE SCHONFELD

Contents

FRIEND V. FRIEND

Introduction

Y OU LOAN A friend $25,000. You don't write up any formal paper-
work because the transaction seems to be predicated on trust,
and you think it wouldn't make sense to formalize the loan
because of the friendship. In any case, she loaned you that much a few
years back. She fails to pay you back even though she seems to have the
money. Are you precluded from suing in a court to get your money
back?

A close friend steals your business idea, runs with it, and doesn't
share profits with you. Do you have any recourse other than ending
the friendship?

You are comatose and have failed to designate an end-of-life deci-
sion-maker for your health care decisions. You have discussed your
desire not to remain in a vegetative state with your friends but not with
your religious family, who would not approve of your preferences.
Should the hospital listen to your family or your friends? Should we
have regulations that clarify which person in your circle of intimates is
the most reliable proxy for your views?

Your best friend is extremely ill. Four different colleagues in your
office got legally mandated time off to care for family members who
had the same type of cancer as your best friend. Should the law require
your employer to give you the same rights as your colleagues to help
your best friend through his illness?

This book helps you think through these hard problems. They
aren't hypotheticals. These are everyday real-world scenarios that
present themselves to us and to our public institutions with frequency.
They are manifestly important because the viability of our legal

institutions and of friendship itself may turn on them. And we have thus far lacked substantial guidance about what to do about them.

Sometimes when I tell people that I'm working on friendship and the law, they quickly tell me that they really don't want to be my friend if it is going to involve any legal obligation! I certainly understand the visceral reaction that there is something wrong with the law nosing into our private lives. For most of us, friends have a place at the center of our lives, and we want to believe that friendship is a special part of our private spheres that the public sphere of the law can't touch. We want to think that friendship is pristine and unadulterated by anything law-like.

In spite of its importance, though, friendship as an institution may very well be in decline. Some sociologists tell us that we have fewer people with whom we can share important matters than we once did, and—the Internet and social networking platforms notwithstanding—our nonkin circles of intimate affection seem to be getting smaller and smaller.[1] We may text our friends regularly, tweet through Twitter, and communicate through Friendster and Facebook, but some social scientists are still finding our networks of truly intimate friends smaller than ever. It seems likely that mass e-mails, 140 characters typed on very small keyboards, and bulletin board postings are not optimal ways to engage in deep friendships. Still, one might think that these technologies should be helping us maintain intimacies formed elsewhere. But friendship may very well be suffering, and no one is doing anything about it from the perspective of public policy.

It isn't easy to say why our friendships are suffering exactly, or even if they actually are. Perhaps we are being spread too thin. As our social networks expand, it is harder to stay close with only a few people. Intimacy suffers at the hands of the need to keep in touch with so many, diluting our ability for focused engagement. Or maybe the undifferentiated nature of our Internet personas, traceable to the interface designs of social networking platforms, makes it difficult to draw people ever nearer to us without alienating too many others who don't want to know that they are only "colleagues" without access to our profiles made available to only our "true" online friends.[2] Some blame TV, atomistic shopping over the Internet, or capitalism more generally. Others might blame the Internet's facilitation of divulging confidences too easily—and anonymously, to boot—leading people to be more cautious with bringing people into their most personal lives. Some might trace our intimacy issues to our high level of mobility relative to older societies: because we can often leave somewhere on a dime, friendship ties might suffer. Good ones probably require some actual time spent together in the same place. If we are always on the go, it is hard to go deep.

One might also draw on an analogy to Anthony Giddens's famous thesis in his book *The Transformation of Intimacy: Sexuality, Love and Eroticism in Modern Societies*,[3] that reproductive technologies led to the "plasticity" of sexuality in modern life, unmooring sex and intimacy from reproduction. One could plausibly say that our communications technologies and social networking platforms have led to the "plasticity" of friendship, disaggregating friendship from real affect, which must always be at its core to function properly. When starting a friendship means only "clicking the link," it is perhaps no surprise that friendship doesn't mean what it used to. We have always had multiple and competing definitions of the friend to contend with, which has always risked diluting the real deal. But perhaps something different really is going on in the current age when friendship has been disaggregated so publicly and so universally from emotion, when "friending" is really just networking. The art, practice, and social institution of friendship has transformed into a verb you can do casually with thousands, sitting alone behind a screen.

Whatever the causes—and no social science will reveal them definitively in any case—is this something to worry ourselves about? And even if it can't be shown conclusively that friendship is being eroded in modern society (for social scientists like to argue about whether there really is such a decline), is it an institution that commands the attention of our policy designers?

I think friendship is a public policy concern, even if it isn't perfectly clear whether friendship is on the decline. Friendship isn't just a good like nice shaving cream; it is an essential part of living the good life and keeping our society cohesive. It helps us psychologically, keeping us from depression and helping us manage anxiety. It helps us physically, nurturing us when we are sick or old. Indeed, studies have shown that friends can do more for our health when we are sick than family does. And friendship helps us individually and collectively in an economic sense, as well: friends provide material support in times of need and they furnish capital to get businesses off the ground and keep them afloat. Friendship of a certain sort oils the wheels of commerce. People with close friends at work are likely to be more productive than their counterparts, and businesses that help coworkers develop close friendships within the organization respond more effectively to change.

Friendship saves the state money by supplying care and services during emergencies. If the state helped friends with small incentives it could potentially make a big impact.

There is another likely structural change in modern society that counsels for more attention and sensitivity to friendship in our public institutions: we are learning to tolerate new structures of intimacy and sociability. Society is steadily moving away from organizing itself solely around the traditional family structure, and we are getting more sensitive to the throngs of people who do not live with partners and kids in the caricatured 1950s setup. Although our laws and policies still generally prop up the traditional family, the gay rights movement, the feminist movements, and other progressive social movements have made real gains in persuading Americans to tolerate and support alternative lifestyles. Although there is no necessary correlation between those movements and a focus on friendship—for social conservatives, too, have shown an interest in the subject matter of friendship[4]—it is worth highlighting that friendship can pick up the slack in our lives when the traditional family is decentered from the core of our collective circles of affection, whether temporarily or permanently. When marriage rates drop, marriage happens later, divorce rates rise, births outside of marriage rise, and more people choose to live unmarried, our circles of care transform themselves in the process. That often can have the effect of making friendships matter more in people's lives. It is thus becoming even more important to protect them.

Think of the elderly retired man whose wife has died and whose children live across the country: his daily routine might consist of talking to his friends and taking his meals with them. Consider the networks of college friends who take one another through developmental milestones that parents cannot because they are not present or not invited. Or the business that only gets off the ground because a group of friends provide the support and capital. Think of adults who aren't partnered—either because they don't want to partner or because they were once partnered but now aren't—and how they structure their circles of intimacy. Think of adults who choose to center their lives around their friends and not their sexual partners, whether they have spouses or not.[5] Think of those who choose to see their friends more often than their relatives. Or those who spend the bulk of their day at work communicating with friends in one way or another.

It doesn't require great creativity to see ourselves or someone we know or love in these portraits. These are the portraits of what we are, who we were, who we will become; they are the stories of friendships all around us. We rarely take stock of this reality. And we don't have a very good sense of what else should change as the social world evolves around us. But once we begin to appreciate the implications of changing realities, we can see more clearly how much we stand to lose if there is a general erosion of or indifference to friendship in our modern society. Even without clear proof that we are undergoing these changes—for these are hard developments to chart carefully and they implicate contentious issues of definition—friendship deserves more attention than it has received from policy-makers.

Libraries are filled with books about the family's role in our lives (and how that role may be changing over time)—but friendship too often falls below the radar. We are doing friendship as a social institution and ourselves no great service by failing to see it, how it structures so much of our modern life, and how badly we ignore it in our public institutions. Journalists in the mass media and sociologists have already noticed the centrality of friendship to our well-being. But few policy designers occupy themselves with the central question: should we be developing a public policy approach toward friendship? Public policy-makers continue to be preoccupied with the traditional family, without giving due attention to the ways we could be doing more to accommodate and promote friendship.

There is, perhaps, good reason that we rarely spend any time thinking about how the structure of our public policies and our law can help sustain and promote our friendships with our nearest and dearest. It is, after all, somewhat ugly to think we need government and laws to help prop up friendship. It seems to be a desecration of the sacred to get lawyers involved in friendship. Yet the choices we make in the design of our public institutions sometimes have the effect of structuring and regulating our friendship networks without any self-consciousness. Could we really do worse than to remain completely indifferent in our policies to friendship?

To be fair, one certainly needs a healthy dose of skepticism that social engineering projects could ever be successful at accomplishing so intractable a task as strengthening what I'm calling the "institution" of friendship. The studies that tell us it is in decline can't be perfectly trusted, for we don't have surveys from the country's founding, and the measures social scientists use to gauge the decline are imperfect at best and at worst exclude unconventional ways of thinking about organizing our structures of care. But many things our public policy designers do—and fail to do—quite plausibly make a difference on a grand scale. Some poverty alleviation programs give poor people housing assistance to move out of high-density poor neighborhoods, the proverbial "ghetto." But by ignoring or underemphasizing friendship in policy design, policy-makers can sometimes fail to realize that the few who move often have to leave their friends behind, which means that these transplants fail to integrate well into their new communities.[6] Greater attention and sensitivity to friendship could help improve these programs and keep friendship networks of support viable. Kin networks of care do get some attention, but friends are often lumped together with kin or are otherwise ignored in design and analysis.

Ultimately, it is too facile to say that law will easily strengthen friendship with an odd doctrine here and some bit of sensitivity there. But it is also unrealistic to assume that the multiple failures of the law to cognize friendship adequately that I shall chart in the book have no systemic consequences we might be able to avoid. So we have to be careful in this terrain. We will have to acknowledge that there are substantial costs associated with trying to support friendship through public policy and law. But just because there will be costs doesn't mean that they cannot be outweighed by benefits. Ultimately, taking this project to its logical conclusion will require cost-benefit calculations, developing a sophisticated way of evaluating each proposed policy for its net effects. Still, it will not always be especially easy to know with any degree of certainty what tangible costs and benefits will be achieved. For that reason, there is also some important function in spelling out the more basic values and normative issues at stake. This book takes on that task, as well as considering some of the more nuts-and-bolts work of imagining what a polity attuned to friendship might look like.

Is the friend, then, really absent from the law? Can it be that the lawyer may have to utter with Montaigne (himself once a lawmaker), "O my friends, there is no friend?"[7] To be sure, there are lawyers who advocate for their clients as friends.[8] There are those who sue as "next friends" on behalf of incompetents with whom there is no real or current friendship. And lawyers sometimes submit amicus briefs, as "friends" of the court. Countries even enter "friendship" treaties with one another.

Yet the status of the friend—the true friend that is not merely a friend by analogy—seems nearly absent from the law, at first blush. There is no clear law governing friendships. And the very thought of a law surrounding friendship makes us even more skeptical of lawyers than we already are. We also tend to think that those who would encode a law of friendship can't themselves know very much about it. There is the general feeling that there is "too much law" in this country, that we are too litigious, that we have to be too careful because of the legal pitfalls all around us.[9] But there are many reasons that require us to be mindful of friendship in the law that I will explore in this book, reasons that are deeply consequential: attending to friendship in the law can lead to a happier society, a more just society, even a more efficient and prosperous society. It is even possible that attending to friendship in the law will inspire more compliance with the law because the law will resonate with our everyday moral sense. By ignoring friendship, our public institutions may be too distanced from our sensibilities of right and wrong—and that keeps our public law more alienating than it should be. Not all ways of promoting friendships require lawsuits, in any case many just require public policy tinkering. If our law got better at calibrating its judgments and protections to the actual relationships we find ourselves in, the law would be a more effective and legitimate mechanism for ordering our lives.

I don't fully understand why the people who react sharply to the incursion of the law into our "private" friendships—my presumptive critics who have a sense that I'm onto something quite wrongheaded here—don't generally have the same reaction to our law's incursion into family and marriage. If it is the private sphere of love and affection you want to keep pure, why not be horrified at the law's regulation of the family and of marriage? And yet we are thoroughly accustomed to the law having an opinion—and an enforceable one, to boot—on family matters. A plethora of laws account for and promote the family unit, notwithstanding its status as the very core of the "private" sphere. It isn't that I sign onto the law's obsessive regulation of sex, family, and marriage; I only mean to note that it can't be denied and that the simple fact that the law butts into our family lives causes few people tremendous anxiety. Sure, gay rights advocates are reasonably furious at how the state decides to regulate intimacy. But the large group of gay rights advocates who want gay marriage clearly desire to partake of the state's apparatus for recognizing and regulating families. Some gay rights advocates and other progressives would rather that the state stay out of this business altogether—but very few in this group are driven by a discomfort about the state in the private sphere, as a general matter. Many of them, I think, would be happy to see the law take more interest in friendship as a way to further decenter the law's commitment to heterosexual marriage and the traditional family that discriminates against large swaths of the population.

We build within our legal system all sorts of preferences for family members—for example, the recognition of marriage in our tax law, spousal testimonial privileges and immunities, and whole areas of criminal law that privilege and punish family members—but we appear not to furnish the friend with any clear legal recognition of consequence. Other relationships of trust and confidence are recognized by the law both through our regulation of intimate relationships and our protection of special professional relationships. Our friends are no less important than our families, our households, and our professional relationships—and friendships would seem to deserve some of the same protections and recognition. Yet friends often seem left to fend for themselves without any possibility for recourse from a legal system that will recognize their special roles in our lives. We seem Pollyannaish when it comes to friendship—it will always take care of itself—but what about when we get really screwed by our friends? What happens if we learn that the benevolent disregard of friendship by society and the law—its routine decision to parcel friendship off into an untouchable private sphere—turns out to have some kind of systemic effect on citzens' ability to form trusting and intimate relationships?

As it turns out, the law is presented with puzzles about friendship and lawsuits between friends and former friends all the time. So even if one wants to keep the spheres separate, it is hard to imagine how that division could fully succeed. One still needs to get into the difficult business of regulating friendships, even if it makes one uncomfortable—just as insurance companies and administrative agencies need to put some market values on lives and limbs, unseemly though it may be. Worlds collide when the public and private intermingle, but there isn't really an alternative.[10]

Given new family structures, geographically dispersed families, and longer life spans, it would seem that more than ever, friends are like family, taking care of us in essential ways. So why should friendship not have the status of other relationships that receive active state support and state sensitivity? New laws and the more capacious interpretation of older ones could elevate friendship's status, respecting it as an essential part of our lives, rather than relegating it to a luxury easily sacrificed to other priorities, a sphere of life that will always take care of itself.

Imagine a group of four friends eager to get its collective hands on some season tickets for the local basketball team. Tickets are hard to come by and they are allocated in groups of four through a lottery system. Accordingly, the friends scheme to get the tickets as follows:

they will each enter the drawing for four tickets and will share their winnings within the group. If too many of them win the lottery, they are confident that they will be able to find someone to take extra tickets off their hands; indeed, the company allocating and selling the tickets will allow them to refuse the offer, so there is no danger of over-subscription.

As it turns out, one member of the group—call her Betty—is ultimately awarded four season tickets, and the informal understanding within the group is that each one of the friends has rights to purchase one of the season tickets each year. Of course, no formal paperwork is drawn up, since they are, after all, friends! And for many years this system works just fine. The tickets come to Betty, since they are in her name, and she resells them, one each, to her three friends Veronica, Archie, and Jughead.

But then Betty makes plans to move cross-country. A colleague of hers—call him Reggie—offers her twice the face value for her four season tickets. Reggie's wife and daughters are huge basketball fans, and the family has had no luck in procuring season tickets through the lottery system. Betty wants to take Reggie's offer. She reasons that no formal contracts prevent her from doing so and her willingness to allow Veronica to transfer her season ticket to her boss some years ago has broken up the feeling that the four of them remain bound by friendship ties into the season ticket pool. Can Betty legitimately resell all four tickets to Reggie?

It isn't easy to answer that question. But the law sometimes has to answer similar friendship ethics questions—and more often than one might think. As the owner of the tickets vis-à-vis the ball club, Betty would have the presumptive right to freely transfer the tickets. The ball club sells the tickets only to Betty—and has a contract of rights and responsibilities executed only with Betty; her relationship with her friends is totally informal and seemingly renewed afresh every year, at her discretion as owner. Since Betty's name is on the tickets, perhaps there is good reason to let her do what she wants. If she offends her friends, that is her risk to take—and the only sanction available for her conduct or misconduct is the reputational harm she might suffer as a bad friend. Many courts see things this way, too.

But not all do: some think the duties of friendship and the implicit deals we make with one another matter and should control our conduct. If the deal we signed up for (even if we didn't sign anything) is to share a pool of tickets, it is not only immoral but an actual breach of a legal duty to sell those tickets out from under the pool. Betty may be holding those tickets "in trust" or as a "fiduciary" for her friends. It may be that friendship's norms can be policed by the law, not just the *Ethicist* page or the *Social Q's* section of the *New York Times*. Small claims courts—as we all know from Judge Wapner's day—have dockets full of everyday problems like this one. But these disputes aren't terribly entertaining for litigants, whose drained emotional lives turn to law when relationships fail. Law should be able to deal with these disputes with some coherence and dignity.

We would still need to ask whether enforcing friendship's duties in such cases could plausibly contribute to helping the social institution in the aggregate. Some people might very well react by assuming that enforcing a law of friendship would threaten to do more to undermine it in society than it would to support it. I try to pursue this line of thinking in this book as well, since my instincts that we ought to do more to support friendship's norms in the law are hardly conventional ones.

But notice, at least for now, how much of your own intuitions about the season ticket scenario turn on how I tell the story: If I tell you to imagine that Betty needs the extra money for her father's care and that she is moving cross-country to take care of him in his old age, it seems much easier to conclude that her friends ought to understand her need and let her resell the tickets to Reggie (assuming the friends themselves agree how to proceed). In such a case, we'd probably be disturbed if a court policed a friendship norm without also understanding that friends need to be generous and forgiving, too, when appropriate. Not everyone would be confident that judges and juries presented with these cases could make a really good determination about what to do. But presuming that judges and juries are incompetent at these common sense judgments might not be charitable enough to our legal system, which often needs to rely on common sense where strict rules produce absurd conclusions. We have lay assessors in our justice systems—a jury of peers—precisely so that common sense judgments of the community can control outcomes to some extent.

Or, go back in time to around 2003 to imagine this hypothetical. What if a group of college kids—close friends, say—comes up with a scheme to get their school's facebook pictures online in a social networking platform, and they all begin planning the launch of their business, UConnedMe. Then, instead of moving the programming along, the main programmer in the group starts dragging his feet when he realizes that there is a much more lucrative venture for which he can write programs on his own, a business that virtually copies the ideas of his friends. He alters the business plan in a few ways that enlarges its scope and potential for generating income. Imagine he pursues such a project without his friends' permission—and purposefully slows down his work on UConnedMe, delaying its launch so he can beat them to market. What if Fakebook, the company based on the programmer's invention, becomes wildly successful and turns the programmer into a billionaire? If the friends who run UConnedMe came looking for some compensation from the programmer, what should be the result?

To be sure, one would need to know a lot more about the structure of the friends' deals with one another to get to a final conclusion here. And although this example is presented as a hypothetical, it is nevertheless the story some tell about Facebook's genesis and ConnectU's failure. The real Facebook and its founder settled with the ConnectU principals when they filed a lawsuit against their former friend. But what principles should guide our thinking about the issues that would have been raised in this legal case if it had not settled? Although this particular example may seem unique, these kinds of problems actually arise frequently we mix business and friendship all the time. Indeed, some argue that the commercial sphere itself could barely subsist without the strong-form trust that friendship provides and models.

For my purposes, I'm interested in the question about whether the nature of the friendship—and the betrayal of a friendship—has any role to play in how we think about what might be a just resolution of such a dispute. My instinct is that it does, and I hope that my meditation on the interaction of our lives in friendships and our lives in law will convince the reader that friendship is a public policy concern in a variety of ways. Even if one concludes that it would be smartest for legal actors to take a friendship-blind approach to deciding cases and writing laws, this book should help one develop that case, too. As the terrain stands now, even those who are skeptical of my interest in friendship and law have not produced careful arguments to explain how to translate the taboo into policies. And we must adopt some policy or other, since there is no way to be completely indifferent when a friend makes a claim in a court of law. It calls for a response of some kind.

The arguments in this book, then, will support two main claims. First, the law must learn to take notice of friendship because friendship matters—to our lives, our law, and the viability of our public institutions. This is not a deeply controversial thesis, perhaps, but it is counterintuitive enough. It turns out that without being terribly self-conscious about regulating friendship, the law does occasionally find a way to make friendship relevant. We need to realize this is happening—that it can happen—so we can intervene well when the law must and does get involved in our friendships. Even if we want to make our public policy a policy of complete nonintervention (a strategy that is likely to fail, I suspect), we have to see how the law and public policy already interact with friendship to support and sustain that conclusion.

Second, and more controversially, I want to convince the reader that our laws, legal institutions, and public policy agendas should be oriented toward promoting and facilitating friendships. Of course, it won't make sense to promote friendship in all contexts: a judge must recuse herself rather than help a friend if she is charged with adjudicating a friend's fate, and a friend on a corporation's board of directors should be looking out for the company's best interest, not her friend's. But many areas of the law and public policy can be better designed to facilitate friendship's role in society.

I doubt readers will agree with all of my arguments about these touchy matters. But struggle with them we must—and we must begin to muddy our mental pictures of purely idealized private friendships, a cleanly public law that stays out of our private lives, and a stranger-based commercial sphere, where intimacies and friendships don't do much of the work holding it all together. This book will challenge easy assumptions. Many liberals—whether of the progressive or the "classical" variety—assume that modern society should design its legal institutions with a firm separation of the public and the private in mind, at least where friendship is concerned. Regulating friendships in one form or another upsets that assumption. And yet the future of both our public institutions and our private spheres may hinge on our willingness to encourage the two to interact in ways liberals have been contesting for centuries.

CHAPTER I

Who Is a Friend?

THE CATEGORY OF "friend" is a hard one to define, and this definitional challenge may be the biggest impediment to the entire enterprise in this book. The vast majority of us know who our parents, children, brothers, and sisters are. But figuring out who constitutes a friend—and when a friendship starts and ends—may be a harder task. A casual definition is usually ready to hand, but it is more challenging to settle on a working definition for more careful analysis.

Indeed, if you asked everyone in the country to list his or her friends, it would be reasonable to suspect that those lists would not always line up: some people would list friends who would not reciprocate. Even friends who would list one another reciprocally in this thought experiment perhaps cannot be relied on to be "true" friends at the core. We all likely operate with varying thresholds, tolerances, and expectations for friendship. We sometimes feel social pressure to call someone a friend. Yet perhaps, if pressed, we all know who our "real" friends are. We think we know when we have reliable ones, but that does not give satisfactory guidance for any form of codification or sustained thinking. Even if we know our real friends when we see them, we reasonably have little confidence that an outside observer without direct access to our emotional lives could have such good judgment to find out who they are.

This is certainly an inauspicious beginning. If I am serious that I want legal duties and privileges to flow from friendship, vague standards are troublesome. If my working definition is not much better than "I know it when I see it," it will be hard to convince lawmakers to bestow duties and privileges up on an unknown class of citizens.

Yet, I tend not to think the definitional challenges are insurmountable, and common sense goes a long way. Most concretely, New York and Florida, to take two examples, *have* legally codified definitions of the friend in the health care proxy decision-making context. Here's Florida's definition:

> "Close personal friend" means any person 18 years of age or older who has exhibited special care and concern for the patient, and who presents an affidavit to the health care facility or to the attending or treating physician stating that he or she is a friend of the patient; is willing and able to become involved in the patient's health care; and has maintained such regular contact with the patient so as to be familiar with the patient's activities, health, and religious or moral beliefs.

This isn't perfect, of course, but it certainly shows that definitions can be codified in certain contexts.

Another way around the definitional problem, perhaps, is to allow people to contract into the friendship relation for the purposes of law and leave the definition of the relation solely in the hands of those who choose to adopt the term. One could, as David Chambers of the University of Michigan once suggested, set up a friendship "registry," so people could sign up to have their friendships recognized.[1] Or we could develop civil ceremonies to concretize the relation. Some Germans engage in a social drinking practice—*Brüderschaft trinken*—that helps signal to the friends and the world that a real friendship has formed.

Yet although these formalizing solutions might help solve the definitional problem, I tend to think this method of *substituting* living in a real friendship with contracts or simple external markers cannot be said to respect or promote friendship itself, as we know it in our daily lives. These methods of "solving" the problem tend to replace friendship with contracts or with a newfangled institution we don't yet know. Friendship is a social institution that will always need to develop organically. The law needs to come to friendship in its organic and fuzzy state, not force it into something else that the state can track more easily. If the only friends who were to count for the purposes of public policy were friends who signed up with the state, we'd certainly be undercounting friends. Even states that have passed something like a "friendship registry"—Hawaii and Vermont have enacted "reciprocal beneficiary" statutes which enable people to confer certain duties and privileges on one another that might resemble the burdens and benefits of friendship—find it used more as a marriage substitute than anything else.

The idea that special duties and privileges should flow to a class of persons that is fuzzy at the edges is hardly revolutionary. Some states and commentators are trying to figure out how broadly to grant intrafamilial testimonial privileges to make sure family members don't have to testify against one another; even the term "family member" is fuzzy at the edges. Fuzziness is part of the law, and not being able to define a class perfectly is not a decisive argument against protection for the core cases in the class.

Nevertheless, I can't leave readers only to work with their intuitive ideas about what a friend is. I must say more about the sort of friendship central to this inquiry, and I start here by suggesting what it must not be, for the purposes of the book, and follow with some general observations about what constitutes friendship, as a practice, an experience, an art, the social institution. The effort here is empirical, conceptual, and theoretical, insofar as it is based both on studies of the social phenomenon from a multitude of different disciplinary approaches and on a long tradition of thinking about friendship. But it is also normative, insofar as this descriptive project should be a starting point for a definition in law, should the status of the friend command more organized legal treatment in the future.

It is important to note at the outset that this early articulation will require refinement in later chapters. When we delve into specific areas of the law, policy concerns internal to those area of social regulation might command a different conception of friendship than the one drawn here—whether more restrictive or more capacious. We might, for example, be very inclusive in a working definition if all we are interested in is giving people a small incentive to be more sociable. But we will want to be somewhat more restrictive if we are going to exact criminal liabilities or sentence enhancements against people who betray their friends. We nevertheless need a starting point to guide the discussion. And although the studies I draw up on throughout the book span the globe, I can only ultimately make my case for friendship as a public policy concern as an American lawyer. That is the political and legal system I know best, and it is the one whose culture I feel capable of remaining sensitive to when I propose policy.

FRIENDSHIP IS NOT KINSHIP

Friendship is not kinship, and if a relationship is one of kinship, it cannot also be classified as a friendship. Friends may not be related by blood or marriage, and they may not engage in any ongoing sexual relationship (though being ex-lovers is no disqualification at all). Although there is something crude and contrived in this narrow version of the friend relation, it is necessary in performing a proper analysis of the category, and necessary if the law is to recognize the status of friend in our culture. This is particularly frustrating because friendship can, of course, be thought to contain a larger set of intimacies. But in the current climate, this approach stands the best chance at success. To be sure, friendship will often be a love relation—friendship is listed most frequently when people are asked to list types of love[2]—and certainly spouses and lovers can think of themselves as friends (even best of friends). But even among those lovers and spouses who tell each other that they are the other's best friend, there is often resort to a "real" best friend to vent about or discuss primary erotic relationships.[3] A study of 1,050 adults in northern California confirmed that although we are pretty promiscuous about how we use the term "friend" in daily life, we tend not to use the term to include kin or romantic partners.[4]

Friends who are not lovers may still pine for one another sexually, whether consciously or subconsciously. There is a long tradition of Freudian thinking that assumes that friendship emerges from sexual instincts and desires—and that same-sex friendships are a form of homoeroticism.[5] Whether that is true or not, an erotic undercurrent to a friendship is no barrier to friendship, so long as there is no ongoing sexual relationship.

It may be worth noting that there are some who argue that once people marry and begin to form their own families, friendships are prevented from forming and the intimacy of marriage shuts out a role for friendship.[6] But others have suggested quite a different interaction between kinship and friendship: that intimate friendship itself developed in parallel to the growth of intimate marriages, where parties learn how to be intimate with others.[7] Others still, drawing on Aristotle, see familial friendship as begetting and training us for more complete and truer friendships.[8] Whatever the interaction effects between kinship and friendship and however they can be seen to overlap, I think it is a good starting point to pull them apart for this project. Nor is this pulling apart particularly idiosyncratic. It is, after all, one of Socrates' most important suggestions in the *Lysis*, Plato's dialogue on friendship: they focus us in that dialogue on the way friendship furnishes a *lysis*—a release—from family bonds. If spouses, lovers, and family members could claim the status of friend, at least four problems might emerge.

First, there is a long-standing and quite common separation in people's minds between lovers and family on the one hand and friends on the other. I am thus tracking a separation that operates fairly broadly in society. To be sure, some queer theorists highlight that "[m]any groups of lesbian and gay friends refer to themselves quite consciously as 'family.'"[9] But this effort to trade on the "capital" of family is a deliberate mixing of categories by those who choose to label themselves this way: they are often merely pointing out that their friends have come to perform traditional family functions and are emphasizing to themselves and to the world that care is being provided in an organized institution that gets none of the respect the traditional family does. That we should come to see friends as doing for many much of what family does only reinforces friendship's centrality. We don't have to put family on a pedestal to distinguish it from friendship.

To the extent that these theorists claim that "[f]or some lesbians and gay men the boundary between friends and lovers is not clear and shifts over time—friends become lovers, and lovers become friends,"[10] I have found precious little evidence to support the idea that this blurring is distinctive of gays: straight people also experience fluidity in these categories over time. Moreover, even gays who prioritize friendship seem to see their sexual relationships and conjugality as a different category, too,[11] so it is hard to insist that the definition I am recommending is insufficiently "queer" or is "heteronormative." It refuses to "trivialize, infantilize, and subordinate" nonmarital or nonfamily relationships[12]— but it also doesn't try to assimilate friendship to family-like or family-lite relationships either.

Second, conceptual confusion might result because it could become much more difficult to isolate the work friendship does in our private lives and in the structure of our social and political lives. If the category of friend were so capacious as to include all our love-based and sexual relations—or even just those that are also "friendly" as well—it could become extremely difficult to ascertain or promote friendship's role in society. We couldn't know as clearly what work friendship was doing by itself and what work kinship and romantic or erotic relationships were doing through their particular forms of love. Romantic love, familial love, and sex might confound an analysis of friendship proper. And it is thus no surprise that sociologists (of both queer and straight orientation) studying people's circles of intimacy routinely draw on the distinction between kinship and friendship.

Third, by our failing to disentangle friendship from sexual and familial intimacy, I fear our public policy concerns about friendship might get subordinated to our public policy concerns in regulating other forms of intimacy, centrally the family.[13] If we fail to distinguish family and friends in some reasonably clear way at the outset of our design project to give special recognition to friends, there is a danger—evident in much of what has been written about friendship in the legal academy—that the entire inquiry into friendship in the law could get tied up with the debates about marriage. To be sure, the gay marriage debate might be usefully informed by thinking hard about friendship and law. But we do both the gay rights movement and friendship a disservice when we run the concerns together too quickly. An argument for friendship and for its legal recognition can be made outside the gay rights context; doing so might ensure that the former doesn't get overwhelmed by the passions prevalent within the latter and might bring into the fold many conservative thinkers who are attracted to the virtues of friendship but are not sold on the gay rights "agenda." Family law desperately needs reform to be less discriminatory against gays. But friendship is a universal value that needn't be co-opted from the get-go by other ongoing debates that could risk adulterating the inquiry. If progress on the recognition of friendship requires full-scale reorientation of our family law, I fear we may not get very far—or as far as we might get with a different strategy—in helping to make friendship itself a public policy concern.

It is not, I should emphasize, that I want to condone here the ways sexual, marital, and family relationships are regulated in our society. Rather, we must acknowledge such regulation and distinguish other forms of intimacy. Indeed, precisely because we regulate sex, marriage, and family so substantially, friendship could get lost in the mechanisms of regulation if we operate with a working definition of friendship that includes sex or family. By keeping the category of friend separate and mutually exclusive from the status of spouse, family, or lover, an approach to friendship can remain more sensitive to the different— and potentially more appropriate—public policy concerns relevant to friendship in particular. If we seek to have a general law of amity that includes all forms of intimacy, our too-obsessive approach to the regulation of the family will bleed into and crowd out a proper appreciation of friendship on its own terms. Studies do, as we shall see, suggest that nonkin networks of friends make a difference in our lives quite apart from kin networks: we ought to keep them separate for now, as the movement for getting public policy to care about friendship is first getting a toehold.[14]

Finally, kinship relationships are routinely friendships of unequals.[15] Parents are not our social equals; neither are our uncles or older sisters.

Although spousal or conjugal friendships might optimally be considered friendships of equality, the structure of our society perhaps recommends against facilely concluding that husbands and wives and sexual partners easily maintain friendships free from distortions of power. Ultimately, the attempt to classify who counts as a friend will get more, rather than less, complex with the inclusion of our full range of intimacies within the friend category. So the exclusive definition is worth taking seriously for now.

When we end a sexual relationship, it is fairly common to hear a lover proclaim: "Let's just be friends." The set of "just friends" in our society is not a null set—and we could do a lot for the institution of friendship by focusing on them and giving them some more attention within our public policies. That there will also be a group of "friends with benefits" who don't get the same legal treatment under my definition is reason to hope, perhaps, for a more inclusive definition down the road. But that will have to await both the firm establishment of friendship in our legal and policy thinking and our giving up on our misguided regulation of sex. Some want to use friendship and its legal recognition to disrupt our current policy focus on regulating sex and the family. But I am not optimistic about this strategy and think it threatens the agenda of promoting friendship to tie its fate to a different movement with a different ultimate agenda. I am hopeful for that agenda in the long run, but I don't want friendship to suffer while we await that sea change.

WHAT IS FRIENDSHIP?

The following set of criteria may be useful in delineating the contours of the friendship relation. These characteristics are not exhaustive, mutually exclusive, or necessary conditions for friendship; rather, they constitute an illustrative composite sketch, drawing on a wealth of analysis from disciplines outside the law. And if the law ever develops a systematic approach to friendship and its privileges and obligations, lawyers, judges, and legislators may wish to appeal to this set of characteristics to help decide who should count as a friend. Nonexclusive multifactor tests are common to the law and public policy, as when courts try to figure out whether a worker is a "servant" or an "independent contractor" for the purposes of agency law. Here's a go at a multifactor test for friendship, drawing together a multiplicity of sources, traditions, and social knowledge.

Voluntariness. Friends perceive themselves as those who voluntarily associate with one another with regularity, voluntarily seek the company of one another, are voluntarily interdependent, and voluntarily seek proximity to one another.[16] Of course, friendships ultimately come with a set of very real ethical obligations, but the association at first is not an externally enforced one. As Joseph Epstein has written in his book on friendship, "Whatever else it has to do with, friendship entails obligation—sometimes ample and demanding, sometimes minuscule and subtle, but always, I believe, present."[17] Friendship is fragile because one may more or less freely disavow a friend; but the bonds are special, in part, precisely because we may walk away at any time. The freedom we all have to draw our own circle of affection does something to help explain why our friends are so precious: they are the chosen ones.

Intimacy. Friends seek intimacy with one another through time spent together developing their relationship. They pursue mutual discovery of one another through conversation and activities. There is often something confessional about conversations with friends—or, at least, friends are those to whom we can relatively easily confess. As Andrew Sullivan once wrote in his beautiful book on friendship, "friendship draws strength from the past, from myriad shared jokes and understandings, from the remembrance of moments endured or celebrated together, especially the small ones."[18] Intimacy is a product of conversations shared, memories created together, and inside jokes, a private language.

Trust. Friends tend to be trusting of one another and develop trust through private disclosures, sincerity, loyalty, openness of self, and authenticity. Our intimacy with our friends creates vulnerability. No one can always be fully honest and open all the time; but we betray friends when we are duplicitous or fail to contribute to mutual trust with some degree of sensitivity, disclosure, and allowing ourselves to be vulnerable. Although Kant, an Enlightenment philosopher enamored with Reason, calls for "reserve" between friends as a protective measure in his *Lectures on Ethics*—he thought we should all conceal our human frailties out of "decency" even with our best friends—most moderns would concede that too much reserve impedes friendship. Trust is risky but essential.

Solidarity. Friends identify with one another and consider one another aligned on some dimensions central to their identities. One routinely sees this dimension of friendship described as "concord" (in Aristotle) or "agreement about all things divine and human" (in

Cicero). Montaigne, a great sixteenth-century theorist of friendship, saw friends as "second selves," having "one soul in two bodies."[19] Of course, not all friends are bound through such tight bonds of solidarity—but friends usually share some important values in common. In a differentiated society, any particular friend probably cannot meet all our needs, but disagreements probably cannot be easily tolerated on matters very important to one's identity.[20]

Exclusivity. There is some debate about whether friendship must be dyadic and come in pairs. Consider C. S. Lewis on the question:

> [I]f, of three friends (A, B, and C), A should die, then B loses not only A but "A's part in C," while C loses not only A but "A's part in B." In each of my friends there is something that only some other friend can fully bring out. By myself I am not large enough to call the whole man into activity; I want other lights than my own to show all his facets. Now that Charles is dead, I shall never again see Ronald's reaction to a specifically Caroline joke. Far from having more of Ronald, having him "to myself" now that Charles is away, I have less of Ronald. . . . Two friends delight to be joined by a third, and three by a fourth, if only the newcomer is qualified to become a real friend.[21]

But even if they come in groups of more than two, they must breed a sense of exclusivity. As C. S. Lewis understood, to claim "[t]hese are my friends" importantly implies that "[t]hose are not." Friendship is "selective and an affair of the few." It requires partiality: if we don't prefer our friends, it is hard to see how they count as friends. We tolerate exclusivity and partiality in friendship because it helps make them feel special. Yet when friendships somehow transition into cliques, they can try our patience or otherwise transform into something other than friendship proper.

Reciprocity. Friends engage in mutual regard and make an effort to reciprocate in the realms of caring, emotional support, and goodwill: they have especial concern for one another's well-being. In addition, friends wish their counterparts well *for their own sake*, rather than solely for any benefit that might accrue to a friend on account of the other's well-being. Each party to a friendship self-consciously engages in reciprocity and is aware of her counterpart's goodwill. Unlike a romantic interest, which can be unrequited, friendship must be shared with an awareness of mutual regard.

Warmth. Friends feel warmly and tenderly toward one another much of the time. This warmth and tenderness frequently manifests itself as a form of acceptance, flaws notwithstanding. Friendship is as much an emotion, involving affect, as it is an activity or art. And it inclines us to be forgiving, to withhold blame for minor infractions, and to serve as a sounding board in a nurturing environment. We can't be too cool with our friends for too long without threatening the friendship itself.

Mutual assistance. Friends help one another practically by offering advice, comfort, networks and connections, material aid (in the form of loans or gifts), and favors of various kinds. "In-kind" transfers or gifts help reinforce the solidity of friendships and help symbolize to parties that they are not mere commercial partners. Yet we cannot ignore the more banal exchange relationship embedded in most friendships. It is only idealism of a misguided form to presume that friendship is not instrumental in part. Although, of course, friendship is something more than a mere relationship of exchange, certainly some exchange must be part of the give-and-take of friendship. Still, there is probably a norm within friendship that prevents parties from being too explicit about keeping tabs.

Consider Robert Ellickson's illustrative example:

> Dinner guests, for example, commonly bring their host a gift such as a bottle of wine. But no dinner guest would, instead of bringing wine, arrive and say, "Here's twenty dollars. I've learned in an Economics course that you'd undoubtedly prefer this to the usual bottle of wine." The tender of cash would signal that the guest thought of the dinner not as an occasion among friends but as an occasion at a restaurant, where diners have a merely commercial relationship with those who serve them.[22]

Thus, although we are rarely up front about the types of exchanges within friendships, they are undoubtedly there.[23] We may not lay out cash beyond covering a round of drinks or a meal in a restaurant (with an expectation of some kind of payback in some form), but we routinely furnish our friends with free child care, free places to stay (to avoid costly hotels), free meals in our homes, and employment information. Usually, we only really become aware of the exchange relationship embedded in a friendship when one person is giving too much or one person is taking too much. We feel for Aziz when he tells Fielding in *A Passage to India*: "If you are right, there is no point in any friendship; it all comes down to give and take, or give and return, which is disgusting."[24] But we also know that there *must* be some give-and-take and give-and-return or it isn't a friendship but rather some more unilateral relationship.

Equality. Between friends, no feelings of superiority are appropriate, and social prestige should be irrelevant. Although friends are rarely equal in all ways, true friends treat one another as if they are. Friends give and take equally, or risk rupturing the bond of friendship. We cannot assume a sense of superiority over a friend without undermining a core attribute of friendship.

There are naysayers on the point, to be sure. Some think that friends end up competitive—and that many cultivate friendships with inferiors in large measure to help their own egos. But I doubt that is a useful way to think about friendship. We may find ourselves jealous of friends, but we know that isn't the right reaction we should be having to a friend's triumphs and accomplishments.

Duration over time. Friendships wax and wane, dissolve, intensify, and become attenuated over time. Nevertheless, the relation of friendship must involve some durability. As Epstein writes, "A relationship with an acquaintance doesn't postulate a future."[25] It may even be that no regular contact is required if a friendship forms in particularly intense ways or at a particularly formative time. For example, two British sociologists report the case of a man who considered his closest friend to be a "childhood companion and co-evacuee during World War II to whom he had not spoken in over twenty years."[26]

Although friendships undoubtedly go through some phases of dormancy, friends usually imagine a future spent sharing life experiences together. And the presumed duration of friendship helps individuals believe that equality in giving and taking, in mutual assistance, and goodwill can be effected over time.

Conflict and modalities of conflict resolution. Friendships of substantial duration will undoubtedly enter phases of tension and conflict. Indeed, Montaigne thought some discord to be at the very heart of frank conversation: Friendship "delights in the sharpness and vigor [of verbal] intercourse....It is not vigorous and generous enough if it is not quarrelsome, if it is civilized and artful, if it fears knocks and moves with constraint."[27] Yet most friendships have resources to mediate even more substantial conflict. Friends must be willing to try to manage conflict because they are invested in the relational enterprise and its future.[28]

To be sure, listing a bunch of attributes, some of which obtain in a given friendship and some of which do not, is a too clinical method of getting at an important social relation that contributes to people's integrity and dignity. There are, of course, more romantic depictions of friendship in our cultural heritage, and they undoubtedly shed some truth on the relation at issue better than a top-eleven list can. Still, this composite sketch of the friend delineates the concept rather well and, in turn, could be the basis of the law's identification of the friendship relation. What we will discover in subsequent chapters is that each domain of the law or public policy may need to operate with a slightly different definition to stay true to the needs of particularized areas of the legal and political system. And the law itself may furnish a unique lens—as we witness the law locking horns with friendship and friends locking horns with one another in legal contexts—that can help us come up with useful ways to rethink friendship and can guide our thinking about friendship's commands and demands. Some legal concepts—like the "fiduciary" and the "relational contract" (explored in chapters 5 and 6, respectively)—will actually help enhance our understanding of the friend; and these are perspectives that haven't been explored thus far in the centuries of ruminations about friendship.

ONLINE "FRIENDSHIPS": FRIENDS VERSUS "FRIENDS"?

Social networking platforms like LiveJournal, MySpace, Friendster, and Facebook trade on the idea of friendship and leverage it to build community (and a sense of community). These sites want you to "friend" your friends—and encourage you to speak about all the people in your extended networks as "friends." It is part of the culture of these sites to add "friends"; after users subscribe and create their online profile, adding "friends" is the next step—and usually a feverish one—to forging one's online self. Yet few think that their online world of "friends" is coextensive with the network of people they consider their true close friends. There is, undoubtedly, some overlap in the membership of people's online "friendships" and their most important friendships, and it seems safe to say the set of criteria adumbrated in this chapter will tend to capture most real friendships, whether or not they have an online presence. Moreover, the criteria would tend to exclude from consideration the sort of friendships that only exist through social networking sites, even though social networking sites help sustain friendships that already exist and can even lead to new ones.[29]

There is already quite a large literature on social networking sites and the differences between friendship and "friendship" (with the latter standing for "friendship" as it is used in sites like Friendster and Facebook).[30] But much of this work reinforces what we already know by intuition: that "friendship" online isn't quite the same thing as friendship as such. To be sure, we can use technologies to aid us in our friendships and we can use technologies to meet new people we otherwise could never have met. Online interaction also enables us to keep up with more people because it can be asynchronous—we can read and write on our own time and don't have to be interrupted by a phone call when it is inconvenient. Although iPhones, Blackberries, and chatting technologies are probably changing norms surrounding the asynchronous nature of e-mail—one is now expected to get back to people sooner, I suspect—social networking sites can support and facilitate offline friendship. But it isn't especially controversial to take notice that online "friendships" really are their own beasts and call for their own analyses. For my purposes here, we can simply say that an online "friendship" can qualify for friendship status in the sense I mean if it meets the criteria enumerated above. Many will—and many will not.

Perhaps this is a good test for the usefulness of the criteria I outlined above: How might Friendsters falter on my proposed friendship index? First, many of these "friendships" will not be voluntary in any meaningful sense. As ethnographers of these platforms have revealed, many people accept "friend" requests because they simply feel it is too mean to say no. Others feel they have to be nice to "friends" of "friends"; peer pressure is always in play within offline friendships, but perhaps it is especially intense online, where reputation can be easily manipulated with campaigns and faceless attacks. Others, still, claim that the status of online "friendship" has no meaning, so they let anyone into their clubs.

That surely is a sign that many people quite simply do not view online "friendship" as especially central to their well-being—but it also implicates the criterion of exclusivity. Although we are in somewhat circumscribed worlds in Facebook or MySpace, insofar as these sites specifically set up a system in which we certainly can and do exclude strangers, it would seem to be a category mistake to call these social networks "exclusive." People routinely are online "friends" with "Fakesters"—representations of people who are not what their profiles claim—or group identities, which are not terribly exclusive. Indeed, in the social networking platforms that do seem to operate with more exclusivity (like certain subcommunities within LiveJournal), it is probably the case that there is more overlap between online "friendships" and offline friendships. There was a time when Friendster limited users to 150 "friends"—relying on the "Dunbar number," the upper limit of people we can gossip with at any given time.[31] But even at that number of "friends" we are forsaking the exclusivity criterion.

The lack of exclusivity also leads to a lack of intimacy. Although social networking sites have probably contributed to people keeping others more informed about the minutia of their daily existences, the very fact that people are doing so in a minipublic in front of a whole network of "friends" (some of whom themselves are "collectors" with enormous networks) tends to make these communications less intimate even when they are about what we might tend to think of as intimate details of our lives. That we feel more comfortable telling people when we are taking a piss as we are doing it in the stall tells us, perhaps, about evolving standards of privacy, but it isn't clear that the disclosure of this fact tells us that we have achieved real intimacy with our "friends."

Trust, too, is implicated by the lack of exclusivity: if you asked people whether they trusted their "friends" on social networking sites, it would be hard to imagine they would—unless the sort of trust you were asking about was a very weak and attenuated brand of it. In small online "friendship" networks, trust is probably in play—but then these small circles probably overlap with offline friendships, too.

There is undoubtedly plenty of mutual assistance on these sites. Many of the sites are used to help "friends" with dating, finding apartments, and finding new jobs. Even the ones that aren't self-consciously instrumentalist—like LinkedIn, for example, which has professional networking as its raison d'être—encourage and support users helping one another in practical ways, whether it is selling a sofa or looking for a good book recommendation.

And all the mutual assistance can lead to reciprocity and a norm of maintaining reciprocal concern for one another. Interestingly, however, most online "friendships" do not have strong social norms of reciprocity, with the possible exception of certain online favors like commenting on blogs or journals, adding personal blogs onto counterparts' blogrolls, or adding testimonials. Indeed, the very idea that "friending" practices are rule-bound on social networking sites offends many users who are asked to articulate a set of norms for their practices. People have a much stronger sense of rules and binding social norms within offline friendships.[32]

There is plenty of solidarity that can arise on social networking sites. Indeed, people seek one another out on the sites precisely because they share interests and gain pleasure sharing their interests with others who are similarly enthusiastic about their interests, whether it is for a band or a political cause. Sometimes the solidarity surrounds the site itself, where the primary focus of enthusiasm is for the networking platform itself and related applications. Ultimately, solidarity isn't a necessary feature of online "friendships," but it often plays a role in "friending" practices and performances.

Online "friendships" sometimes show durability over time, and sometimes they don't. When Friendster became uncool, many of the networks built by the site collapsed over a short period of time. When people came to realize that their activities may be mined for data and sold to third parties, some soured on the platforms and ended their online "friendships," albeit for reasons having nothing to do with the relationships themselves. Many users switch platforms and lose online "friends" in the transition. And sometimes drama—conflict—can lead to "de-friending" (or "unfriending," Oxford English Dictionary's 2009 word of the year!) people. Unfriending is usually the result of a conflagration and is instantaneous, a much cleaner way of terminating a relationship than is usually experienced in friendships offline, where petering out over time is a much more common form of breaking up.

Indeed, programmers of MySpace essentially invited drama by encouraging people to choose "top friends," whose names all could see. Some use this feature as it was intended—by listing their closest friends—but then find the drama associated with the lists too much to bear. Accordingly, many opt out by including only family or groups and bands in their "top friends" slots. Adults rarely rank their friends— with the possible exception of a best friend—and creating public "friendship" hierarchies can inflame and offend people when they find they are not included in such lists. The listing function helps exclusivity but creates more conflict than most people can manage productively.

It is hard to say, ultimately, how durable online "friendships" are, since most adults who have close friends have had them for longer than any of the social networking sites have been in existence. Moreover, because it is always hard to say which platforms will prevail or be cool at a given moment—Facebook looks like the current leader as of this writing, but who knows what the future will bring—it isn't easy to know too much about the long-term durability of online "friendships." Many people also lose steam with their online presences at these sites once the excitement of finding old lovers and old high school friends subsides. That said, teens growing up with these platforms as central to their lives may simply see acts of online "friendship" as a component of

their offline friendships and have more fluid online and offline existences. Some kids say quite seriously that you don't exist if you aren't
on MySpace. It is hard, then, to say for certain what will become of
online "friendship" for the next generation. Yet even if online "friendship" turns out to be coextensive with old-school offline friendships, it
seems unlikely that our cultural idea of friendship itself would change
substantially. Time will tell.

Just as with durability, equality also does not seem easy to gauge
without more careful study, nor does it seem easy to see it as central to
online "friendships." Quite the reverse often seems true: people seek
out higher status individuals to "friend" on social networking sites to
make themselves seem more popular and impressive. People also seek
out celebrities and bands to project and develop their identities, but
also to raise their own status. Professors and students, parents and children, managers and employees, faculty and staff find themselves
connected by social networking sites—and many struggle with exactly
how to navigate these unequal "friendships" online. Yet equality may
well be quite common in our online "friendship" worlds, even if not
essentially so. Most people's networks are quite likely composed of
people alike in status, as generations of research on the "homophily"
phenomenon—that people tend to associate with similarly situated
and educated people—would predict.[33] But it doesn't seem to be *normative*, as it is in the basic case of friendship offline.

Perhaps much comes down to warmth. How warmly do people feel
about their online "friends"? The answer to that question could be the
key to unlocking the core of friendship itself; it seems like the canary
in the coal mine that signals when we are dealing with people who are
real friends or just Friendsters. Affection is what matters so much in
friendship, and online "friendships" do not easily translate or transmit
warmth. Emoticons are not hugs. Love happens in friendship; less
often in "friendship," especially if the "friendship" involves people that
have never met face to face.

There is nothing disqualifying about being Facebook "friends," of
course, but when people are just Facebook "friends," it really is hard to
call that a friendship in the sense I use it in this book. There is such
heterogeneity associated with why people become online "friends"—
whether it because you want access to written material or photos
reserved for "friends"; because it is cool to have a "friend" with such a
cool profile; because you want to keep all Haitians together (a reported
reason a sixteen-year old named Ono accepts all "friend" requests from
Haitians); because it is hard to say no to a "friend" request; because you

like collecting "friends," since sheer numbers enhance your sense of self or your attractiveness to others—that it seems inappropriate to treat online "friends" as friends per se. Admittedly, there is a fair bit of heterogeneity even in offline friendship practices too (and social pressure in offline friendships clearly exists, even if we like to think of our friendships as voluntary in important senses). But we can at least say with some confidence that online "friendships" are really different sorts of relationships, notwithstanding the fact that we can certainly have online "friendships" with our offline friends. One court that was put in the position of assessing the relevance of parties being Facebook "friends" (because friendships do, as we will see, sometimes matter in the law) had this to say in 2009:

> The Court assigns no significance to the Facebook "friends" reference. Facebook reportedly has more than 200 million active users, and the average user has 120 "friends" on the site. The fastest growing demographic is those [who are] 35 years old and older. Regardless of what Facebook's apparent popularity or usefulness may say about the nature of 21st century communications and relationships, the site's designers' selections of icons or labels offer no substance to this dispute. Indeed, the Court notes that electronically connected "friends" are not among the litany of relationships targeted by [our laws]. Indeed, "friendships" on Facebook may be as fleeting as the flick of a delete button.[34]

Lest you think, however, that all lawyers think Facebook "friendship" irrelevant in the law, take note that Florida's Judicial Ethics Advisory Committee recently decided to issue an opinion disfavoring lawyers' "friending" of judges because it could evidence a potential conflict of interest. The *New York Times* provided some helpful perspective: "In practice, of course, actual friends and Facebook friends can be as different as leather and pleather, and the committee did recognize that online friends were not the same as friends in the traditional sense. A minority of the panel would have allowed Facebook friendship, which it characterized as more like 'a contact or acquaintance' without conveying the notion of 'feelings of affection or personal regard.'"[35]

None of this is to say that online "friendships" aren't also embedded in our offline social worlds and interact with them in multifarious ways; they are not completely distinct. Allowing ourselves to be broadly vulnerable on Facebook—updating 120 or 1,200 people about our private lives as they are developing—may have ripple effects in how we deal with our most intimate friends. Some sociologists have suggested that as our marriages and primary erotic relationships got more intimate, we got more capable of developing deeper friendships; the same dynamic might be hoped for with online "friendships." And just as our physical spaces for "hanging out" can be sites of real friendships or just places to congregate with a bunch of acquaintances, so can social networking platforms. "Defriending" in an online context can have trickle-down effects in the real world—and vice versa: defriending in the real world, when it does happen, can change our online "friendship" networks. These are worlds that are interlocked.

Still, it remains safe to distinguish online "friendships" from their namesakes. The real McCoy has people caring about each other for their own sakes, at least in some substantial measure. Social networking is rarely that way, at least in part because most seem to have an unspoken convention that one should accept almost all requests from known peers, irrespective of the quality of the preexisting relationship. It is no surprise, then, that new participants in social networking sites often complain about the loss of distinction in the online world between "friend" and acquaintance. Ultimately, people adjust. But the online "friendships" just don't coalesce around the same social norms (or arguably, any social norms other than inclusion) or characteristics that govern offline friendship.

There remains the question of whether the social networking platforms that are growing ever more present in our lives are eroding friendship itself. Certainly, in the early days of the Internet, some worried about the influence it would have on our social relationships. There was widespread speculation that interacting online would overtake our offline relationships and risked destroying them. That scenario never quite came to pass. In fact, most researchers studying how the Internet affects people's personal relationships find that, over time, whatever alienation people feel going online subsides once people grow comfortable with the technologies, learn how to mediate between online and offline selves, and learn how to incorporate and integrate Internet functionalities into their personal relationships.[36] Just as acclimating to the telephone and the ease of world travel required adjustment within personal relations, so, too, does acclimating to the Internet. We already learned, before the Internet came around, to have intimacy over long distances and without constant face-to-face communication; the Internet isn't obviously a new and radical challenge to our personal networks. In fact, Jeffrey Boase and Barry Wellman suggest that it was our appetite for long-distance communication that in some measure "caused" the Internet, rather than the Internet being the cause of our long-distance friendships.

Ultimately, there is plenty of evidence that the Internet enhances our ability to maintain networks by, among other things, easing our ability to plan meetups and coordinate activities. The Internet builds social capital and gives it a place to sustain itself and needn't be charged with causing its erosion. People use the Internet to make important decisions and gather critical information. And when people turn to online interactions, they are largely interacting with people they know offline. To the extent that the Internet is taking people away from things they did before its advent, it is breaking into the time they used to spend sleeping or watching TV, hardly the most social activities. It is facilitating local neighborly relations just as it is helping people stay connected globally.

Indeed, the widely publicized elegy for our nation's loss of social capital, Robert Putnam's *Bowling Alone*—which found substantial evidence that we aren't quite as civically involved as we once were (in the 1960s)—has been roundly criticized for failing to take notice that the 1960s were probably an especially fertile time for civic involvement and for failing to realize that much civic engagement and social capital has just migrated to different places.[37] We may not bowl much in leagues or go to the Elks Lodge—but we might participate in listservs, chatrooms, and online activity collectively. We give money to causes more easily and more often; some of the credit for that goes to the Internet, no doubt.

But for all the empirical studies that tell us not to worry much about the Internet generally, social networking sites can be disquieting nevertheless, for they interact with our friendships and our very conception of friendship in a way, perhaps, that e-mail and web surfing does not. Although it is undoubtedly true that people can and do use social networking sites to enhance and sustain their offline friendships, there is more reason to be concerned that online friendships are having some negative impact on people's offline friendships for two basic reasons.

First, as I suggested in the introduction, online friendships can tend to disaggregate friendship from affect in people's minds: friends stop being those whom one loves and start being casual acquaintances with whom one shares an occasional 140-character update. There is some concern about "nipple confusion," if you will: that contact with our "friends" will pacify us with ersatz intimacy and keep us from seeking out the real thing. Although most people, after a period of adjustment, can distinguish between those who are only online "friends" and those who are their real friends, friendship itself would seem to lose something in our using the term and its power promiscuously.

Second, the way most social networking sites encourage large networks can require social energy from us that simply gets used up, leaving us unable to engage in more intimate contact offline. Although this hasn't been shown to be an especially realistic concern about the Internet as such (it seems TV and work may be the things most people cut from their schedules to make room for it), there is still plenty of investigation to be done analyzing the effects of social networking sites more specifically. There is reason to worry that trading on the institution of friendship might be having detrimental effects, as might the sheer expansion of people's sets of "friends." More research is necessary to test these hypotheses. But they are plausible and have some anecdotal support. Even if there is some evidence of what some sociologists call "media multiplexity"—that contact in one medium tends to correspond with contact in others, so that more Facebook updating is likely to lead to more rather than less face-to-face contact with your friends— surely more work is warranted to figure out the systemic effects of having a multitude of "friendships" that are not friendships at all.

ARISTOTLE ON FRIENDSHIP

It may be that moderns will think more about online "friendships" and be more naturally interested in the Internet's role in transforming Americans' friendships than they will think about or be interested in classical philosophy. But it is still necessary in modern discussions of friendship to compare one's account with Aristotle's canonical treatment of friendship in books 8 and 9 of his *Nicomachean Ethics*.[38] Although he was not the first in the West to get his philosophical thoughts about the matter into a written form that has made its way to the current generation—that distinction might belong to Socrates, as chronicled by Plato in the *Lysis* and the *Symposium* (and perhaps the *Phaedrus*)— our modern conception of friendship owes much to an Aristotelian legacy that has traveled through Cicero, Montaigne, Emerson, and others.[39]

Aristotle's inquiry into friendship begins by asking some very basic questions about the relationship: (1) if friends must be similar or if opposites attract; (2) whether friends must be virtuous in order to maintain friendships; and (3) whether happy people need friendship, too, or whether the happy are self-sufficient without friendship.

Aristotle concludes that friendship "is most necessary for our life" and that "no one would choose to live without friends even if he had all the other goods."

These preliminary inquiries help Aristotle separate true friendships (sometimes called "character friendships" or "virtue friendships") from other kinds. Indeed, Aristotle's main legacy to contemporary discussions about friendship is his tripartite typology of friendship, which isolates a pure or true form. For Aristotle, there are three degrees or species of friendship: friendships that are useful, friendships that are pleasant, and friendships of the good. Even if these types are oversimplifications, they cast a large shadow over the way Western civilizations think about friendship.

Friendships that are useful bring personal gain, and pleasant friendships bring pleasure. Aristotle insists that these species of friendships deserve the title of friendship more than, say, the "natural friendships" we have for animals, our children, and our fellow human beings generally; however, these lesser species of friendships are friendships, Aristotle claims, only by "similarity" to the most complete friendships, not in "the primary way." Aristotle considers the useful and the pleasant forms of friendship incomplete because they are easily dissolved. Both friendships are used as a means toward some intermediate end, and friendships sought merely for pleasure are likely to disintegrate when the end in question is achieved or when pleasure is achieved and then dissipates.

Good friendships, by contrast, endure. They are constituted by "good people similar in virtue," so need does not tarnish the friendship. Thus, true friendships are relatively stable because virtue is enduring, and good people tend to stay good. An oddity of this account—to be clear—is that only good people can have true friendships. But it is not a fully idiosyncratic one: Etienne de La Boétie—a very good friend of Montaigne—writes, "Friendship is a sacred word; it is a holy thing. It never occurs except between honorable people.... It maintains itself not so much by means of good turns as by a good life. What renders a friend assured of the other is the knowledge he has of his integrity."[40] Obviously, Aristotle's and de La Boétie's conception of friendship could not be adopted into our laws; among many other reasons, we do not like our laws taking a stand on who is a good or virtuous person.

Nevertheless, Aristotle is still careful to note that true friends may, on occasion, be useful or advantageous or pleasant to each other.[41] And although he is clear—as I am trying to be—that erotic and romantic love is another breed of relationship entirely, Aristotle does not preclude, as I do here, spouses from being friends of the highest sort.

Aristotle's canonical account of the highest form of friendship ultimately confirms many of the characteristics adumbrated in this chapter. For example, he requires friends to have a substantial level of equality and a degree of concord between them. Also, he observes that friends must share "distress and enjoyment," spend time together, and trust each other. Friendship, furthermore, must be active; distance does not necessarily dissolve friendships, but prolonged absences will tend to do so. More, Aristotle requires that friends must wish their counterparts well for their counterparts' own sake. His account focuses on reciprocity, and he claims that unreciprocated goodwill is not constitutive of proper friendship. Finally, he requires that friends be mutually aware of one another's reciprocated goodwill.

There is, of course, some material in Aristotle that might seem, for lack of a better word, weird, and its features have not been adopted in the foregoing account. For example, Aristotle seems to be of the view that there is never any conflict in true friendship; that older people cannot be true friends because they are unpleasant; that true friends must live together; that the paternal and maternal relations in and of themselves are forms of friendship; that friendship is a form of self-love (which might be narcissistic); and that all friends are good people.[42] Aristotle also devotes pages to puzzles that seem downright odd: whether it is better to have friends in good fortune or bad fortune (not surprising, perhaps, he concludes that it is "choiceworthy" to have friends "in all conditions") and whether we can befriend ourselves in any meaningful sense. To be sure, some of these less familiar thoughts about friendship that fail to resonate emerge from Aristotle's focus on the Greek concept *philia* (or *philos* or *philein*), a relation that potentially includes a much broader set of relations than our modern conception of friendship.[43] But, all the same, we can trace our modern conception of intimate friendship to Aristotle's categories—and especially to his elevation of a virtue or character friendship above other, lesser, forms. Even if our own typologies differ from Aristotle's—and how could they not, given obvious cultural differences?—we will always be indebted to his account and can learn much from his insistence that there are different forms and species of friendships that command different types of attention.

Some final lessons from Aristotle continue to ring true: Aristotle thinks one can befriend too many people—and one can only imagine what he would have thought about those with twelve hundred Facebook "friends." Because friendship is the product of tremendous effort and requires true sharing of grief, distress, and celebration, a person can spread herself too thin. As Aristotle puts it, it "seems impossible to be an extremely close friend to many people.... Those who have many friends and treat everyone as close to them seem to be friends to no one, except in a fellow citizen's way. These people are regarded as ingratiating."

Perhaps even more insightfully, Aristotle also notes that when disputes arise in friendships, the tension is often traceable to a transition within the friendship from one species to another; indeed, he writes that "friends are most at odds when they are not friends in the way they think they are," when one party misleads the other into thinking a different kind of friendship exists. We would do well to remember all of these insights as we endeavor to construct a workable concept of the friend that our public policies could employ.

So much for what we can do by way of defining the friend as a general matter. As should be obvious, although much of my account of friendship here draws from Aristotle, my working definition of the friend here does not classify itself neatly into the Aristotelian category of the virtue or character friendship. It makes sense not to have the same expectations of the friend's virtue as Aristotle did. Contrary to Aristotle's account, my account here excludes from consideration spousal friendship, familial friendship, erotic friendship, and a generalized civic friendship.

Still, Aristotle's discussion furnishes a nice segue into the normative inquiry that makes up chapter 2: Should the law recognize the status of the friend? Aristotle does not have a well-developed response to the question, but he does offer some stimulating thoughts that may help to introduce the topic.

First, he suggests that friends have "no need for justice." It is not perfectly clear what he means by this, but it might mean that the law and legally-enforced justice have no place between friends.[44] Support for this reading can be found in Aristotle's approving citation of the practice of some cities where "there are actually laws prohibiting legal actions in voluntary bargains [presumably between friends], on the assumption that if we have trusted someone we must dissolve the association with him on the same terms on which he formed it." Similarly, in writing about "rules friendships," Aristotle distinguishes between rules friends who use explicit conditions for their contractual and debt arrangements and those who allow grace periods, transacting much less formally. In the latter cases, Aristotle observes, "some cities do not allow legal actions…, but think that people who have formed an arrangement on the basis of trust must put up with the outcome."

Ironically, perhaps, Aristotle appears to endorse a legal recognition of the friend precisely by denying friends any benefit of legal enforcement to their arrangements (even if they are traditional transactions that look commercial, it seems). This is a provocative thought, endorsing the idea that friends should live outside the law—or at least under their own special legal regimes. Chapter 2 argues that the law should protect the status of the friend in a more substantial way than merely denying friends access to the legal system, though the rest of this book is more generally a response to these fragmentary thoughts about the legal relevance of friendship from one of the most important thinkers on friendship who has ever lived.

CHAPTER 2

Why Should Friendship Matter?

RIENDSHIP IS so obviously a good in the world that it is hard to justify allocating trees to defending its goodness. Indeed, to define it is already to embark on a normative project of explaining why it is a central good in most people's lives. Yet to argue that the law should recognize the status of the friend requires more carefully specifying the role friends play both in private and public life.

But even that will not be enough to justify legal recognition, of course, because the law is not designed to protect and recognize all human goods. Juicy and ripe red plums are very good, but they obviously should get no special legal protection. Well, maybe we would take some formal action to avoid their extinction from the planet, come to think of it. Lollipops are goods for children (from their perspective, anyway), but it would be odd to argue that the law should protect and develop children's rights to lollipops. And even if it could be shown that social networking platforms were detrimental to friendship, regulating them with the blunt instrument of the law hardly seems like the first-best solution to reinforce the contributions real friendships make to our ability to flourish. In short, there is no neat translation of good and bad into the law. But I still hope to convince the reader that the law should be doing more for friendship than it does—and that it can do so in ways that do not altogether make us bristle with disgust that law is involved in social engineering projects of Orwellian proportions.

Ultimately the panoply of friendship's benefits I expose here illustrates that friendship is not just any old good. It is a central feature of what we think of as the good life: lives with deep private and personal connections. If one believes that our legal system should develop and facilitate the acquisition of capabilities that render our lives dignified and meaningful, the law should find a way to support, recognize, and promote friendship, whether through legislative initiatives, public policy sensitivity, or judicial decisions. But there are many other reasons for the law to respect friendship. I survey some in this chapter and then turn to countenance some early objections to the project of making friendship matter in the law.

BENEFITS IN OUR PERSONAL LIVES

Friendship confers a series of personal benefits in our daily lives. These benefits are not necessarily available exclusively through friendship, but friendship furnishes them plentifully.

First, friendship is central in the exploration, formation, development, and maintenance of identity. "Shopping" for friends and trying to get along with various people in intimate ways allow us to learn more about who we are and who we most want to become. One's sustained friendships ultimately constitute, in some measure, one's very identity, and maintaining relationships through time helps the continuity of one's identity through different life stages and substantial life challenges. Healthy friendships allow us room to develop our identities further and provide opportunities for a sense of self-selected identity outside of our institutional affiliations through work, education, and kin. More, friendship can be "the most fertile ground for acquiring the moral sensibilities."[1]

Second, friends confirm one's sense of social and moral worth. As one commentator puts it, "[s]elf-esteem, the most important disposition associated with happiness and a prime protector against depression, is...closely related to friendship."[2] Friendlessness causes depression, and friends help us avoid deep sadness. To be sure, our families and extended kin networks also provide many of these benefits, but friendship is perhaps an even greater confirmation of social and moral worth because friendship relations tend to be chosen in a deeper sense; we usually feel more stuck with our families. Obviously, most people choose their spouses, too. Still, we can dispense with friends more easily, and our larger family circle is not chosen in the way our friendship networks are. Some have found that it is friendship rather than money, commodities, or family that buys people happiness.[3]

Not only do friends help us avoid depression, but they are also more generally good for our health: Although there was a time when sociologists concluded that "friendship plays a very small part in the overall pattern of support and care" of the "chronically ill and handicapped"[4] and that kin was more likely to perform these tasks, more recent evidence suggests that those with close friends and confidants live longer than those without them and that "close family ties... ha[ve] no discernible effect on survival."[5] Indeed, this finding is so robust that journalists have occasion to report this fact on an almost annual basis because new studies keep coming out exploring how important friends are for one's health. Despite one recent study that finds that friends might make us fat if they are fat themselves, most of the evidence points to an important correlation between physical survival and friendship. Here is a sampling of the conclusions: Older people with a large number of friends are less likely to die than those with fewer friends; strong friendships can promote brain health as we get older; you are four times more likely to survive breast cancer with ten or more friends (and having a spouse makes no difference to your outcome); friendships can stave off heart attacks and coronary heart disease—only smoking is as big a risk factor as not having good friends; and friendships make one less likely to get the common cold.[6]

More, friendship can furnish important emotional and financial aid in times of crisis when public services are overextended: "The closer and stronger our tie with someone, the broader the scope of their support for us and the greater the likelihood that they will provide major help in a crisis."[7] So close friends are critical in the provision of care and keep one healthy and safe. All things considered, one might be more likely to survive disasters—natural or not—with the support network that friends provide.

Finally, friends can inspire innovation and creativity, giving rise to new modalities of thought. Friendship is thus generative, not only supportive. In this vein, C. S. Lewis noted that the Romantic movement, communism, abolitionism, the Reformation, and the Renaissance were all pioneered within friend groups before they surfaced on the world's stage.[8] Whatever one thinks of these contributions to cultural and political life, it is an interesting lens into them to see them as sustained by, nurtured by, and made possible by friendship. By serving as a respite from other more formal social roles and obligations, friendship facilitates our sense of control over our own lives, helps us to be authentic, and furnishes us with a greater sense of individual autonomy. This freedom can open up for us new ways of thinking. Friends help us remain the same, but they also help us grow. Although the confirmatory studies of friendship's importance that I draw from here (and in the rest of the chapter) hardly delimit the term "friend" the way I did in chapter 1, the point remains the same: Friends aren't just around for a good time; they sustain our lives and our society.

PROFESSIONAL PERQUISITES

Friendship also yields some real dividends in the workplace, as generations of research on labor patterns in sociology and labor economics have revealed. Employees with friends at the workplace are more efficient than their peers, suffer less stress at the office, tend to stay at their jobs longer, and experience less job dissatisfaction. Having sources of emotional support at work helps gets us through the day, helps us feel like we have a stake in the institutions we work for, helps us feel comfortable getting creative with our work product, and generally enhances team morale. Friends help us find new jobs, help develop our skill sets, help us find opportunities for promotion, vouch for us to higher-ups to smooth our evaluations and reviews, give us warnings about coming layoffs and grumblings about aspects of our performance, and help us think through our professional options as they present themselves over time.[9] Even when we choose to transact with friends—which studies show we do more often than we probably assume and which can cause unique stresses, too (making that rent payment to a friend rather than a stranger may make us more stressed out about making rent on time rather than less stressed—and having to make a choice about whom to promote, a friend or a more productive underling, can cause emotional turmoil)—we are more likely to be satisfied with our outcomes.[10]

Managers, too, benefit from friendships in the workplace and seem to promote friendships within their organizations actively; they tend to think organizations will reap rewards from friendships and see them as a net good.[11] Those rewards include the very same benefits employees themselves will gain: support to help get the job done efficiently, good communication within the organization, high morale, low stress, a sense of loyalty and confidence in the organization, increased productivity, and innovation. The more managers create a feeling of impersonal bureaucracy, the less they can depend on their workers: absenteeism, turnover, and low levels of motivation can result. There was a time when some managers encouraged employees not to develop social relationships with one another, but but the pendulum has clearly swung to the other side. The conventional wisdom is that friendship ties within an organization will help the organization deal with crises because they help organizations adapt to uncertainty and changes.[12]

None of this is to say that there aren't some risks associated with mixing friendship and business.[13] Just as with online "friendships" that might be causing some erosion in Americans' conception of friendship itself, business friendships may also be too "fictive" to take seriously because they are often highly instrumental—and they may do damage to the very concept of real friendship. Moreover, workplace friendships can cause conflicts of interest and more intense jealousies when people's friends get promoted above them. Much has been made of the possibility of awkward romantic liaisons, tension surrounding how close friends in the workplace really are, the professional dangers of exposing too much vulnerability in the workplace, concerns about sexual harassment, distractions from work, too much gossip, the undermining of independent judgment or merits-based decision-making, the wasted energy that goes into inevitable friendship deteriorations, and the cronyism and nepotism that can result from mixing work and friendship (to say nothing of the racial and gender bias that can result when we allow employers to prefer their friends with special office perquisites and pay and status raises). Real costs—psychological, cultural, social, distributional, economic, cognitive—certainly offset some of the advantages of developing close friendships at work. Competing firms can use friendships to collude with one another to keep prices high at the expense of customers. And managers can use friendships as a mechanism of control to keep employees in line and compliant, encouraging them to keep the hierarchy as it is.

But most of the evidence (and most managers' behavior) points to the benefits outweighing the costs.[14] And there is some evidence that people are increasingly intermingling their social and work lives, so it might be sensible to pay attention to this fact as a public policy concern, even if we don't want to welcome the development with wide-open arms. Actually, friendships between managers at competing firms seem to improve firm performance through enhanced collaboration, better information exchange, and less time wasted on competitive behaviors that undermine effectiveness: one study about friendships among competitors in the hotel industry estimates that "each friendship with a competitor contributes approximately $268,000 to the annual revenue of a typical hotel," and that "[i]n total, the observed friendship network augmented the annual revenue of the 40 hotels...studied by roughly $70 million."[15] Talk about social capital! And the increase in capital is not always coming at the expense of the customer: sometimes the customer is getting better service and useful referrals because of the ties (though, admittedly, not enough has been done to figure out just what portion of the enhanced firm performance is a net social gain for all and how much is not). Some important businesses actually seem to need friendship ties to survive: one study at Columbia Business School found friendship ties essential for the survival of shipbuilding companies on the Clyde River.[16]

Friendships among buyers and sellers (often called "vertical ties" in contradistinction to the "horizontal ties" between competing firms) also seem to promote effectiveness through enabling cooperative efforts that might not get off the ground between strangers who have less trust through facilitating communication to solve sticky problems as they arise, and through the goodwill that allows simple solutions to problems that might set strangers off into adversarial conduct.[17] Exchange between those tied by friendly relations can lower transaction costs and create an environment of especial trust, which can lead to good economic outcomes.

All this tells us little about what the law ought to do, of course. But to the extent that we use our legal system to help businesses function efficiently and to the extent that we see more systemic benefits to friendships, we might think it makes sense to have the law modestly push us or nudge us in an efficient direction. We'd also have to pay attention to the costs, of course, for they are real: if friends are using their friendships with members of competitor firms to collude in ways the current antitrust regime cannot contemplate, that is an argument for reform. But it is a reform from within an orientation of sensitivity to friendship in the professional sphere; ignoring this major component of people's professional lives wouldn't seem to serve our working lives at all. We regulate trans-fats to save ourselves from eating badly— and getting a little more sensitive within the law to how friendships operate in the workplace would seem to be less paternalistic than legally controlling what people are allowed to eat.

PUBLIC ADVANTAGES

Many of these personal and professional benefits create a windfall for society more generally. There are public health implications as well as ramifications for our economy. For example, the state clearly reaps a public health benefit from friends who take care of the sick and handicapped, a cost that Medicaid or Medicare need not absorb if there are able-bodied friends willing and able to pitch in. Friend networks help sustain the Red Cross and volunteer services that help us muddle through and survive disasters.[18] And friendship networks save the public money because friends can step in and serve a variety of care functions that the state might otherwise need to provide. If Robert Lane is right, "[a]dvanced societies are likely to increase 'utility' if they maximize friendship rather than the getting and spending of wealth."[19]

Even if the accumulation of wealth turns out to be one of the central desiderata of our society, the avoidance of depression that friendship can accomplish has ramifications for our capital markets and may help the state with economic growth. Alienation and disconnection are clearly drains on the economy (though they are also perhaps generative of some great books and pieces of art too)—and promoting friendship may help ameliorate some of that drain.

Friendship facilitates economic growth in a few other ways as well. In the first place, as noted, close social networks promote individual freedom and creativity, which have real market effects. Innovation is a driving engine of our economy—and to the extent that friendship contributes to such innovation, it is supporting important sectors of our economic development. Second, broad friendship networks facilitate business because one is more likely to contract with those whom one trusts.[20] Friendship is, as one anthropologist put it, "closely related to contractual agreement and reciprocal behavior"[21]—and contracts and the collaborations that make them work lie at the center of our liberal market institutions. Third, and related, friendships establish paradigmatic examples of interpersonal trust, central to the smooth operations of a market. Friendships are especially well-suited to the creation and reinforcement of the interpersonal trust that is critical to helping the market function.

There are even more public benefits that could accrue to the state if it promoted friendship more directly. In particular, friendships have the potential to save the legal system enforcement costs (in short, the costs of contracting, lawsuits, and long negotiations) because transactions based in friendships often do not require the law to monitor them. Norms internal to friendship can successfully police party behavior and save the legal system effort in the process. The values of friendship and its commitments to reciprocity and goodwill lubricate and underwrite economic transactions.

To be sure, friendship also has its very real economic costs: In Andalusia, for instance, some farmers complain that friendship makes sellers feel obligated to sell at a loss or to sell things they otherwise would prefer to keep.[22] Yet these costs are arguably counterbalanced by the costs friends save in not needing to rely on the relatively more expensive norm-enforcement techniques furnished by the law.

Of course, it cannot be that the law should provide room and recognition for all extrinsic norms that could potentially save a legal system enforcement costs. Many nonlegal regimes of social organization can furnish this benefit, and surely the law cannot give special status to all extrinsic norms. But friendship's norms are especially useful for the law because those norms are centrally ones the legal system should stand ready to endorse. The law needn't interpose its own norms if it can piggyback on friendship's internal ethical structure—especially when the trust, reliance, equality, and reciprocity that friendships demand are the very same desiderata the law pursues. This is not dissimilar from the law's strategy to accommodate customs in commerce (commercial norms and practices) and culture (religion), so long as the customs can be shown to be well entrenched and inoffensive to public policy more generally.[23] The law need not impose its own foreign norms when they are so readily attended to through an external norm system that it can endorse and underwrite.

Aside from some basic utilitarian reasons for taking on a more sensitive treatment of friendship in the law, at least a few other reasons seem important. First, it may very well be that our sense of justice requires us to treat different sorts of predicate transactions differentially, depending on whether they are between strangers or between friends. If we wrong a stranger by accident, it may be less blameworthy than wronging a friend in the very same way: our standard of care to our friends would seem to be higher, and it is more disturbing to wrong our friends. If moral justice demands different results in the law depending on whether a perpetrator or victim is a friend or stranger, it would seem rather important for the law to develop a regime for friends and what we expect of them. Pretending all transactions happen between strangers—as much private law presupposes—would seem to lead us into injustice quite frequently.

In a related vein, it might be that citizens will embrace their polity and be more likely to comply with the law more generally if the polity adopts a legal system that caters to the collective sense of moral desert in the community. If we do have a different sense of justice as between friends, it may benefit our society more broadly to have a legal system that doles out merits and demerits on the basis of that more calibrated and differentiated sense of justice. Some empirical evidence has shown that the community's agreement that the legal system punishes conduct that "deserves" sanction breeds general compliance with the law.[24]

Some scholars go even further and suggest that vast swaths of our legal system are themselves predicated on friendship, and that our law would not be possible without a conception of friendship undergirding it. Perhaps certain norms within contract and tort law, for example, themselves had their genesis in friendship's commands: act in good faith, take due care, keep your promises. This is Peter Goodrich's provocative idea. And although he sees friendship as a "special kind of law," he thinks it "introduces *caritas* into the practice of legality, and it is precisely from this concept of care that comes the primary private law bond of community—the 'duty of care' that we owe to our neighbor in the law of obligations."[25] If the law is parasitic on the friend for its own normative structure, perhaps the law owes the friend the privilege of being recognized. This is, to be sure, getting more and more abstract (though chapters 4, 5, and 6 try to make all these considerations concrete as I try to develop a "law of friendship"). But there are a few more things to be said about friendship's benefits for the political sphere more generally, beyond its contribution to public health, our economic system, and the law.

Friendship can also be a resource for social integration and political cohesion.[26] Citizens can be made to care about their polities and contribute to public life when they realize and experience that their friendships and their friends' lives are at stake within the same polity. I might not participate in public affairs or care much about the commonweal if it cannot touch my "private" life. But if I see that politics affect my friends, I might be more likely to become involved and feel a general solidarity with my broader community. As Aristotle understood, friendship ultimately contributes to the moral worth of the state: "[F]riendship would seem to hold cities together."[27] In interpreting this credo, Anthony Kronman reads it this way: "[T]he best safeguard against political revolution is a stable spirit of friendship among the members of the *polis*. . . . This is why, for the continued existence of the *polis*, justice is not enough. There must also be friendship among its citizens."[28] One can be more locally focused about this, too: sociologists have for some time been interested in and have been studying "neighborhood effects," how certain communities foster social behaviors in their borders. Friendship ties can contribute to and alter these neighborhood effects, helping to mobilize citizens into political participation through voter registration and turnout, helping to build institutional resources like libraries, schools, churches, and clubs, facilitating social integration, and supporting social order.[29]

PARRYING SOME OBJECTIONS

There are some who might object to protecting friends because there are too many of them and because the class is too expansive to warrant protection. Yet the most recent study on friendship in the sociology literature confirms that most people in the United States think they have only two close friends, and one in four people say they have no one with whom they can discuss important matters.[30] Even the now-classic counterstudy that people like to cite for the proposition that we are somewhat less isolated than this result would suggest still finds very few nonkin friendship ties, in particular; we may have a reasonably sized group of people with whom we consort, but few are what we would think of as close friends: the bulk are family members, relatives, coworkers, and the like.[31] In short, "friends" is not a hopelessly large class of people that would get special treatment in a regime more sensitive to the friend.

This recalls, of course, how I started in the introduction: it is worth taking note here again that friendship may very well be in decline (albeit we now have many more reasons to support friendship besides that finding).[32] Friendship sorely needs and deserves the support of our public institutions to help it flourish. As a recent newspaper report observes:

> Weakening bonds of friendship, which [many] studies affirm, have far-reaching effects. Among them: fewer people to turn to for help in crises such as Hurricane Katrina, fewer watchdogs to deter neighborhood crime, fewer visitors for hospital patients and fewer participants in community groups. The decline, which was greatest in estimates of the number of friends outside the family, also puts added pressure on spouses, families and counselors.[33]

This commands the attention of the public, lawyers, public policymakers, judges, and legal scholars. The law can indeed help protect friendship, but the law has thus far failed to take friendships sufficiently seriously and appreciate its role in sustaining them (and regulating them, even if unconsciously). Of course, it is not obvious that legal recognition will lead to an increase in the actual number or quality of friendships within society—and if policy designers are too clumsy, the law's recognition might lead to further decline (assuming the decline found in recent studies is not artifactual). But at the very least, we need some account of the law's relationship to friendship. We need to remain mindful that legal rules will have some effect on this most important social institution and social resource that allows people to function and furnishes them with dignity, integrity, and well-being. The benefits of friendship for private and public lives haven't quite gone unnoticed, but that they collectively support an argument for some attention by public policy designers has really never been put on the agenda. I want it there now.

Admittedly, my thesis is somewhat counterintuitive. Nevertheless, here I give some form to the sorts of objections that likely structure people's intuitions that this is a bizarre—and really quite bad—idea. I will hope to show here why such intuitions may be wrong. Although I will revisit some of these objections in chapter 7, once I have provided a better sense of what it really means—in practical terms—to buy into my project, I do want to address readers' concerns in some substantive way here, because I want readers to persist to the final chapters, where I show the potential of bringing careful thinking about friendship to law (and vice-versa). It gets a tad technical later, and readers will need some motivation to slog through legal doctrines with the confidence that the project isn't radically wrongheaded from its inception.

To be sure, there is good symbolic reason to keep friendship out of law and the law out of friendship. Goodrich is illustrative:

> [T]he judge must recuse him or herself from judging friends, the attorney cannot properly represent or act for a cause in which he or she has an interest or amity, and affect indeed is supposed to play no part in the concatenations or elaborations of law. The order of law is predicated upon a refusal to deal with friendship and so it institutes a nonrecognition of the friend.[34]

Indeed, keeping friendship out of law helps keep the law impartial and free from affect and eros, an obvious Western liberal good. But the law's appropriate posture of impartiality to repel criticisms of "cronyism and nepotism" (as Goodrich puts it) does not justify a complete nonrecognition of the relationships of friendship in society, and it is hardly clear that the law can rid itself of cronyism without some theory of when a friendship triggers a partiality to which the law must respond by a demand for recusal, if nothing else. While later chapters of this book should rebut the case that the law is or could be successful in any thoroughgoing campaign of "nonrecognition," here I develop four more potential theoretical objections to my enterprise.

Keeping the Private Sphere Private

Most basically, perhaps the law and friendship should not intermingle because we tend to think of our friendships as quintessentially voluntary and the law as quintessentially coercive.[35] Allowing the law to penetrate friendship in any way might threaten friendship's core and undermine its defining characteristic. One could go further yet: Friendship and keeping it private may be central to our freedom. Without friendship's privacy we might have no authentic personal relations outside the control of the state.

Indeed, according to a widely discussed reading of the thinkers of the Scottish Enlightenment (David Hume, Adam Smith, Francis Hutcheson, and Adam Ferguson),[36] both a healthy commercial society and friendship itself function much better when the public economic system takes no special notice of friendship. The logic is as follows: Friendship prospers best when there is a separate sphere of public commercial transactions because such a separation helps demarcate friendship as noninstrumental. Before there was a public commercial sphere, it was more difficult to tell who was a true friend and who was being befriended for commercial gain. Once a public economic sphere emerged, however, it became easier to signal who is a true intimate and who is a mere business partner.

As applied here, one might agree with the Scots and argue that keeping friendship private helps keep it unadulterated: commercial interests can rule the public sphere and be "liberated" from the sympathy and love in the private sphere. Keeping the market (and, by extension, the law that governs it) free from considerations of friendship serves friendship best. A market society that ignores friendship makes it more likely that one will be able to form authentic friendships because one can credibly signal to others that one's friendship with them is not fundamentally about exchange.

From another perspective, keeping friendship private also serves the economy best at the same time. Adam Smith imagined this dynamic functioning in two ways. First, natural intimate friendship *in the private sphere* helps to generate sympathy and trust in society, facilitating the market economy without overriding it.[37] Second, friendship helps to establish and reinforce "strangership" in the public sphere, which is useful to the economy as follows: When intimate friendships emerge in the private sphere, people no longer see those with whom they do not do business as enemies or competitors but begin to see them as strangers with whom they can have disinterested transactions. Strangers in commercial society are not, as Allan Silver has argued, "charged with uncertain and menacing possibilities" but are "authentically indifferent co-citizens—the sort of indifference that enables all to make contracts with all."[38] Thus, private friendship is aided by the market and, in turn, aids the market's functioning.

These are serious challenges to any project that tries to get the public sphere to do more to facilitate, recognize, and promote private friendship. Such intervention in the private sphere risks unsettling the balance between private and public that allows our liberal society to function. There are, nevertheless, a few things one can say in response—though a fuller reckoning with this challenge will have to await chapter 7.

In the first place, many of these arguments merely serve to highlight again the very significance of friendship to our economy and society, to remind us how urgent it is to protect friendship and enable it to flourish. Even if we choose to try to keep friendship's core as a private relationship rather than one with public recognition that carries duties and privileges, good reason remains to give the legal system competence to recognize friendship—even if only to keep a hands-off policy toward it most of the time.

One must also, however, challenge the basic supposition that friendship is *purely* voluntary, that friendship lies exclusively in the private sphere of personal choice.[39] We sometimes stumble into friendships without quite intending that result: We make choices not to avoid someone, choices to indulge the habits of friendship without affirmatively seeking companionship, choices not to have dramatic break-ups— and these indirect choices lay upon us real obligations of friendship that we wouldn't choose in a purely abstract sense.[40] More, much of the sociological literature about friendship seeks to establish that friendship is relatively constrained by social structure and stratification. As one of the most famous sociologists of friendship writes: "[F]riendship is not just a voluntary or freely chosen relationship. It is one which is patterned and structured in a variety of ways by factors which can be recognised, at least to some degree, as genuinely...outside the individual's immediate control."[41] I explore the details of this stratification and the limitations imposed on friendship in the next two sections, but the central point is nevertheless important here: fetishizing the voluntariness of friendships is misguided because structural stratification—governed by rules of state and society—predetermines many of our friendships and their concomitant commitments. This is not to say that we ought to stop thinking about the voluntariness of our friendships as a source of their value, only that we cannot simply assume that the voluntariness in friendship is complete. As friends, we may see ourselves as free—but there is much predetermined work going into that perception.

Given this sociological reality, the idea that the law should stay out of our friendships is at least naïve. The law makes possible and structures friendships, whether it does so consciously or not. Accordingly, pretending that the law has nothing to do with our friendships is not a plausible posture. As cultural environments and their enabling conditions within the law change, so do friendship patterns and processes. And the forms of intimacy friendships display in any cultural context are no doubt affected by the law and legal categories.[42]

Moreover, consider the family (as I will do more extensively in chapter 3). It is something we tend to think of as a quintessentially private relation; indeed, it constitutes the very core of the private sphere. Yet one does not need elaborate citation to know that it is heavily regulated by the state. Despite the family inhabiting the private sphere, the law takes notice of the family, confers legal recognition on it (marriage is a legal union, after all), and erects a series of duties and privileges that flow from familial status. From this example, we might conclude that legal recognition hardly invades and demeans the private sphere if there is authentic affect there; it can often help protect it from infringement. As Robert Brain writes: "As in marriage, which is also superficially a practical and businesslike affair, the signing of a contract and the existence of sanctions do not preclude love."[43] Arthur Stinchcombe once summarized a similar objection to the one I have outlined here as follows: "The notion is that the more formal, impersonal, technical [and legal] social relations there are in a group, the less intimacy, charity, and mutual faith there is likely to be." His response: "There is...not a shred of evidence for this proposition, and a good deal of evidence against it."[44] I'll revisit some of the evidence in chapter 7—there is even more evidence to evaluate now than there was when Stinchcombe wrote—but the bottom line is the same: the weight of the evidence does not support the objection.

Finally, as for the theory of friendship and economy rooted in the thinkers of the Scottish Enlightenment, Robert Lane offers reasons to disagree. He forcefully argues that modern commercial (and capitalist) society, which is insensitive to the role of the friend, will not ultimately promote personal relations. Lane believes that the free market has a "destructive influence on friendship...through elevating instrumentalist and materialist values over social values, by eroding communities and neighborhoods, and by intermittently increasing the demand for overtime labor." He finds some evidence that "markets, themselves, are an inherent cause of social isolation" and that "the increased impersonality of shopping and the increased use of individually, as contrasted to socially, consumed goods have played modest roles in the loss of a therapeutic community of friends."[45] This decline leads to a culture full of depressed and anxious people, and market inefficiencies follow.

One way to fix the decline might be for our legal system to find some way to have our public sphere give friendship its due. This could lead to the repair of both friendship networks and the economic networks that can be sustained by them. Lane knows the agenda is a tall order: "[P]eople are chary of governmental intrusion in their most private lives." But he has a strategy that policy designers would do well to pursue: "[L]est governments become invasive and paternalistic, the authorities...have to focus on creating a 'scaffolding' within which individuals [can] find new opportunities for the companionship and...solidarity that [could] genuinely increase their sense of well-being."[46] This book aims to begin constructing that scaffolding to support the foundation that could let friendship flourish, leading to the well-being it generates. There is no doubt that we will have to be modest in what we can expect of the law—there will also be serious costs associated with supporting and sustaining friendship in certain areas within the law that could undermine the speculative benefits. But it is urgent that we gain some sensitivity to the problems associated with the lack of attention to friendship in public policy, so we don't have to harm it unnecessarily.

Gender Dynamics in Friendship

Some may be opposed to the state's subsidization or endorsement of friendship for the same reason some oppose the state's deference to and substantial protection of the family (a theme I will investigate more elaborately in the next chapter): It is a potentially patriarchal and male-dominated institution with a history of gender hierarchy. Many who have studied friendship patterns confirm that men and women have different kinds of friendships,[47] and the friendship literature in many disciplines tend to use male friendship as a model.[48] Jacques Derrida in his classic treatise on friendship suggests that the "ethico-politico-philosophical discourses on friendship" have excluded friendships between women and between men and women.[49] Not just high school students or movies like *When Harry Met Sally* question whether guys and girls can be friends: Serious researchers of the social phenomenon question the viability of cross-gender friendship and investigate which kinds of friendships serve as stronger social ties. It is a robust finding, in any event, that friends tend to be of the same gender.[50]

Perhaps it is hard, in practical terms, to see how the support of friendship would contribute to patriarchy. Surely in the current age, friendship is an equal-opportunity institution. However, there is at least one way that it is imaginable for the state's endorsement or protection of friendship to reinforce gender hierarchy: To the extent the friendship gives one access to information, knowledge, networks, and clubs, supporting friendship might contribute to helping men retain power over certain domains of society.

In the final analysis, I do not think this objection has power in condemning the enterprise of getting our law and policies to take seriously the support, facilitation, and maintenance of friendship. Although it undoubtedly remains true that many friendships occur within the same gender, that our cultural heritage probably displays more prominent examples of male-male friendship, and that male friendships are used to pass along "secret handshakes" to help other men maintain positions of power in our society, it is just as surely the case that the battle for gender equality can be fought without sacrificing the worthy project of developing a public policy sensitive to friendship generally – and gender dynamics within friendships specifically. Any contribution of friendship as an institution to patriarchy can be countered in other ways without needing to dispense with the protection of the institution itself.

There are a few other things to say on the matter. First, very recent evidence suggests that women are closing the gap and have as many nonkin confidants as men.[51] With "friendship equality," women can similarly help one another hold open the door of opportunity and claim friendship as their own. Second, if the law recognized the status of friend in the manner outlined in chapter 1, our public institutions could potentially contribute to the gender neutralization of friendship because nothing in the multifactor test developed last chapter is gender specific (though I concede that its emphasis on "equality" may give *same-sex* friendships an advantage, hardly a boon to men over women per se).[52] Finally, just as with the institutions of family and marriage, keeping the law out of the private sphere may do more to enable the replication of patterns of domination within the institution. Interposing the law within friendship could further help break the cycle of male domination by disfavoring secret-handshake male friendships. If a benefit for friendship is created, certain classes could be excluded from protection—and, more generally, in a desirable public friendship regime, patriarchal nepotism and cronyism would be disfavored. Once the law adopts a working conception of friendship, it can self-consciously exclude the sort of friendships that do little else than serve the gender hierarchy.

Obviously, marriage promotion, too, can contribute to gender inequality—and most people are complicit in a regime that privileges marriage in our society. As Laura Rosenbury argues, friendship recognition and promotion *instead of the recognition and promotion of marriage* could help undo the contribution marriage may make to gender inequality. That could, assuredly, help address the normative objection to my enterprise that emanates from the perspective of gender.[53] Still, I steer clear of embracing this strategy as a general matter (though I will embrace a more muted version of it in chapter 6, decentering marriage in certain models of contract) because it is not my intention here to pit friendship *against* marriage. I think we can do a lot for friendship even if we are going to continue to have marriage—as we are likely to for the foreseeable future. We can fight for both the reform of marriage, to make it less gendered, and for friendship side by side. If we collapse those two fights, there is a worry that we will not make as much progress as we might if we instead choose to promote friendship even while family continues to occupy its current place in our political and legal culture.

There is a different sort of challenge to my enterprise. One might suggest, as some have, that friendships in the gay community take on different characteristics from those in the heterosexual community.[54] Accordingly, it may seem plausible that my research agenda and the way I am carrying it out may disadvantage friendships within the gay community. That is certainly not my intention—and precisely by cordoning sex out of friendship, I am hopeful that sexual identity can be rendered irrelevant to qualification for friendship protection. Yet if the queer boundaries between friends and lovers are not distinct—or are less distinct than they are among straight people—there may be a substantial problem with separating sex and friendship. Since it is, of course, not my agenda to privilege heterosexuals in friendship promotion or regulation, if it turns out that gay and straight friends are quite different, I am open to refinement of the concept of the friend over time to be more sensitive to the way friendship presents itself in gay and straight communities alike.

To be frank, however, and as I suggested in chapter 1, I'm not sure it is correct that gays sexualize friendship in a manner that heterosexuals do not: both straights and gays can, do, and don't. We all—sexual orientation notwithstanding—sometimes "slip" and have sex with our friends, court "friends with benefits," feel there is a taboo against having sex with our friends, and become good friends with former lovers.[55] I'm not yet convinced that separating sex and friendship is a particularly "straight" thing to do—and that blurring these particular boundaries is a particularly "queer" thing to do. What's more, I worry that developing policy with the assumption that gays routinely have sex with their friends but heterosexuals do not could have detrimental and unintended consequences for the gay community. For now, I remain of the view that there is nothing "heterosexist" or "heteronormative" about promoting friendship in the way I suggest. I am all for developing a friendship policy that is sensitive to how gays and straights use the institution differentially. But as far as I am aware, nothing implicates my affirmative argument here that friendship should matter in the law (and, indeed, the queer community has been at the forefront of urging us to give more attention to it)—and that we ought to take friendship seriously, even if we have to cordon off sexual relationships to get the project off the ground.

Race, Class, and Friendship

It is not only that most friendships remain within one gender; a more general "homophily" pervades the social phenomenon. It is one of the most robust findings in the sociological friendship literature that "friends are normally of roughly the same age and class position. They also tend to share similar domestic circumstances[,] to have similar ethnic backgrounds and, where it is of social consequence, to belong to the same religion."[56] Accordingly, friends arguably further entrench differences of class, race, age, religion, and ethnicity. In addition, blacks and other minorities are more likely than whites to have very few close friends and confidants; thus, to the extent that the law gives any privileged status to friendship, it may be preferring whites. Although friends must be similar on some important dimensions to sustain the friendship (as chapter 1 makes clear), their socioeconomic and racial homophily might be of greater concern for a society committed to full-scale integration and desegregation.

The differences in friendship patterns in different socioeconomic classes are widely studied. Researchers study whether intimacy is the same among working-class and middle-class people; whether only the middle and upper classes have time for friends; whether "buddies" and "mates" are different forms of friendship existing predominantly among the working class; and whether kin plays a larger role in the lives of the working class. There is at least some consensus among those who study the sociology of friendship that the poor and the working class are not able to form and maintain the same kinds of friendships as the upper classes, at least in part because the members of these social classes have less time for leisure and fewer resources for the gift giving and entertaining that help sustain friendships. Moreover, certain friendship-forming activities—such as clubs, gyms, team sports, neighborhood watch groups, political party work, and parent-teacher associations—have lower participation rates within the disadvantaged classes.[57]

Is this an argument against the public recognition of friendship in our law? Consider the entire research agenda triggered by Mark Granovetter's theory of the strength of *weak* ties:[58] he highlights that most *bridging* relationships—relationships that will lead to new information and opportunities not already available within closed communities of close friends—are going to have to be weak rather than strong ties. Close friends, precisely because of the dynamics of homophily, will already have all the same information and opportunities at their disposal: close friendships create closed systems, but weak ties (generally something less than friendship) can more easily expand our exposure to new things. If this is right, should we be focusing on weak ties rather than strong ties in our public policy? Perhaps. If one is especially interested in dismantling our class-based and racial hierarchies, it is plausible for one to resist giving friendships any special privileges in the law on account of friendship's contribution to maintaining and reproducing such hierarchies and social stratifications.[59] As Granovetter urges when revisiting his thesis about weak ties, friendship's exclusive networks "may be one reason why poverty is self-perpetuating."[60] Accordingly, if one's core commitments include fighting poverty with every reasonable tool, perhaps one should be against friendship generally and against any public recognition of the friend.

Moreover, beyond redistributive concerns, even if all one wants is an efficient marketplace, homophily may cause market distortion.

Enlightenment thinkers, for example, attacked idealized notions of friendship because keeping transactions within an elite class tended to inhibit efficiency. As with the concern about gender, "old-boy" networks may contribute to the parceling of occupational and financial resources to those already in an "in-group" and the diverting of opportunities to friends when they could be more efficiently allocated to others.

Finally, the reality and robustness of homophily may expose friendship's roots in narcissism and self-love. Since we tend to enjoy friendship only with those similar to ourselves, one might think that friendship itself is an indulgent institution where we get to lavish ourselves with self-love, projected through a similar other. This idea is not unprecedented in discussions about friendship[61]—and, indeed, Aristotle himself found the relationship of friendship and self-love noteworthy. If friendship is really about self-love, perhaps it is not sensible to encourage narcissism through the legal promotion of the institution.

Ultimately, I do not think these objections are sufficient to deny legal protection to the status of the friend as a matter of first principle (even if these considerations will affect "street-level" design and counsel for particular implementations of the more general commitment to get public institutions to take friendship seriously). The reproduction of racial and class-based hierarchies is undoubtedly a serious matter. But most people—irrespective of race or class—see friendship as a central good, too important to be ignored completely on account of a potential contribution to hierarchy or inefficiency. If friendship is indispensable to our form of the good life, we ought to protect it and encourage it, even if we are also simultaneously committed to combating hierarchies and maintaining market efficiency. Indeed, to the extent that the law fails to recognize friendships and continues to keep friendships immune from the law, the law actually further entrenches stratification through friendship. If the law got involved in friendship and recognized its role in our lives, the law could actually do more to encourage cross-class and cross-race friendships through educational design and other modest "nudging." At the very least, it bears noting that ignoring friendship does nothing to stop the reproduction of hierarchies that friendships might accomplish. More, even if the encouragement of weak ties in public policy can accomplish a lot of good in educational policy design and urban city design, that hardly is an argument against also trying to reap the clear benefits of strong ties, its weaknesses notwithstanding.

Homophily is analogous to a similar finding in marriage patterns: "homogamy." Homogamy (marriage between individuals with similar social characteristics) is routine and robust. Indeed, marriage is *more* homogamous than friendship is homophilous.[62] As Peter Blau and his colleagues observe: "Disproportionate numbers of spouses are members of the same group or stratum. Catholics tend to marry Catholics; whites, whites; persons of Greek descent, other Greek-Americans; and members of the upper-middle class, others in the same class."[63] Yet we do not use homogamy as a reason to condemn or ignore marriage and deny it legal privileges and duties; accordingly, homophily should not be used as an excuse to ignore friendship. Of course, the law ought to do what it can within its regulation of intimacy (whether of friendship or of marriage) not to reproduce racial and class-based hierarchies. But these intimacies are too important to be marginalized in service of diminishing the potentially pernicious forms of balkanization that these "loves of similars" can engender and sustain.

It is also relevant to note that the hold of homophily in the context of friendship may not be ironclad. Although we are undoubtedly attracted to friends who are similar to us (as measured by some important register), it may be that homophily is merely a product of a failure of social mobility in times past. Indeed, as higher education becomes more accessible to people regardless of class or race, friendships may cease to display the characteristic of homophily. Higher education furnishes opportunities for class mixing and forms of friendship irrespective of class and race. There is also evidence that people now have more confidants of another race.[64]

Finally, it is not clear what to make of the connection between homophily and narcissism. Whether people's potential narcissism is any business of the state is certainly contestable. And narcissism is at least as troublesome within marriage and parenthood, where people also often seek to reproduce themselves. Still, there may be a way to turn the narcissism objection on its head: As John M. Cooper distills Aristotle's argument about friendship and self-love, friendship facilitates self-love and inspires confidence; friendship is not ultimately about narcissism but helps us love and value ourselves.[65] On this view, homophily contributes to one's own ability to value oneself and is perhaps yet another advantage friendship confers rather than a basis for objection to its legal protection.

Subversive Friendships

Friends' special obligations to one another may undermine duties and responsibilities that flow to co-citizens or to the state more generally— and this may be reason for the state not to confer on friends any special standing. The subversiveness of friendship—to state and to morality—is actually a recurring theme among those who think seriously about friendship (and is a counterpoint to Tony Kronman's belief, introduced earlier this chapter, that friendship will keep regimes stable, keeping revolutionaries at bay).

First, consider C. S. Lewis:

> It is…easy to see why Authority frowns on Friendship. Every real Friendship is a sort of secession, even a rebellion…unwelcome to top people….Each therefore is a pocket of potential resistance. Men who have real Friends are less easy to manage or "get at"; harder for good Authorities to correct or for bad Authorities to corrupt….Friendship (as the ancients saw) can be a school of virtue; but also (as they did not see) a school of vice….[T]he element of secession, of indifference or deafness (at least on some matters) to the voice of the outer world, is common to all Friendships….The danger is that this partial indifference or indifference to outside opinion, justified and necessary though it is, may lead to a wholesale indifference or deafness.[66]

The idea that the state might try to combat friendship rather than support it seems to follow from this portraiture.

Lewis's notion has been given a more explicitly political valence by other writers on friendship. For example, E. M. Forster famously said in the late 1930s, "[I]f I had to choose between betraying my country and betraying my friends, I hope I should have the guts to betray my country." Montaigne also suggests that the obligations to true friends could dissolve all other obligations to the city; he writes of a paradigmatic friendship that the parties were "friends more than citizens, friends more than friends or enemies of their country."[67] This theme is also prevalent in Allan Bloom's treatment of friendship: "[Friends] are more dedicated to each other than to the polity, the goals of which they may not share." Bloom continues: "The pair of friends is a community of its own, which may or may not be in accord with the body of citizens as a whole. Friendship helps to explain what is wanted in politics but also leads to an awareness that politics cannot arrive at that desired end."[68] States may reject friends because friends do not share their goals and because friends can expose the impoverished nature of mere civic bonds. More concretely, friendship can support and sustain underground organizations that focus themselves on antigovernment activities. And friends, precisely owing to their high level of trust, are candidates for the bonds that spur criminality.

Apart from challenges to the political establishment, friendship also poses potential ethical problems. For example, "Christian theology has long been concerned with the problem of 'preferential friendship'—friendship offered to one or some but not others or to all—in light of the Christian obligation to love all humanity."[69] Indeed, Søren Kierkegaard thought that friendship can too easily lead to despair and jealousy and consequently threaten our moral lives.[70] Others have suggested that friendship can lead to "aristocratic isolation,"[71] "elitism,"[72] or "corporate superiority"[73] that is incompatible with Christian commands to love all humankind.

Although the state and our laws may not need to concern themselves with the particulars of Christian ethics, a number of secular moralities are also challenged by friendship's partiality. Indeed, contemporary ethical theorists expend substantial energy trying to ascertain whether "associative duties"—special ethical duties that flow to friends and seem to arise from the friendship relation—are reconcilable with general ethical commands of equal treatment for all. As Niko Kolodny puts the problem, the worry about "differential treatment"—that I might give prior and better treatment to my friends rather than to strangers who may be in equal or greater need—stems from a concern about "distributional effects:" that our associates will gain more than they deserve.[74]

The "problem of friendship" obtains especially, it seems, in ethical systems that issue universalized commands, such as Kantianism,[75] utilitarianism, consequentialism, welfare liberalism, and other systems that demand strict forms of impartiality.[76] And even if friendship does not challenge the entirety of an ethical system (because philosophers have been able to construct successfully a system that allows us to prefer our friends), friendship can lead to what some philosophers call "moral danger": by lying for friends, covering for them, helping them escape capture by the authorities, or helping them violate substantial moral violations, actors implicate themselves in their friends' misdeeds.[77]

Such is the case for friendship's subversiveness from a variety of perspectives. Although I certainly cannot undertake extended engagement with all of these claims, none firmly makes the case against promoting the legal status of friend within the law.

In the first place, the authorities—threatened as they may feel by particular friendships—ultimately have the power of coercion. Any friendship that leads to true rebellion can be stopped in its tracks; cells that are brewing serious trouble can themselves be subverted through the mechanisms of the criminal law. More important, it is the hallmark of a free society that members are entitled to develop their capacities and identities with their intimates, so long as no harm comes to others. This may be at the core of our purported "freedom of association," with roots in the First Amendment of the U.S. Constitution.

Subversive to public authority as friends have the capacity to become, they remain central elements in a full and flourishing life (even if we occasionally tell little white lies and help cover for friends who lie to their parents, for example). Refusing friends any status in the law seems like a severe response to an attenuated possibility of threat to state and society. Friends who are friends principally to commit crimes and wreak havoc need not be respected in their status; a wholesale legal ban on recognizing friendship seems like an overinclusive and draconian response to a very low-level threat that can be managed with other techniques. Indeed, the prevalence of these kinds of friendships may help us with the second-generation questions about what sorts of legal protections for friends are appropriate. If the law discovers too many friends who are co-conspirators, that will have effects on how the law treats friends in certain areas of the criminal law. But it is no argument that the law should ignore friendship entirely.

Arguably, friendship is important to develop precisely because it furnishes freedom from the state. That "authorities" feel threatened by friendship may actually be a good argument for finding ways to make friendships flourish through public policy.[78] The citizens of the Soviet Union were said to treat friendships as precious in large measure because they helped develop personal integrity and dignity when the state otherwise could not.[79] A free society like ours should welcome the dignity that can be conferred through friendship, not fear it. As Lewis understood well: "[I]f our masters . . . ever succeed in producing a world where all are [c]ompanions and none are [f]riends, they will have removed certain dangers, [but] will also have taken from us what is almost our strongest safeguard against complete servitude."[80] Similarly, political theorist Jason Scorza argues, "[T]he proliferation of personal friendships . . . serves as an independent check on the possible civic corruption of the state as a whole."[81] Of course, there is always the danger that friends in high places will only help one another out—and nepotism and favoritism still need policing—but this is simply another area where friendship potentially needs to be regulated, not ignored.

To the extent that the bonds of friendship will expose civic bonds to be thin, it can hardly be the place of a free society to ban friendship to reinforce patriotism. Such bans are the sort of actions undertaken by totalitarian societies. The ties modern liberal states create and need for regime maintenance need not be especially strong or tight to perform their functions. No one seriously considers policies and laws that would aggressively subvert familial ties because of the potential role the family plays in exposing mere civic ties to be weak. Neither should we consider having the law undermine or ignore the importance of friendship to prop up the co-citizen relationship.

It does not seem especially pressing to worry about Christian ethics and whether our public policies and public laws are consistent with Christian commands (though I'm pretty sure my Christian friends have friends, too). And this is probably not the best place to try to tackle the interesting ethical challenges philosophers have developed. Still, as Peter Railton argues:

> [W]e must recognize that...friendships...are among the most important contributors to whatever it is that makes life worthwhile; any moral theory deserving serious consideration must itself give them serious consideration....If we were to find that adopting a particular morality led to irreconcilable conflict with central types of human well being...then this surely would give us good reason to doubt its claims.[82]

This general theme is consistent among the philosophers who see friendship as a challenge to this or that ethical theory: The partiality of friendship may be problematic if it bleeds into territories where we have a strong requirement of impartiality. It is likely the case that moral actors have no thoroughgoing requirement to be impartial all the time in every context. To be sure, one must be careful not to let the partiality of friendship overwhelm one's general duties, but the idea that the friend is not a morally relevant category itself may be seriously misguided. We can say with certainty that we should not allow a judge to prefer (or even sit in judgment over) her friends because there is, in the judicial context, an especially stringent duty of impartiality. Even a law committed to encouraging friendship could not admit or tolerate such forms of improper partiality. But the idea that I have to share my licorice with everyone impartially borders on the laughable; preferential treatment for my friends in licorice distribution is not morally problematic. Again here, a sophisticated regulation of friendship can help distinguish when friendship is problematic to the state's core and appropriate commitments, and when it is not.

In any case, for the most part, philosophers do not present friendship as a challenge to morality to argue in earnest that one ought not to have close friends to whom one is partial. Rather, through inquiring about friendship's relationship to morality, they aim to refine our understanding of what makes an ethical system plausible and to refine conceptions of ideal friendship. Accordingly, public policy designers should not utilize these potential "shortcomings" of friendship to argue against people having friends or against having the state support and facilitate those relationships that are central to people's lives. Indeed, ignoring friendships completely is a sure way to trigger high legal-compliance costs and to maintain a polity with little affective resonance among citizens.[83]

In any case, whatever moral challenges friendship presents, the state's commitment to equal regard could be manifested in multiple ways (and ways that still protect friendships). There is much more the state could be doing to bring about the equal regard of all citizens, and friendship's distributional effects must be seen as a relatively minor contribution to social and economic inequality. Families undoubtedly also challenge the moral command of equal regard, and they also potentially contribute to economic inequality through inheritance laws. Yet the law clearly confers priority on the family with respect to status—you can't fully disinherit a spouse, and when you die without a will, your assets go to your family, even if distant emotionally, not your friends who may have been the ones caring for you until the bitter end. Friends potentially deserve real and practical respect in the law.

Here ends my extended case for taking seriously the project of incorporating some consideration of friendship into the law. These arguments need much more refinement, but that refinement must await further development of what it might look like to have a legal system more sensitive to friendship and what it would really mean to have a public policy oriented toward promoting friendship. Still, I must first take a brief detour, in the next chapter, into the subject of the family before moving on. Many of the arguments and parries to objections I have offered here clearly rely on an analogy to the family, so I must discuss that analogy more explicitly before getting to the nuts and bolts of how to make my proposed project work.

CHAPTER 3

The Family Analogy

A<small>T MANY JUNCTURES</small> in my affirmative argument, I revert to an analogy with family: If families get special protections in the law, so should friends. If friends are becoming more like family now that the traditional family is on the decline, we should help friendship through our public policy. If legal regulation of families doesn't give us the heebie-jeebies, neither should we be especially concerned about the regulation of friendships. If we are okay with regulating the core of the private sphere of family, we should be similarly copacetic with the law's incursion into our friendship circles. If people's tendency to homogamy—coupling with those who are basically like themselves—isn't a reason to stay out of the regulation of marriages, people's tendency to homophily—befriending people who are basically like themselves—shouldn't be a reason to stay out of friendships. If family ties aren't subversive enough to make us leery of state promotion of the family, neither are friendship ties subversive enough to make us leery of state promotion of friendship. If we aren't going to disincentivize reproduction within families because having kids is potentially narcissistic, we shouldn't ignore friendships because they might display some narcissism, too.

But let me be clear: I feel extremely awkward about this constant invocation of the family analogy. More than awkward, I feel downright guilty. Although I have some confidence that the analogy *is* especially helpful in illuminating and dispelling some inappropriate criticism of my theses, the use of the analogy makes me feel like I am colluding with the way the law regulates family. No matter how many disclaimers and proclamations I make to distance myself from that law's regulation of familial intimacy because I think it is wrongheaded and unfair in so many different ways, the very fact that the regulation exists (and is on the whole not especially controversial in most people's minds) still forwards my arguments.

This short chapter continues my discussion of the family analogy. I shall briefly survey the odd ways the law regulates the private sphere of the family through the criminal law (the subject of my last book).[1] I will then briefly explain some things that are wrong with this apparatus. I hope to show, however, that many of the problems with the way we regulate family do not implicate my own theses about friendship. If anything, they reveal further reasons to embrace my proposal, better direction as to ways to incorporate friendship-protection within the law, and ring warnings of inappropriate ways to promote friendship with law and public policy.

Most basically, our regulation of family is essentially discriminatory and too patriarchal—and giving more legal and policy respect to friendship could mitigate some, though not all, of those problems. But that is a by-product or another reason for promoting friendship rather than the primary reason to engage in friendship-promotion. As I have been suggesting throughout, trying to use legal recognition of friendship primarily as a vehicle to undo the law's approach to family is a very steep climb, and there is a lot one can do by way of promoting friendship that doesn't require such radical reorganization of the state's orientation to the family.

THE FAMILY AND THE LAW

It is beyond cavil both that the family can provide many of the same benefits to state and society as friendship does—and that our public policy orientation is one that goes out of its way to accommodate and promote the family unit in multifarious ways. And despite the fact that friendship furnishes many of the same benefits as family does, the law is much less sensitive about its regulation of the friendship relation and is much less protective of friends. Similarly, the family creates some quite serious internal vulnerabilities, just as within friendships we must be vulnerable with one another. But the law is much more protective of family members who are disadvantaged because of those vulnerabilities and often ignores the vulnerabilities created by friendships.

One doesn't need to be a lawyer or public policy-maker to be aware of many ways the law regulates and promotes (a certain traditional conception of) the family. Marriage is, after all, a legally recognized union with obvious perquisites and responsibilities. Parenthood confers both discretion and obligations. In short, the family gets special privileges, and the members of families often have special duties of care to one another on account of the special vulnerabilities within families.

The criminal lawyer especially would be able to find a plethora of subsidies for families in the criminal justice system.[2] In fourteen states, for example, the state cannot prosecute family members for harboring fugitives. These states tend to exempt spouses, parents, children, grandparents, grandchildren, and siblings. Four other states mitigate liability for immediate family members without fully immunizing them. These laws are at once respectful of the reality that we might be incapable of saying "no" to a family member in need (so outlawing such help would fail to deter the conduct anyway) and that we might have mitigated culpability or blameworthiness when we are helping a family member. But it is all the same a privilege family members get that friends do not: if we harbor our friends, we are guilty of a crime, however hard it would be to say "no" to a best friend in need and however mitigated our blameworthiness for helping a friend.

Many states also make life easier on criminals whose victims remain within the family (surely an odd way to promote the family, allowing it to erode from within from violence and inattention). Parents sometimes get reduced liability for or immunity from assaulting their own children when they invoke a "parental discipline defense": a father in Hawaii was given the latitude to use a belt to hit his fourteen-year-old daughter's legs for ninety minutes and forcibly cut her hair—as a punishment for her inviting friends over.[3] Men can sometimes more easily avoid rape charges if their wives allege "marital rape," and spouses can more easily avoid murder charges if they kill a spouse in response to certain provocations. A man can get a mere eighteen-month sentence for shooting his wife in the head after catching her in bed with another man.[4] Domestic violence is notoriously difficult to prosecute. Sexual assaults within the family are often subject to certain sentencing loopholes in statutory regimes and fall outside the ambit of sex offender registration laws. Sexual misconduct within the family is often prosecuted as "incest" rather than assault or rape—a strategy that carries substantial discounts in penalties. These laws protect family members and recognize the private ordering of individuals within the family unit but are not extended to friends.

Families also get subsidized (unlike friends) when courts must decide whether a particular defendant is to be released on bail or remanded to custody to await trial. Family ties are explicitly considered during bail hearings to assess whether someone should get the benefit of returning home before being proven guilty of a crime. Federal law requires courts to consider family ties at the bail stage—and many states do as well. Unlike the protection of violence within the family, which seems hard to justify—and which we certainly wouldn't want extended to friends—the consideration of family ties in bail hearings might not be so pernicious: it proxies for the state's interest in not harming third parties unnecessarily (because those with family ties need to provide care and cannot if they fail to make bail) and proxies for the defendant's flight risk (under the plausible assumption that those with strong ties to the community are less likely to flee while out on bail). Of course, the care one provides to friends and one's friendship networks would seem just as important to the bail inquiry but do not receive as privileged a position. To be fair, stories abound about people who get out on bail to take care of ill family members, only to commit more crimes on bail.[5] So it isn't obvious that this would be an appropriate extension to promote friendship.

At trials, families often get the benefit of not having to testify against one another. Spouses are generally protected from testifying against one another—and in certain states, the privilege has been extended to a broader class of family members to include mothers, fathers, daughters, and sons. But best friends never get the benefit. As unseemly as getting best friends to testify against one another feels, prosecutors do it (or threaten to do it) all time.

Even at the sentencing phase, despite the fact that the federal Sentencing Guidelines discourage the consideration of family ties when issuing punishment, courts at both the state and federal level have given certain privileges and discounts to family members that nonfamily members do not receive. "Downward departures" from otherwise applicable sentences are not rare. For example, in the 1999 case *United States v. Johnson*,[6] two defendants were convicted of participating in the same crime; and the court found that they warranted the same offense level. But Johnson, the defendant with caretaking responsibility of four children, received a significant departure from the guidelines based on his family responsibilities: he didn't get any jail time, just home detention. His codefendant, Purvis, who had no children and who was also found to have played a more minor role in the scheme, was sentenced to more than two years in jail. Now that the Supreme Court has effectively found the federal Sentencing Guidelines merely advisory rather than binding on federal judges, there is an even higher likelihood that family circumstances will be considered by sentencing courts in lessening punishment. When was the last time you heard of anyone getting a sentencing discount to take care of their friends? But if we are going to let caregivers get a break, why limit caregivers to family members, who may be no better at caretaking than friends? As we now know, friends do more to ensure survival than kin.

Lest I leave you with the impression that the law categorically privileges family status in the criminal justice system, there are plenty of laws that would seem to do just the opposite: self-consciously punish or tax family membership by making life more difficult for family members within the criminal justice system.[7] But one could say that even these laws remain sensitive to and respectful of the family, in ways that the law does not remain sensitive to and respectful of friendship.

For example, family members who fail to prevent certain kinds of harm from befalling their counterparts can be found criminally guilty of "omissions liability," a type of liability that is only rarely imposed against nonfamily members. To be sure, only certain familial relationships tend to trigger omissions liability: parent-child and spouse-spouse are the standard examples. Courts can be sensitive to differing circumstances, but status does a lot more work; only very infrequently will paramours or unmarried couples qualify for omissions liability. Generally, spouses for a day will be expected to suffer the consequences of omissions liability, which can be quite severe, whereas friends for years usually will not. Perhaps this is not truly a way to "punish" the family as an institution, since it seems essentially calibrated to support it and protect internal vulnerabilities. All the same, however, this is one central way the law takes a stand on the level of care we expect of families, using the blunt instrument of the criminal law to make its point. This is no legalistic subtlety: mothers go to prison for leaving their children with unreliable boyfriends who turn out to beat the children.[8]

Another burden on the family in the criminal law is the set of laws known as "vicarious liability." We often hold parents responsible for the acts of their minor children under a theory of failing to supervise them properly. An Oregon statute is illustrative: It holds that parents are guilty of a crime if their children violate a curfew law or violate a truancy law.[9] No showing of the parent's knowledge of or contribution to the child's criminal wrongdoing is necessary for a finding of liability. This is extraordinary stuff and shows the criminal law going quite far out on a limb, because in these crimes, Oregon dispenses with what the criminal law usually takes as a most basic set of prerequisites for liability: *mens rea* (some bad intent) and an *actus reus* (a bad act). Again, the law taxes family members because it expects more from their behavior than it would from strangers to the children at issue.

Similarly, if you fail to pay your debts to the electric company or to your car leasing company, the law doesn't consider your failure to pay a crime. There may be collateral consequences and civil liabilities, but you won't be going to debtor's prison any time soon, most likely. Not so if you fail to pay child support. When it comes to certain debts within the family, the law considers them sacrosanct—and sensitivity to that fact has the law seeking to jail debtors in the child support context. If you owe more than $5,000, you are guilty of a federal crime.[10]

And twelve states also require you to provide material support for an indigent parent.[11] Talk about enforcing familial duties—and with the criminal law, no less! It is one thing to try to make sure families don't con Medicaid and convey assets away from parents and toward their children to get the state to pay for expensive health care—and thus to create *civil* liability requiring children to provide for indigent parents. But many states make it a *crime* not to pay for your parents if you can. At least Massachusetts adds a proviso (as some other states do) that absolves children who were not themselves supported materially by their own parents and mitigates responsibility to allow children in multiple-child households to pay only their fair share.[12] Our laws do not passively hope that people will do right by their families; our legal system enforces a particular vision of moral conduct within relational obligations.

There are, of course, many other areas within and outside the criminal justice system to which one can point to substantiate the claim that the state promotes and supports the family through the law and public institutions. It would take me too far afield to survey them all or to provide a comprehensive account of why we do what we do when we give special consideration to the family within our law. Ultimately, whatever one may think of many of these policies (some of which seem more offensive to fair play than others), one must take note that friendship obviously receives substantially less attention and respect in the law. Let me pause here, though, to explain how and why many of these methods of promoting the family are, in fact, troublesome, so that we may have a better idea of how to build a legal system that is attuned to the needs of intimate associations without running afoul of some basic principles required by a liberal justice system. After all, the idea that we ought to impose vicarious criminal liability for friends' misdeeds or that we ought to jail those who fail to pay their debts to friends seems very unappealing. The law surrounding the family shouldn't thoughtlessly be applied to friendship circles. Indeed, much of the state's orientation to regulating family behavior through the criminal law is severely misguided.

WHY PROMOTING FAMILIES IN LAW CAN BE UNFAIR AND UNWISE

Before going on the attack, however, it is worth saying something about why as a general matter it might make sense to give the family some attention in our public and private law.[13] There is something more than empty rhetoric and hypocrisy going on when we talk about "family values" in our public policy: the vast majority of us are also constituted and situated within families, and it is very hard to imagine a law seeming relevant if it simply ignores how the selves that make up the polity identify themselves.[14] We have loyalties, role responsibilities, and deep personal ties that may be morally prior to the state[15]— and the state would be foolish not to appreciate, respect, and facilitate our authentic expressions of ourselves. Indeed, the state risks irrelevance, illegitimacy, and broad-scale lack of compliance when it refuses to acknowledge people's special associative duties in some way.[16] The sources of persons' individuality are thus very important concerns of the state. Of course, this general argument could underwrite recognition of friendship in the law, too.

There is still another argument, familiar from chapter 2. Families provide all manner of services in preparing citizens for contributing to the stability and the flourishing of the state. The state cannot pay for all the services and education families render as part of their collective contributions to the daily lives of citizens. So the state subsidizes the work of the family to help it help the state. The tools we need to become good citizens capable of democratic self-government are costly to instill—and the family does it economically, reliably, and without much coercion.[17] Another good reason to have the state support families— and friends, of course, who perform many of these functions as well.

A third reason to furnish families with special privileges and attention in our public policy and law is also resonant with some of the arguments I have just offered for greater attention to friendship: an ethic of care could serve our society well.[18] As Deborah Stone has written in *The Nation*:

> Caring for each other is the most basic form of civic participation. We learn to care in families, and we enlarge our communities of concern as we mature. Caring is the essential democratic act, the prerequisite to voting, joining associations, attending meetings, holding office and all the other ways we sustain democracy. Care, the noun, requires families and workers who care, the verb. Caring, the activity, breeds caring, the attitude, and caring, the attitude, seeds caring, the politics.[19]

To be sure, it is necessary to be somewhat critical of the idea that care *only* happens in families, which is what the law projects when it focuses on care there and not elsewhere. Feminists and queer theorists rightly emphasize that an ethic of care can be sustained in a very gendered manner, ensnaring primarily women into the often undercompensated work involved in caregiving.[20] Our caregiving networks are much more nuanced than simple attention to the traditional family would suggest—and the care we want may come from wholly outside the family and from friends (where that care, as we saw in chapter 2, is actually more likely to lead to good outcomes).[21] But all the same, and with the relevant provisos in place, we can see how fealty to the ethic of care can be marshaled to support the state's subsidization of the family—and of friendship.

A final suggestion. Since most people order themselves in recognizable family units, it isn't altogether surprising that the law takes notice and uses convenient shorthands: because most people probably want to leave money to their families on death, why not save them some costs and create a default for where people's money should go when they die without a will? Or consider the rule that married couples share their property equally: It is a convenient shorthand that saves people time and money by selecting the rule most of us would probably select, forcing people who want different rules to make their preferences known. Thus, we recognize families in the law because the social cost of using that default is cheaper than alternatives.

So much for the general argument to support the family. This isn't exhaustive but gives a flavor for why those who seem to embrace "family values" in our political and legal life might have some actual arguments to support their creeds and mottos. And those arguments also tend to support an embrace of "friendship values" in the design of our public institutions and law.

But the general argument isn't enough: it takes much more to get from "we ought to protect families" to "we ought to protect families in these particular ways within our criminal justice system." Although there is a lot to say about this, let me focus on a few major ways the law goes astray in implementing the general argument for state support into specific benefits and burdens. These family-protective strategies will show, I hope, how *not* to translate the general argument I have been offering in favor of legal protection for friends into certain specific rules geared to provide friends with duties and privileges. And pointing out the ways the law goes astray will also reinforce still another set of reasons for getting the law into the business of growing more sensitive and protective of friendship: Taking these steps might help cleanse some of the more odious things the law does when it regulates families.

First of all, there is clearly an overinclusiveness problem in our use of family within the law. Using family status to privilege and punish members of our society will tend to award benefits and exact costs on members of our society whose family ties are not especially relevant in their lives. That we should have "omissions liability" to protect spouses who live across the country and who are clearly separated from one another, whether formally or not, seems an odd way to promote the family unit. That we should allow a spouse to prevent testimony from being offered by another spouse who wants to testify seems like a strange way to grant the family special respect within the criminal justice system.

At some level, overinclusiveness is the cost paid for the ease of administration of using family status. Even if we wanted to extend some of these benefits and costs to friends (and we may not want to for other reasons: support obligations for friends punished by the criminal law surely seems hard to stomach, even for the staunchest supporter of friendship obligations being made enforceable in the law), it would be hard to administer who would count as a friend. Still, it should be mentioned that "family" is quite variously defined for the benefits and burdens surveyed above. In the support context, parents and children have obligations where siblings do not, but in the evidentiary privileges context, only spouses get the benefit (with parent-child privileges applying only in a few states). Vicarious liability applies only to minor children, but the harboring fugitive exemption applies quite broadly within the family and can include grandparents. In sum, the law is doing a fairly inconsistent job in drawing the contours of the "family" for the purposes of various laws; ease of administration sacrifices a lot of precision and consistency.

So to say that we should limit the law's application to family and not friends because there are bright lines in the "family" is mistaken. The law usually needs to calibrate better who should be included and excluded more carefully anyway. If we decided that friends ultimately should qualify for some of the same treatment as "family," policy designers would actually have to get more explicit about which relationships really deserve protection and why. We always need clearer specification of who should count for special treatment—all families and all family members is overinclusive; capturing the right relationships to protect in a given policy space is paramount for good design.

More important, there is a serious underinclusiveness problem with the use of family status in the law (which greater sensitivity to friendship might also improve, though couldn't fully fix). When the law picks out of the world "families" for special treatment, it is making an expressive judgment about who matters in the eyes of the law. To the extent that there are other groups who see themselves as caregivers but do not get counted—whether same-sex couples, polyamorous unions, or groups of friends—the law discriminates against them. There is thus good reason to oppose the law's use of family status in many of the aforementioned benefits and burdens because they disrespect and treat unequally large swaths of the population that do not organize themselves into the traditional state-sanctioned family unit.

It is ultimately inadequate to use generalized arguments for the promotion of the family to counter the very real discrimination that is effected on the ground when using these categories. If we think we want "omission liabilities" between people in small circles of care where one party is made very vulnerable to another, same-sex couples and friends would seem to qualify. If many of the family ties burdens are really in our law to promote relationships of voluntary caregiving (as they seem to be), it makes little sense to discriminate against large numbers of people in relationships of voluntary caregiving that do not conform to a simplistic notion of the family that is increasingly outdated in modern society. If evidentiary privileges promote strong couple relationships, same-sex couples should get that protection, too.[22] Since the law has to do more than draw the line at family—some families (mafia families, say?) really shouldn't count, and we don't tend to see siblings as responsible for one another in quite the same way as parents are responsible for their children and each other—the failure to include relationships like gay unions and others is an act of discrimination that a liberal society cannot tolerate. We are using morally arbitrary categories when we simply adopt family promotion as a policy goal without more sensitive attention to what family is serving as a proxy for. Other values of equality and nondiscrimination really trump the simple talk of family values, and failing to treat like cases alike is a stain on any liberal legal system—a criminal justice system, especially, which exacts coercion from citizens most directly and violently.

Beyond the moral wrong of discrimination, there is also the failure to think about the actual systemic consequences of drawing the lines to exclude untraditional "families." Consider sentencing: if we want to give people discounts so that they are able to provide care in their networks of caregiving, why not allow those who can show they are actually caregivers—whether for friends or family, gay or straight—to benefit? Or omissions liability: If a gay couple is raising a child with a group of friends, why shouldn't that child get the benefit—and the couple the burden—of special duties to care for the child? Why is vicarious liability any less pressing for the gay guardians of children, assuming it is the vulnerable children whom we are most interested in protecting? Again, to say that using the heteronormative family is more easily administrable is just cover for unnecessary discrimination and inadequate policy design.

Seeing how badly our laws do in the regulation of the family helps support the argument for friendship-recognition even more, because it could supplement many modes of family protection in a somewhat more inclusive and honest-to-their-purpose ways. That recognition also cautions us not to implement an agenda of friendship-promotion in discriminatory ways that threaten the morality and efficacy of our legal system. However, since my definition of the friend is not calibrated to take in the entire gay rights agenda (in partial fear that I will lose both the war and the battle if I make friendship-promotion and friendship-recognition coextensive with and dependant on the dismantling of the discriminatory acts of state in denying gays all the benefits and burdens heterosexual families get), buying into my friendship agenda will not automatically solve these problems with the law's regulation of families. Those discriminatory laws will have to be changed, even if one is willing to take on the friendship-promotion agenda I offer in this book. But in the interim, the protection of friends should mitigate at least some of the harms of exclusion.

The failure of equal treatment that we can see as soon as we peer deeper into the way we promote family values in our legal system is really not a great surprise. That is because many of the benefits and burdens surveyed here arose in historical contexts in which they were used to perpetuate patriarchy, gender hierarchy, or domestic violence.[23] That historical legacy too often lives on in the design and implementation of family benefits and burdens in the legal system— and the legal system must be cleansed of these stains. Friendship-recognition could help here, too, though it won't solve all our problems.

With respect to evidentiary privileges, patriarchal origins are clear: women were not able to testify against their husbands because they lost their claim to any separate legal existence on entering into marriage. Women used to be held completely incompetent to testify, and some see the roots of the evidentiary privilege in the idea of "petit treason": People within a household should not treasonously be allowed to testify against the head of the household, a man.[24] The privilege is a vestige of a dominant legal theme that a man's home is his castle—and domestic privacy is paramount.[25]

Even in the modern age, where the privilege is equal opportunity, men get most of the benefit: they commit more crime, and they are more likely to be batterers in the home. The fugitive-harboring exemptions also have similar patriarchal origins—wives were supposed to do their "duty" and protect their husbands from the state—and patriarchal effects, because more men reap the benefits.[26] These are not decisive arguments (using bad history and gendered effects as reasons for getting rid of laws might condemn too many laws, some of which aren't malign), but they certainly help us grow somewhat uncomfortable with what we are doing without thinking it through very deeply.

The parental discipline defense has served to perpetuate child abuse and neglect. It emanates from the cultural assumption that the "natural bonds of affection" within families will protect our children.[27] But reality is less romantic: what we really have is a culture of relative indifference toward violence in the family, particularly against children.[28] And women largely pay the price when we do seek to clamp down on violence in the home: mothers get punished most harshly and are commonly held to a higher standard of care for children through the criminal law.[29]

These days, thankfully, we have been making some headway in undoing the patriarchal immunization of violence in the household. Police officers are expected to enforce the criminal law when they arrive at the scene of a domestic disturbance rather than protect the family from the entrance of law.[30] Admittedly, some scholars contest whether that role is desirable because the implementation of "no-drop" or "shall-arrest" policies—policies that try to bring the household and spaces of intimacy within the law's reach, where the home was once protected or immunized from law—might end up alienating victims from the criminal justice system; victims' preferences might not align with state consequences for domestic disturbances.[31] But whatever the result of those difficult debates, we have mostly moved beyond the malignant rhetoric that uses the excuse of protection of the "private sphere" to facilitate exploitation and domination within the home.

Not that we aren't still suffering from exploitation and domination in the private sphere. As a society, we tolerate way too much elder abuse, domestic violence in heterosexual and homosexual[32] relationships, marital rape,[33] and corporal punishment against children. But at least we are growing ever more conscious of these problems. A completely hands-off approach to the regulation of the family risks allowing too much immoral conduct there.

Our regulatory apparatus's prior experience with immunizing the home from the gaze of the state furnishes serious caution in how to think about interposing the law in our friendships: we shouldn't do it in any way that allows private violence, hierarchy, exploitation, or predation—and we shouldn't keep the law out by using the excuse of the privacy of the private sphere, because that strategy failed us and continues to fail us in the context of regulating the family.

WHAT WE CAN LEARN ABOUT REGULATING FRIENDSHIP FROM OUR REGULATION OF THE FAMILY

In sum, the very reality of our regulation of the family gives the lie to those who would tell us that we simply cannot have the law involved in the private sphere. Insisting on the firm distinction between the private and public—and suggesting that the law stay out of the private—is something old wives would be sure to remind us was mythology that only worked to their detriment; feminists today help us continue to see how malignant that trope can be.[34] Moreover, investigating *why* the law chooses to give the family a special place within its operations—the special services, support, ethic of care, vulnerability, and voluntary caregiving that goes on there—has also revealed that some of the same concerns that animate our law's sensitivity to regulating the family are clearly in play within friendship as well, suggesting that it should be brought within the ambit of at least some of the ways the law recognizes and remains respectful of the family.

Exploring *how* the law chooses to promote and protect the family unit, however, has helped us see that the general argument to support, sustain, recognize, and promote friendships still leaves us with the need for more specific attention to the actual areas of the law where we will apply these insights. "Promoting the family" seems okay some of the time (so long as we get more inclusive about who counts as a "family"), for example when we try to help reintegrate prisoners with their families on release from prison or when we use family ties as a way to rehabilitate prisoners. Yet it seems mostly wrong-headed when we immunize sexual predators by giving them sentencing discounts for committing "incest" rather than child rape. So, too, policy designers will have to be careful about how they go about the task of recognizing friends, remaining quite sensitive to the policy arena in which they find themselves.

Finally, whatever policy space they find themselves in, they will have to take care to avoid some of the most serious problems that the protection and recognition of the family has wrought. They will have to take care not to be overinclusive, not to be underinclusive, not to discriminate against people who do not organize themselves within the heteronormative family, and not to reinforce hierarchy and patriarchy in our regulation and promotion of intimacies. As it turns out, friendship protection and promotion can help mitigate (though not undo) some of these problems with the regulation of the family: attention to friendship, giving it parity or priority in many policy areas, can undermine discriminatory and patriarchal dimensions of our regulation of family as currently organized. Still, I very much doubt we are likely to see family status become irrelevant in the law anytime soon, and much more will be needed beyond a prioritization of friendship to undo all the ways we discriminate against gays and those who perform untraditional scripts in the organization of their private lives, whether by living as a single or in a group. But with the addition of sophisticated approaches to friendship recognition, we might just cut some of the sting associated with many of our more discriminatory policies that use the traditional family as a proxy and as an ideal.

To be sure, friendship, too, can be gendered, exploitative, collusive, and heteronormative in certain manifestations. But if we have learned well from the family analogy, we won't be so squeamish about disturbing the privacy of friendships when untoward things happen there. If there is anything to be learned from the family analogy, it is, perhaps, that the private isn't private—and it's a good thing, too. To support institutions central to our well-being and to root out discrimination, patriarchy, heteronormativity, and exploitation of vulnerability sometimes requires the scaffolding and the arm of the law.

In the next three chapters, I'll provide a taste of what such a regime could look like, moving a bit away from the controversial issues surrounding the family, where we are likely to see contestation for some time. The truth is that I want to see our family benefits and burdens liberalized and made more friendly to gays, alternative lifestyles, and singles because it is the right thing to do, quite independently of my friendship agenda. And, as I've repeatedly suggested in earlier chapters, using the friendship agenda primarily and principally as a way of opening up the law's approach to family risks stalling the friendship agenda before it gets off the ground. It also might distract attention from the real reasons we should liberalize our approach to the family to include alternative circles of affection: we should do so because it coheres with our values of equality and liberty, not because family is a subset of friendship, which is the real value to protect. Friendship is also a value to protect besides—and the family analogy helps us see both why and how we should proceed.

CHAPTER 4

How Can the Law Matter?

Friendship and Our Legal Institutions

N<small>O ONE SHOULD</small> be left with the impression that the law actually completely ignores friendships. Even if one is resistant to the general idea that friendships should matter in the law, one has to acknowledge that friendship presents itself as relevant all the time, as I hope to show more extensively in the remainder of this book. The federal Bureau of Prisons gives most criminals a right to see their "friends" when they are incarcerated.[1] Sentencing guidelines often contain enhancements for abusing a position of trust like friendship (consider how many people thought Bernie Madoff's Ponzi scheme was particularly blameworthy because of the way he preyed on friendships to keep the fraud alive). And sometimes friendship, though not as often as family, might be used as a mitigating factor if it is part of the motive for a crime (consider how we sometimes have sympathy for and think less blameworthy those who commit crimes to save their friends).

Corporate law also has a law of friendship of sorts. In corporate law, director "independence"—central to all sorts of prerogatives available to management on corporate boards—can be affected by the friendships in which directors are engaged. If directors are friends with each other or friends with officers, it can threaten the board's ability to act independently—and courts are given the task of policing levels of friendships within corporations. The recent kerfuffle with the litigation surrounding Martha Stewart's trading of ImClone stock is illustrative: Shareholders, in trying to sue Martha Stewart Living

Omnimedia for Martha Stewart's behavior as CEO, wanted to take a shortcut in the litigation process and avoid the "presuit demand" phase, where aspiring derivative lawsuit plaintiffs ask the board to take on the case on behalf of the corporation. The shareholders argued that it would be "futile" for them to bother with a demand because of the deep friendships between Martha Stewart and several members of the board of Martha Stewart Living Omnimedia. Although the court ultimately found the directors to be independent enough of Stewart to dismiss the shareholder lawsuit, they could only make this finding by assessing the nature of the friendship between Stewart and her directors; courts were passing on the qualities of the friendships and developing a common law of friendship, of sorts.[2]

So it is undeniable that the law is sometimes willing to consider friendship an important form of intimacy that deserves attention—and that courts sometimes must consider just how some friendships should be regulated by law and how others shouldn't. But the largely latent, underemphasized, and undertheorized interactions between law and friendship need to be more carefully considered, made more salient, and made more widely known. The fact that the latent attention to friendship exists at all, though, helps reveal that an agenda of friendship-sensitivity may actually be consistent with our current legal regime.

A PRO-FRIENDSHIP POLICY AGENDA

But if you have made it this far with me, you probably know that I think we could—and should—be doing much more for friendship. There are many important ways we could more comprehensively seek to promote friendship through our public policies. Consider a few at the legislative level: We could, for example, provide for some tax deductions for "friendship expenditures." Our tax law is solicitous of marriage, home ownership, and business expenses, so why shouldn't our friendship activities be tax deductible, at least in part? To be sure, a deduction could be too easy to get if it were available for all sorts of expenditures like nachos and beer on Super Bowl Sunday. But such deductions could be limited to expenses in connection with providing care—driving a friend to and from a colonoscopy, serving as a custodian during a serious illness, and the like—and could be subject to a cap. The tax code does a lot for charities and small businesses by allowing people to deduct some of their contributions to these enterprises; it can help friends, too, by giving similar respect to these important relationships in people's lives. Notice that this doesn't require enmesh-ing the law into friendships in any direct way: it just provides some "scaffolding" to incentivize people to develop and deepen their friendships.

So, too, could we—as some states have done—open up health care decision-making opportunities for friends. Again, this method of friendship-promotion doesn't require regulating conduct within friendship directly. We could establish a default rule to make sure doc-tors ask friends rather than only kin what a patient might have wanted if and when the patient becomes unable to make medical decisions. We often tell our friends more than we tell our families; they can know us better and be more up-to-date on our thinking about certain sensitive medical and end-of-life ethical matters.

We allow spouses to sue wrongdoers for loss of society and com-panionship when a defendant wrongfully kills a spouse. Why shouldn't we enable friends to collect for loss of companionship as well?[3] Our friends are often our most important companions, whether or not we have spouses and close family. Why, then, exclude someone from recovery who suffers severe loss at the wrongful death of a friend? Again here, we would need some cap: too many people grabbing at the pockets of defendants could become unmanageable. So we'd need some legislatively defined class of friends who would count for these types of actions. But people who choose not to marry and create tradi-tional families shouldn't become targets of defendants, who might have to pay less for wrongfully killing unmarried people or people without "idealized" families that the law recognizes. In this sense, friends could serve a deterrent effect, if only they had standing to complain.[4]

We could also establish a "Friends Medical Leave Act" to allow friends to leave work to take care of one another during sickness.[5] It seems odd, arbitrary, and discriminatory that one cannot take off from work to care for one's best friend but can take time off to care for a dis-affected family member. Even if we'd have to require an administrative hearing to determine that it is really a close friend for whom someone wants to provide care (since the law probably uses "family" for administrative ease), that would still be better than what we have now. Here, I would certainly hope that we would not force gays into the "friend" box to get this benefit; we should just liberalize our definition of the "family" for the purposes of these laws to make sure we are properly inclusive and nondiscriminatory.

Or consider property regimes. We often allow family members to benefit from rent control laws: they get benefits as owners and as tenants. Owners can vacate units to allow family to live in otherwise price-controlled units—and tenants can give some of their family members the benefits of their lower rents relative to the market by assigning leases or letting surviving spouses remain in controlled units. It would seem that we could similarly afford this benefit to friends. Of course, we would want to make sure that people aren't using "friends" who are not really friends to undermine the rent control system (assuming it is a rent control system we want—and here I'm merely assuming that acceptable democratic processes created that system)— but we have more respectful ways of doing that than the simple denial of such privileges to friends.[6]

It is, moreover, interesting to consider how we could design our cities and towns with friendship in mind. We might use well-placed public spaces to encourage people to gather and converse, and we might incentivize foot traffic rather than car traffic to encourage people to interact face to face, something that seems important within friendships. Suburban sprawl might also be targeted for reform to help promote friendship. When we think about integrating schools and communities to include more racial or class diversity, we should do so with sensitivity to enabling friends to remain together (if they choose) rather than enforcing their "desegregation" thoughtlessly. Leaving people in "better" aesthetic surroundings but without their friendly networks of support might not be the best recipe for development (unless friends seem to be holding some people back with their excessive demands).[7] We might even take a cue from the city of Port Phillip in Australia, which posts signs warning people of their entering a "10 smiles per hour zone" to encourage people to smile at one another, ostensibly creating a safer environment for friendship formation. At least more people are smiling at each other there.[8]

To be sure, these last ideas seem aimed more at reinforcing *civility* or *weak ties* than at promoting friendship per se—but there is at least a loose connection between them, and it is useful to consider very cheap ways to achieve our policy ends. More, as we saw in chapter 2, weak ties furnish their own quite impressive benefits.[9] In these lean times, trying to squeeze limited budgets for friendship-promotion might be a waste of time. But small interventions and a little sensitivity might go a long way. There are relatively unobtrusive ways we could design our public policies to give more respect and help to the very important institution of friendship. And these ways really don't implicate the worry of those who don't want judges and legislatures meddling in friendships.

FRIENDSHIP CEREMONIES AND REGISTRIES?

To be sure, as I suggested in chapter 1, we could establish legal rituals to solidify friendships just as we solemnize the status of marriage and citizenship—our other associative duties—through public oaths and legal documents. Or we could maintain a registry of real friends—think Facebook for your actual friends!—that would allow you to clearly indicate to others and to the state that this small class of people deserve special treatment in any legal matters that relate to you. Indeed, some scholars have considered the ritualization and institutionalization of friendship in this manner and think such ceremonies and registries could have a potentially salutary effect on the law's difficult task of assessing who counts as a friend, an inquiry that presents itself as necessary both under our current laws from time to time and under a more friend-sensitive regime.[10]

Consider the German custom of *Brüderschaft trinken* (literally, "to drink brotherhood"), in which two male friends decide to use a more informal mode of addressing each other, going from the *Sie-Sie* or the *Sie-Du* relationship (formal) to the *Du-Du* (informal). They self-consciously share a drink while bringing each other close (often, interlocking arms) to signify the change in the mode of address. Such a ceremony could help to signal to the law that parties, in fact, consider one another friends. Although this tradition was once reserved for men, the contemporary instantiation of the practice seems to include women as well. And one German lawyer has suggested that this ceremony can have some "evidentiary importance in labor law."[11]

David Chambers has proposed that certain kinds of friends be allowed to register with the government as "designated friends." Here is how he describes his proposal:

> [C]ouples would come to a government office and register as "designated friends." The form for registering would tell them that by doing so they are accepting a set of mutual responsibilities. They are empowered to make and undertake the obligation to make financial and medical decisions on behalf of the other in case the other becomes incapacitated; they are entitled to family leave, or the same terms as married persons to take care of the other if the other becomes seriously ill; they are entitled to the same testimonial privileges as spouses in civil and criminal cases if they enter the designated friend relationship at least two years prior to the event giving rise to the case; if the other dies without a will, they are entitled to some specified modest share of his

or her estate; and, finally, if they are government employees, they will be subject to anti-nepotism rules that apply to employees who are married to each other.[12]

This idea draws from "reciprocal-beneficiary" statutes in effect in Hawaii and Vermont, which permit variants of this idea.[13]

Although creating more ceremony surrounding friendship might not be a terrible thing—and could have some benefits for the law—my basic trouble with this strategy is that designated friends do not necessarily designate the organic social relationship of friendship. Forcing friends to appeal to the state in advance to receive legal recognition seems to miss the point of protecting friendship as a social institution: the law is supposed to grow sensitive to and promote friendship as a social relation, not convert it into a purely legal relation. The law should come to friends, not force friends to sign up with the state.

FRIENDSHIP AND LAWYERING

So how can this work? I have already suggested a few ways to make friendship matter more in our public policy. Many of these proposals for reform, however, would likely require mobilization and legislation. Common law lawyers, by contrast, can also help shape the fabric of the law to focus attention on friendship-promotion without the same effort at broad-scale mobilization. There is nothing exhaustive about the domains of the law investigated in the remainder of this chapter; they are merely meant to provoke discussion and lay a foundation for further work in developing a law of friendship. To the extent that they can be organized thematically, they divide into two classes of ways the law could take account of friendship: first, by exacting special duties on friends (the duties of rescue, disclosure and fair dealing, and confidentiality), and second, by furnishing friends with certain privileges (the privileges of informality, care-giving, privacy, and vindicating rights). What follows is a mostly a survey of ways friendship could be made to matter more in the law. I reserve for next chapter a more sustained case study that gets into the nitty-gritty of the law and the particular policy space that recommends having the law meddle in friendship duties.

But first a word of caution as I introduce ways to get law on the friendship scene: we need not see the law solely as a tool to repair broken relationships. Many of the sorts of cases I treat here are, indeed, cases of friendship breakdown and cases where friends sue friends. And perhaps the legal regimes of contracts, torts, and property—when looked at as bodies of law to address particularized disputes between contesting parties—seem like tools to repair broken relationships. But when viewed through these regimes' capacity to incentivize behavior in the future, there is much the law can do to support and facilitate relationships prospectively through the adjudication and administration of cases. We can and should protect the invocation of friendship and the trust it entails so that people who try to trade or prey on the trope in the future will be deterred.

Moreover, as Aristotle understood, dissolved friendships still ought to get some special treatment on account of friendship past.[14] It is natural to think that the category of "ex-friend" also carries with it a status worthy of recognition and may be relevant to ascertaining appropriate legal remedies as well. The fact that many friendships dwindle is well known, and it is not necessarily the symptom of a flawed friendship. People move away, get married, have kids, get rich, become poor, change jobs, change interests—and all of these circumstantial changes can affect their friendship networks. It is quite obviously ex-friends who find themselves in court more often than people engaged in a friendship while they are litigating against one another (though even *that* is not unheard of). Having once been friends can aggravate disputes and enhance feelings of betrayal when the law enters the dispute. These facts help us see that the law's approach to friendship needs not only to embrace sensitivity about litigants and actors within the courts but also to attend to furnishing the right incentives for friends in the future.

The Duties of Friendship?

The Duty to Rescue

As everyone who has gone to law school in this country knows, Americans do not have a general duty to rescue strangers. This fact has been a matter of debate among scholars and legislators, some of whom reject the rule and aim to create a more general duty of helping one's fellow citizens avoid trouble. To be sure, there are a number of exceptions to the rule, most of which draw on some *status* of one of the parties: A special duty tends to emanate from a special relationship.[15] Special relationships can include that of employer-employee, school-student, and business-customer, but the list is open-ended.[16] It is plausible to imagine that a duty to rescue friends could and should be recognized by the law. This may, of course, be one of the areas where legal protection is least needed—after all, it is a pitiful friend who would not undertake a rescue. But for just that reason there would be little cost to recognizing such a duty in law.

The case most on point—and one where such a duty was arguably already recognized—is *Farwell v. Keaton*.[17] In this famous case, a defendant watched his friend undergo a beating, resulting in substantial head injuries. He then drove his friend around for a few hours and noticed that the friend passed out in the back of his car. Ultimately, the defendant parked the car in the driveway of his friend's grandparents' house and left him there after failing to awaken him. The friend died as a result of both his injuries and failing to get medical attention on time. The dead friend's estate sued for wrongful death, and the court upheld a jury verdict against the defendant.

The court made it clear that a variety of factors were relevant in reaching its conclusion and did not make explicit that its judgment was based on the duties of friendship in particular (although the friendship is mentioned more than once). The parties were, the court says, "companions" on a "social venture." Indeed, the court aims to reason by analogy and fit the social relationship between the parties into an already-recognized "special relationship" exception.

Other courts, however, such as the one in *Webstad v. Stortini*,[18] limit the *Farwell* case to its facts, highlighting both the fact that the plaintiff was an invitee in the defendant's car (because the status of invitee rather than friend tends to trigger special duties of rescue on hosts) and the fact that the defendant's leaving his friend in his car disabled the friend from getting the help he otherwise might have gotten elsewhere (another traditional factor in duty-to-rescue cases that tends to trigger liability).

One could recommend that more courts adopt the approach of the *Farwell* court and be clear that people have a duty to rescue their close friends. Perhaps we do not need the law to tell us to save our friends. But why shouldn't the law confirm what we already know to be true? It is perfectly sensible for the law to reinforce people's well-accepted duties; it contributes to the law's affective resonance (our feeling that the law is, after all, our own, which proceeds from our collective sense of justice) and may have broader effects in facilitating compliance with the law's commands more generally.

To be fair, some more careful thinking and evidence would be needed before anyone should feel comfortable signing on to this specific friendship duty. In particular, we really would want to know whether people would stop hanging out with their friends and involving themselves in co-ventures (or whether parents would try to stop their children from friendship activities, for it is often parents of minors who end up litigating some of these issues) before adopting this proposal, so as to avoid such liabilities. It could be counterproductive to try to help friendship by creating duties that disincentivize people from engaging in it. But there is good reason to think this concern is over-blown: we don't really think the duty to save your spouse or child is a major disincentive to getting married or having kids. It is just one of the costs of an activity or relationship with pretty high payoffs.

In some sense, we've already learned this lesson in another area of the law. Most states once had "guest statutes" that disabled casual guests in automobiles from suing their hosts, if the host should happen to get into an accident. Guests in the car could sue if the driver was grossly negligent, wanton, or willful—but for your average accident, states didn't want friends suing friends (or family members suing family members) over bad driving that led to injuries. Some states claimed they did not like the guest to be "ungrateful" for the free ride and did not want the host driver to be punished for doing someone a favor. There was a concern that if we forced drivers to shoulder liability for driving friends, we'd disincentivize friends driving around together.

There were other policy considerations, too. Some states seemed primarily concerned about collusion against insurance companies that would be paying for more injured parties: friends might collude to maximize multiple claims against insurers. (And it is no surprise, then, that insurance companies funding state legislators' campaigns were more than happy to have these laws on the books, which limited their liability.) Still others were worried about insurance coverage for the people in the other car that was not occupied by a group of friends; and they didn't want the limited pool of money to go to the victims in only one driver's car.

Nevertheless, only three states (Alabama, Indiana, and Nevada) retain any form of guest statute today, and only one—Alabama's—would apply it to friends sharing a car ride.[19] Notwithstanding the concern about the disincentive to drive our friends around these days in forty-nine states, it seems we do it plenty. Indeed, even conceptually, something about the idea of the guest statute is at odds with common sense: there would seem to be a plausible case that we ought to be driving *more* carefully when our friends are in the car rather than being given license to drive without the basic duty of care we'd have to those who are not our social guests in our cars. That we have abandoned the idea of guest statutes quite broadly isn't pure evidence for my case here, of course, since so many other policy considerations are in play. But it does suggest that potential worries about friends colluding or disincentivizing friendship did not win the day in this domain (anywhere but Alabama) and probably should not win the day in the duty-to-rescue context either.[20]

The idea of a "duty to rescue" also probably implicates "social host" laws that impose liability (sometimes civil, sometimes criminal, sometimes both, depending on jurisdiction) on those who serve alcohol to others, when the recipient of that alcohol goes on to injure third parties. The literature and cases surrounding this form of liability very much consider questions of friendship. Although the laws are often designed quite generally to apply to all of a host's intoxicated guests, judges and lawmakers are quite focused on the application in friendship contexts: Is it reasonable to expect hosts to supervise their friends' alcohol consumption? Should we have a society where hosts may be chilled from having parties to develop their friendships because of extra potential liability that might befall them? Can we expect friends to take a paternalistic posture with their counterparts, lecturing them instead of refilling their tumblers?

I don't know all the answers to these hard questions of social policy. But they are good ones to be asking. Learning more about how friendship operates without making prior assumptions about how law and friendship interact would seem to be good for the judges who must consider or apply these laws. The laws are considered in a whole range of cases (to social hosts of friends, family, business associates, acquaintances), but the application of those laws to social hosts of friends in particular both has gravitational pull on how courts think about the other classes of cases and is important in its own right for my project here.[21]

Ultimately, my instincts are that a bit of civil liability in the friendship context could be a good thing, because it could help reinforce our collective sense of responsibility for our friends, their well-being, and their safety. Reasonable people could disagree, especially since much else is in play in the design of these laws, which routinely focus on our drunk driving problems, especially among minors. In any case, I wouldn't expect a friend to do more than put forth a reasonable effort to disable his counterpart from drinking too heavily and harming others as a consequence. If we aren't our brothers' keepers, we can't be our friends' keepers either! But we can try to control them when we know or reasonably can expect that they are prone to hurt someone else.[22] And I would think common sense laypeople who sit in judgment on these cases—jurors—could be trusted to dole out justice in the circumstances under which these issues arise.

The courts that allow these cases to go forward to judgment are very conscious of competing public policy concerns and the demands of fairness and justice. Suggesting a rule that allows a cause of action predicated on a failure to supervise a friend's irresponsible behavior that causes needless injuries to others seems to be a modest way to reinforce what we owe our friends and what we owe the world with respect to taking care of our friends. Most courts that impose the duty are principally focused on deterring drunk driving and providing ample compensation for victims of negligence. But the duty can also be used to reinforce the institution of friendship and its commands. Rather than a free-for-all where we permit ourselves to enjoy irresponsible drinking and driving so as to promote a private space of friendship, we might actually think friendship demands some responsibility among friends.[23]

The Duty to Disclose and Deal Fairly

In the average fraud case, courts do not generally impose a duty to disclose specific facts leading up to a transaction or a duty to deal fairly on anyone. But there is an exception to this general principle for people known as legal fiduciaries or those in relationships of trust or confidence.[24] Although some courts would never treat friendship as capable of triggering such duties, other courts take a different approach. In this area—the focus of chapter 5—courts sometimes find themselves entangled in friendships and could, perhaps, benefit from a more systematic approach to them. But the recommendation here is consistent with the general theme of this book: friendship can and should matter in assessing whether special duties to disclose or deal fairly should be imposed.

Wilson v. Zorb[25] is the classic treatment of friendship and fraud in which friendship is held not to trigger special duties. The factual background is as follows: The plaintiff and defendant, both doctors, "had been close friends for many years, intimately associated in social activities." They spent much time together (with their wives) and stayed at each other's homes often. Then the defendant negligently shot the plaintiff. After several weeks in the hospital, the plaintiff recovered in the defendant's home over a number of months. The defendant gave the plaintiff a payment as further compensation and got the plaintiff to sign a release of all claims stemming from the shooting. Ultimately, the plaintiff sued because he claimed he was induced to sign the release on the basis of false assertions that the defendant made about his financial situation. At issue in the case was whether the friendship constituted a special relationship, which would have triggered special disclosure duties from the defendant to the plaintiff. Here is what the court had to say:

> Warm friendship, confidence and an affectionate regard for each other were mutual with the parties, and yet each was self-sufficient, competent and independent. At times each attended and prescribed for the other's patients and they consulted with each other in professional matters. Such relationships happily are common, but they are not confidential relationships in a legal sense. It takes something more than friendship or confidence in the professional skill and in the integrity and truthfulness of another to establish a fiduciary relationship.[26]

This approach was endorsed more recently in *Kudokas v. Balkus*,[27] a fraud case in which the court refused to find a duty to disclose despite a lifelong friendship between the buyer and seller of a motel. The court did not deny that close ties of friendship might be found within certain "confidential relationships" in which a duty to disclose would be required of a seller. But the court was careful to indicate that friendships do not *create* confidential or fiduciary relationships that trigger duties to disclose and deal fairly.

A similar conclusion was reached in *Vargas v. Esquire, Inc.*[28] The plaintiff, a foreign artist, had entered into an employment contract with the defendant corporation, which published magazines and calendars. The president of the corporation was a close personal friend of the plaintiff and his wife, and the plaintiff claimed not to have been aware of the compensation terms in the agreement and that his friend had unfairly and fraudulently induced him to sign the contract. At issue was whether the friendship between the parties triggered any special duties on the part of the defendant. The court concluded that it did not. In particular, there was no liability put on the defendant, notwithstanding the trust between the two men.

Not all courts, however, have reached such conclusions—and chapter 5 is devoted more particularly to mining this area of the law for how we might make friendship matter. Ultimately, many courts have held that friendship may be a relevant factor in establishing a party's right to rely on certain representations.[29] And an underlying friendship between contracting parties may excuse a party from carefully investigating form contracts for exculpatory clauses, relying on the goodwill of a friendship.[30] These are all ways that courts have—albeit inconsistently—enabled friendship to matter in the law and, indeed, promoted friendship by enforcing its special duties of disclosure and fair dealing. Before recoiling in horror about the law interposing itself in friendship, we should ask ourselves whether it doesn't, after all, make good sense to modestly encourage friends to treat one another with some specialized degree of care when they find themselves transacting with one another.

The case of *Cox v. Schnerr*[31] is especially instructive on the friend's duty to deal fairly. The plaintiff commenced an action to clarify whether he in fact had title to a property purportedly transferred from the defendant. The defendant claimed that the transfer was invalid, owing to the plaintiff's "undue influence" over the transferor—the defendant's deceased wife—a trusted friend and advisor of the plaintiff. After noting that the burden of proving fraud usually rests with the one asserting it, the court held that the burden should shift to the one resisting the claim of fraud to prove she "exhibited the *uberrima fides* [utmost good faith] which removes all doubt respecting the fairness of the contract."[32] The court made clear that this burden-shifting regime should apply not only to parties whose relationships are traditionally considered to be confidential, such as physicians, attorneys, and clergymen, but also to those parties "who by the very force of their...relationship are presumed to be in the class of persons bound to act with the utmost good faith."[33] The friends in this case were held to be included in this class, and the transfer was held invalid.

A duty to deal fairly might be discharged through heightened punitive damages for friends who wrong one another. Take the case of *TVT Records v. Island Def Jam Music Group*.[34] The fact that members of the litigating parties were friends influenced the court's determination about whether an unusually high punitive damage award was appropriate. The jury awarded the plaintiff approximately $132 million in compensatory and punitive damages in a dispute involving breach of contract, tortious interference with contractual relations, fraud, and willful copyright infringement. The defendant—a division of the world's largest record company, Universal Music Group Recordings—objected to the award, arguing that its conduct was not sufficiently reprehensible to sustain the punitive damage award. In adjudicating the defendant's motion (and ultimately granting it), the court noted that social relationships and friendship underlying the transaction may counsel for the award and can help assess the reprehensibility of the conduct. In particular, the court found it relevant that TVT's principal owner and CEO considered a certain high-ranking official at Universal "one of his closest friends in the industry" and "a personal mentor and confidant." Although this consideration was one of many factors, it highlights how friendship may, after all, trigger special duties of fair dealing that are enforceable through punitive damage levels.[35]

Finally, one also might imagine that an abuse of a friendship might figure into a criminal sentence by subjecting a defendant to an enhancement for an "abuse of a position of trust," as I mentioned at the beginning of this chapter.[36] This is another way to reinforce a duty to deal fairly—but through the criminal law. The central idea here is that an enhancement may be appropriate because those who take advantage of friendships may be more culpable than those who do not. These are ways to enforce the duty among friends and give friends incentives to behave with a certain degree of care with respect to each other in acknowledgment of the vulnerability that friendships establish.

The Duty of Confidentiality

One can imagine several ways of enforcing a friend's duty of confidentiality. First, consider insider trading prohibitions interpreting Securities and Exchange Commission (SEC) rule 10b-5.[37] Under the "misappropriation" doctrine of insider trading liability, an investor commits fraud "when he misappropriates confidential information for securities trading purposes, in breach of a duty owed to the source of the information."[38] The U.S. Supreme Court has made clear that there is no duty not to trade on material nonpublic information unless one gets the information through a confidential relationship, like attorney-client. And courts have found misappropriation liability in other classically trust-imbued relationships such as "executor-heir, guardian-ward, principal-agent, trustee-beneficiary, or senior corporate official-shareholder."[39]

The influential Second Circuit Court of Appeals decision in *United States v. Chestman*[40] guides the law in this area. The court held that one may not misappropriate information in breach of a "relationship of trust and confidence." Yet the court simultaneously held that a family relationship, standing alone, is insufficient to trigger liability. A natural question posed by the project here is whether a friendship should qualify as a relationship of trust or confidence to trigger misappropriation liability.

Friends would seem to lack *inequality*, a prerequisite for misappropriation liability in *Chestman*. *Chestman* requires qualifying relationships to be "characterized by superiority, dominance, or control,"[41] the inequality presumed not to characterize friendship in chapter 1. Nevertheless, the SEC has recently called certain holdings in *Chestman* into doubt. For example, the SEC has written more recently:

> [T]he *Chestman* majority's approach does not fully recognize the degree to which parties to close family and personal relationships have reasonable and legitimate expectations of confidentiality in their communications. For this reason, we believe the *Chestman* majority view does not sufficiently protect investors and the securities markets from the misappropriation and resulting misuse of inside information.[42]

This dissatisfaction with *Chestman* led to the SEC's promulgation of rule 10b5-2, a regulation that makes clear that family relationships of "spouse, parent, child, or sibling" will be presumed confidential unless a party can show otherwise.[43] Friends, however, were not similarly named in the nonexclusive list offered by the SEC. Yet nothing should necessarily stop a court from taking notice that strong personal relationships of friendship can be presumed to be confidential and can be the basis of misappropriation liability under rule 10b5-2. The SEC has rejected *Chestman*—and those interested in having the law protect friendship could urge courts to recognize friendships' duties of confidentiality in the 10b-5 insider trading context.[44]

One could reasonably contest whether this is a useful way to prosecute securities fraud. After all, the friend who was tipped within a confidential relationship doesn't necessarily have an obligation to the corporation or shareholders to keep the information to herself, or an obligation to the corporation not to trade on it. But misappropriation liability is still a way to protect a friend's duty of confidentiality and reinforce a culture between friends that information disclosed is private information that can be misappropriated and should not be the source of profit.

There is still another remedy that could be used to promote confidentiality within friendships—and it is one that may be gaining importance in the age of the Internet, where it is notoriously easy to violate confidences, ruin reputations, and cause grave psychic harm to friends anonymously or seemingly anonymously (before service providers need to divulge where an anonymous message came from).[45] Our friends, like our doctors and lawyers, have very sensitive information about us at their easy disposal. We are vulnerable to that information's disclosure, yet revealing that information is the only way to get the relationship off the ground and keep it productive and honest. We can't get really good legal advice or health advice unless we answer touchy questions; likewise, we can't form friendships without giving our friends something they might hold over us. But at least in the case of doctors and lawyers, we regulate the disclosure of that information without resort to all sorts of "free speech"–related objections. Why not within friendships, too? If people start divulging their friends' sexual habits, fantasies, or ailments on gossip websites, why shouldn't they be held accountable, just as therapists are held to account for disclosing such private information? We don't leave our private medical and psychiatric information to the free market and to "free speech" fetishism, so why should we leave our secrets shared in friendship to them?

This issue is, of course, embedded in larger debates about whether we want those who can easily collect our sensitive data like our banking, shopping, and Internet surfing habits regulated, whether we want the "Wild West" quality of talk on the Internet regulated, and whether regulation of speech on the Internet can only lead to a world of many lawsuits, censorship, and mainstream media takeover over the whole of cyberspace. Some very well-known disputes have recently come to light about "trolls" on message boards slandering and embarrassing students in colleges and law schools, triggering some of the aforementioned larger debates in a very disconcerting context, in which careers, lives, and reputations are on the line in a palpable way. I can't survey exhaustively here the voluminous literature about these matters, with vocal and coherent advocates on both sides.

And although the approach I suggest here—that a friend's (or ex-friend's) deliberate disclosure of private information that causes real damage to a friend's psyche, pocket, or reputation should be legally compensable—interacts with those debates, surely it is a more modest remedial approach than full-scale regulation. Indeed, this suggestion is not specific to the Internet, since people could divulge their friends' private information even without the Internet (though perhaps off-line it cannot be done as easily, as anonymously, and with as wide a distribution). It seems fair to say that changes in technology routinely shape people's conceptions of privacy and the types of privacy that ultimately need legal protection—reproductive technology as much as communications and photographic technology. But whatever technologies we have at our disposal shouldn't lead us to betray our friends. I don't have to take a position on strangers' right to snap photos of people, reveal publicly available information about them to larger audiences, out them as pseudonymous bloggers, or criticize them vociferously on the Internet to embrace the more narrow view that we ought to have a legal remedy for certain kinds of disclosures of private information that people possess about their friends. When a friend blogs about his or her intimate's private life, perhaps there is something more the betrayed friend should be able to do than just break up.

Saying that there should be some recovery for people betrayed by these types of wrongdoings, however, doesn't mean that we have to buy into a regime in which we give wronged friends access to unlimited awards from their friend-betrayers. Even conceding that it is important to have such a remedy that protects people from their friends doesn't have to mean that limitless or easy liability is appropriate. In the first place, it is essential to remember that allowing such lawsuits as a matter of law does not mean juries will find liability in all cases: they can be instructed to use their common sense to determine whether liability is warranted based on the norms of the community, with sensitivity to circumstance and to the implicit deal the friends had about how such information could be used appropriately. We could also require a potential plaintiff to show some quantum of loss (a jurisdictional minimum) to avoid "honor" lawsuits that are really about getting even rather than being made whole. Or we could require that a defendant's conduct be intentional so that mere negligence with private information would be punishable only through the informal channels of "defriending" or "unfriending."

I'm not particularly committed to any of these methods of remediation, but they give a flavor of the way society can respect friendship, enforce its norms, and not completely replace it with legal rules. We tend not to want law to be perfectly coextensive with moral norms, so as to give them some space to do their own work and to prevent law from being too moralistic. But it is not adequate to say that the risk of disclosure is just built into the relationship and that risk serves to give the friendship value only if no remediation can be awarded: we can provide some legal remediation and still preserve that value. Disabling full remediation leaves some room for that risk to go unrepaired (and so maintains the intrinsic risk and fragility of disclosures within friendships), all while defending those made vulnerable and preyed on by "friends" who turn out not to be very good ones at all.

There is, nevertheless, good reason to be concerned about some silly scenarios that could arise if we go down this path, especially if we don't delimit the cause of action for "breach of confidentiality" carefully enough. Consider Eugene Volokh's hypothetical: "Let's say you are talking to your new []friend about past relationships.... You tell her you've been hurt by an ex-[]friend, and she asks you to tell her about it. You then have to say, 'I'm sorry, but I'm legally bound not to reveal anything about that relationship.'"[46] Volokh has a point, of course, but it is hardly the final word: requiring the friend not to have had a malign intent to hurt the ex-friend seems simple enough to prevent liability here—or, perhaps, we could build some "fair use" defense for people who use the information for benign purposes, like developing new friendships. Juries charged with deciding these cases will be able to use good sense with some useful instructions about the kind and degree of betrayals between friends that we wish to tolerate or not. Using the information to develop new friendships seems like fair use; selling lurid details to a newspaper for fast cash seems more obviously troublesome. If the newspapers are already reporting your secret from a different source or independent investigation, the betrayer might not have caused any compensable harm, since the information was effectively in the public domain already. The betrayal of idiosyncratic taste in undergarment preference seems like a private fact with little public interest in disclosure and so might be actionable; the betrayal of a fact about the friend's criminal or fraudulent conduct to the police is somewhat less troublesome, perhaps, because there are real and substantial interests in disclosure on the other side of the ledger.

Unlike some of the other duties I have offered for consideration here (like the duty of rescue, the duty of fair dealing, the duty of disclosure, and the duty of confidentiality through securities fraud law), U.S. law does not provide much legal support at all for this theory of liability for friends (though the breach of confidentiality tort I am describing here has actually reemerged in American law for a certain class of other relationships like physician-patient). The standard line in American courts is that friends "necessarily assume the risk that a friend or acquaintance in whom [they] confided might breach the confidence."[47] Former lovers have the right to write a tell-all book about ex-lovers for profit, so it would be a pretty hard sell to get courts to take these causes of action seriously. Moreover, U.S. courts often allow the disclosure of private information without tort liability when the information is "of legitimate concern to the public."[48] However, Britain, Australia, New Zealand, Canada, and other countries[49] have more developed "breach-of-confidentiality" causes of action and could serve as a guide should U.S. courts wish to go down this path—at least for egregious and intentional disclosure of private information for profit. We could also imagine a more robust negligence standard with personal and private information with some modest remedy, like a $5,000 fine or "disgorgement" of the profits the betrayer makes.

I say more about the duty of confidentiality in chapter 5, too, since it is part of the more general idea of fiduciary duty, which I investigate in more detail when I try to move beyond suggestion and try to offer a more comprehensive analysis of a way to bring the law into friendship to protect it in a useful and unobtrusive way.

Undoubtedly, legally enforceable duties of friendship will tend to make some people wince. I think they will be uncomfortable for the wrong reasons—but I am pleased to offer them some ideas about giving friends some *privileges*, too. Although I think there are sound reasons to build both legal duties and privileges into the relationship of friendship (as we already do with "family," as we've seen in chapter 3), it is probably easier for people to swallow the idea of privileges, as a general matter. Here are some suggestions.

The Privileges of Friendship?

The Privilege of Informality

Friends deal with one another with some degree of informality. Friends are not usually mere business partners and are likely to have enhanced levels of trust and reliance between them. Although many business partners are "fictive friends" in the sense that they have no real affect for one another but just act as if they were social friends to smooth transactions, there are a whole range of circumstances where there is a real friendship that lies beneath a transaction and where a transaction leads to real friendship. This reality and the reasonability of friends' reliance on one another may counsel for different treatment by the law. I shall offer a whole chapter on friendship, business friendship, and contracts in chapter 6; for now, some basic observations are appropriate.

Perhaps one could argue that friends need not require "consideration" for their promises to be binding. Of course, nearly all contracts require consideration, the law's formal requirement for making sure there has been a real bargain or exchange made between parties, a quid pro quo. But there are clear exceptions for certain kinds of "donative" promises or other seemingly unilateral promises that trigger acts taken in reliance by the promisee that the promisor should have reasonably expected.[50] Because we might think most friends can be presumed to rely on one another, perhaps their promises to one another should be presumed to be enforceable through the law, even without a formal showing of a bargain or exchange. The presumption could be defeated, perhaps, for there are certainly occasions when we do not mean for our promises to be enforceable. But as a general rule, showing that an active friendship existed at the time of the promise could be useful evidence that would be probative of the promisor's expectation of inducing reliance, which gets around the consideration requirement. At the very least, it should be easy within friendships to find donative intent in making gifts, one of the requirements of gift-making; as in family relations, a friendship should establish a presumption that there is such intent.[51] There is even an argument to be made that in friendship contexts, *promises* to make gifts—which under U.S. law are presumptively unenforceable because they quintessentially lack consideration—should be enforceable because of what we already know about the exchange relationship and the reliance implicit in most friendships.[52]

A ready example of the sort of situation I have in mind comes from *Stukas v. Muller*, an Iowa case from 2005.[53] Muller was a close friend of an elderly couple, Burton and Doris Stukas; the three began their friendship in the 1970s. In 1995, the couple transferred money and property (their farm and home) into Muller's name, opened a joint account with him (from which he withdrew $20,000), and named him executor of Doris's will. The court found that consideration was paid for the farm, but that none was paid for the Stukas residence or for the establishment of the joint account. In rejecting the claim of Stukas's conservator for unjust enrichment, the court noted that the closeness of the relationship among the parties warranted concluding that the joint account and residence were, in fact, gifts given to a "close friend" who was "liked" and "trusted." Thus, the friend was able to keep the farm, the residence, and access to the joint account. The court understood that these transactions occurred somewhat informally within the context of a friendship, which was central to understanding how they arose and central to picking a just remedy in the case.

Or take the 2005 New York case *Schwartz v. Houss*.[54] The plaintiff and defendant were close friends and neighbors. The plaintiff allegedly transferred property to his friend to hold while the plaintiff's house was being converted to a different use. The plan was for the defendant to give the property back on completion of the work. When the plaintiff died, the defendant informed his friend's children that he intended to sell the property rather than return it to the estate. The plaintiff's children sued for a permanent injunction to prevent the sale. There was some factual dispute over whether any "consideration" for the original transfer had changed hands and whether the purported agreement was formalized in any writing. The core of the legal dispute was whether there was a confidential or fiduciary relationship between the parties, which was a prerequisite to the sort of remedy the plaintiff was seeking. The defendant believed that no such relationship could be predicated on "mere" friendship.

Nevertheless, the court firmly held that such a relationship could be found "in appropriate circumstances, between close friends."[55] And the court viewed the informality of the agreement itself as proof that the close friendship was one of trust and confidentiality: "Thus, contrary to defendant's argument, plaintiffs have adequately alleged that [parties] were not merely social friends, and that the absence of a formal written agreement was a consequence of the close relationship between [the parties]."[56] Although this case is also relevant for chapter 5 (on fiduciary duty law), here I emphasize the way the court allowed friends to deal with one another informally and still found their transactions valid, even though they didn't meet formal requirements for legal enforceability. The plaintiffs won—and the defendant who had transacted with his friend informally was held to his informal deal, disabling him from selling the property for his own profit.

The case is similar to the New York case *Cody v. Gallow*,[57] in which a party claimed he casually gave money to his friend (a woman), expecting the money to be returned. After the plaintiff-friend married a different woman without telling the defendant, she denied ever having received the money to hold for him. There was no formal documentation or writing, and the defendant opposed the plaintiff's application to get his property back. The court, in awarding the plaintiff's claim, noted the "close, harmonious and trusting relationship" between the two "close friends" (prior to their falling out over the plaintiff's marriage), finding that the "court of equity should interpose its powers to remedy the wrong" between friends. The court was not deterred by the informality of the transaction between friends.

It is, perhaps, not surprising that these actions for unjust enrichment and "constructive trusts" (the fancy name for the remedies asked for and received in *Schwartz* and *Cody*)—actions expressly predicated on "equity"—seem more sensitive to friendships and the privileges and benefits that should accrue to them. Still, it is useful to expose this heightened sensitivity in the equity context to show how friendship's norms may be given legal effect.[58] It is also instructive that even though the law has no organized approach to its regulation or promotion of friendship, regulation and friendship-promotion are not wholly anathema. But they are happening below the radar of legal academics, lawmakers, and judges, who have not shown especial interest in developing a systematic law of friendship or a legal framework that recognizes the status of friendship as one worthy of attention.

The Privilege of Caregiving

Family members are not the only care providers—nor do they seem to be the most effective care providers—when individuals get sick. Accordingly, as I suggested earlier in this chapter when considering legislative efforts on behalf of friendship, state and federal legislators might consider a "Friends Medical Leave Act" in recognition that, just as we feel it is appropriate for our governments to force certain employers to give us leave to take care of family members, we should similarly be given leave from our jobs to help our friends in need—especially friends who do not have familial resources nearby.[59] One of the privileges of friendship should, perhaps, be the privilege to give care, and the law could endorse this privilege through a series of legislative initiatives. Quite obviously here, it simply will not do to exclude friends who are also lovers if our conception of "family" for the purposes of the Family and Medical Leave Act continues to discriminate against gays: this is one place where we should and must allow the more inclusive definition of the friend, so long as the use of family in this context remains discriminatory.

Yet there are also judicial forums where the issue of caregiving for friends arises. Consider *In re Conservatorship of Estate of McDowell*.[60] The court there held that a decedent's friend who helped care for her in her final stages of life should not be presumed to have exerted undue influence under California's Probate Code § 21350, which would have disabled the friend from inheriting under the decedent's will. The code requires that all "care custodians" be presumptively disqualified from being a named beneficiary in a will unless they can show that the will was not the result of undue influence. The court, applying the earlier case of *In re Conservatorship of Estate of Davidson*, found that the statute was intended to limit *professional* caregivers' ability to receive donative transfers from their elderly patients but not to limit an elderly person's ability to "recognize and reward services performed for them ... by close personal friends, intimates, and companions."[61] Friends, *Davidson* held, should be allowed to help one another in old age without the presumption against being a beneficiary attaching, recognizing an inchoate privilege for friends to provide care without getting screwed in will administration. In *McDowell*, the court found the decedent's friend to be "well meaning," even though the friendship was of relatively short duration. The court took on itself the task of assessing the quality of the relationship, understanding that its quality matters for the law.

However, more recent case law in California has called *McDowell* into question, and has held that close personal friends who provide care *do* come within the statute and are presumptively disqualified from being recipients of a donor's largesse. *Bernard v. Foley* now makes clear that the Probate Code's statutory scheme does not allow for a "preexisting friendships exception" to the "care custodian" provision, the standard that had been articulated in *Davidson* and applied in *McDowell*.[62] The *Bernard* court's exercise of statutory interpretation on the custodial care was, at the least, respectable in its careful analysis of what the legislature intended and what the text most probably means.[63] Yet it was arguably insensitive to the role the law can play in supporting friendship and the way statutory construction can incentivize the behavior of friends. The thoughtful concurrence of Chief Justice Ronald M. George was more attuned to the importance of the law's role in respecting genuine friendship: In agreeing with the majority's construction of the Probate Code in the particular case before the court, he called for legislative modification to help support and promote friends' roles in the provision of care, hoping to limit the *Bernard* decision so it could not be used broadly as precedent in the future. His approach may be the preferred one, and state legislatures would be well advised to carve "preexisting friendship" exceptions to statutes like the one at issue in *Bernard*.

The Privilege of Privacy

The relationship of trust and confidence that is friendship also could be granted a different range of privacies from the one it has under current law. This issue was recognized over twenty years ago by Sandy Levinson: he attempted to find a way to give the status of friend the same respect that evidence law confers on certain relationships with members of the family, the bar, and the clergy.[64] Our relationships with our spouses (and our children and parents in some jurisdictions), our lawyers, and our rabbis and priests are protected from discovery in public proceedings, but our communications with our best friends have no such protection. Levinson's particular proposal—allowing people to issue a finite number of "privilege" tickets to whomever they want, including friends and family—has gained little traction and no adherents.[65] Yet Levinson highlighted an interesting problem, whose solution may lie in further consideration of how the law could protect a friendship's privilege of privacy. If the law developed a recognizable category of friend, perhaps we would not need to distribute tickets to figure out who is entitled to the privilege of privacy. Here too, we'd need a nondiscriminatory recognition of friends and families so that gays and nontraditional groups of people who live together with conjugal bonds or otherwise do not get left out.

The Monica Lewinsky affair may be the most recent highly publicized example where intimacies between friends were required to be exposed to the state: Kenneth Starr got Monica Lewinsky's best friend, Catherine Allday Davis, to testify and share intimate e-mails with his grand jury.[66] Surely this goes on all the time. Friends are pitted against friends, threatened with indictment for failure to cooperate—and no testimonial privilege can protect them as it protects spouses. Chapter 3 covered this.

But should the law of evidence allow us to claim a testimonial friendship privilege? That is not a question I can answer here, for that would require a much more elaborate investigation of the costs and benefits of testimonial privileges and how they can serve to obstruct justice. At the very least, however, if courts or legislators were to begin to recognize a friendship privilege, the descriptive effort in chapter 1 might guide a relevant multifactor test to figure out which friends can qualify without relying on the complexity of a "ticket" regime, an online database, or social networking platforms to ascertain who counts. And thinking about why friends deserve testimonial privileges helps us see the way our regime somewhat arbitrarily picks out some relationships for protection and excludes others that might serve very similar functions in our lives.

Still, some features of the potential design for testimonial privileges seem critical, if the law is to go down this path:[67] First, not all communications could be privileged, only "matters communicated in the context of promoting mutual understanding, trust, closeness, [and] intimacy." Second, the privilege could be limited by overriding it in co-conspirator contexts. Third, we could allow the privilege to be waived by the recipient of the information so the choice to betray a trust resides with the potential discloser, disabling the one who wants confidentiality from forcing his friend to maintain his loyalty in the face of a demand from the state. Finally, we might wish to limit the privilege only to "best friends" or "very close friends," who show a level of intimacy that extends beyond the average friend.

There is another general area within the law where a friendship's "right to privacy" might also be vindicated: Fourth Amendment jurisprudence. If the law were truly interested in protecting people's friendships, we might have different Fourth Amendment rights from the ones we have under current doctrine.

It is undoubtedly the case that police searches routinely disrupt shared spaces where friendship occurs in private. For example, friends often spend time together in one another's homes or cars. Yet police searches need not currently respect "shared" privacy and are only bound to respect the privacy of an individual. As Mary Coombs explains, "Most lay people ... are probably not aware that the law would not recognize their claim to privacy in a friend's car."[68] Current Fourth Amendment law has no room for a privacy claim that would emerge from the privacy within friendship. But it doesn't have to be that way; litigants can keep pushing courts to appreciate that shared friendship space is often very private space that should be treated with respect and immunized from state scrutiny.[69]

There is also the Fourth Amendment issue of "false friends,"[70] which seems relevant to the subject at hand. False friends are government agents who extract information from defendants by pretending to be their friends. Alas, "[F]ourth [A]mendment challenges to this law enforcement method, in all its forms, have inevitably fallen on a majority of deaf ears."[71] The logic behind the rejection of these challenges turns on the idea that victims of the false friends "voluntarily" disclose any secret information and have no reasonable expectation of privacy in such disclosures. But perhaps the false-friend problem cries for a different solution in a polity properly attuned to the needs of friendships and their success. If we want a polity where people's intimate disclosures to friends are given some respect, it would seem worth maintaining the privacy of such disclosures even if a friend turns out to be false and a government informant. Although it isn't altogether obvious that we should go down this path (because sometimes the public interest in law enforcement will have to make other values give way), it is still critical to put the disruption the law may be causing to friendships on the policy agenda as well.

The entrapment defense could similarly be made sensitive to a friend's privilege of privacy. In *Sherman v. United States*,[72] Joseph Sherman claimed that the government's informant abused the friendship between them, inducing him to commit a crime he likely would not have otherwise committed if he had not been so concerned for his friend's well-being. Sherman met the informant at a doctor's office where they were both being treated for drug addiction; they quickly bonded, owing to their similar struggles to overcome the addiction.

Ultimately, the informant tried to get Sherman to obtain drugs for him, which Sherman did (after refusing several requests). He did so without profit and was subsequently arrested.[73]

A jury rejected Sherman's entrapment defense, finding that Sherman was "predisposed to commit the act and exhibited only the natural hesitancy of one acquainted with the narcotics trade." The Supreme Court reversed the jury, finding that the entrapment defense was established as a matter of law: The informant's "resort to sympathy" was exactly the "evil which the defense of entrapment is designed to overcome." Justice Felix Frankfurter, concurring in the reversal of the jury's decision, was particularly disdainful of the government's appeal to friendship in ensnaring the defendant, and argued that Sherman's entrapment defense should have been predicated on the informant's appeal to friendship rather than on Sherman's supposed lack of criminal predisposition.

Justice Frankfurter's sensibility on these issues was also given expression in *Pascu v. Alaska*.[74] Gordon Pascu raised the defense of entrapment because his friend of five years, a government informant, induced him to buy drugs to alleviate his pain. The informant repeatedly reminded Pascu of their long-standing friendship. The court was thoroughly disgusted with this abuse of friendship and the informant's appeals to Pascu's "sense of obligation and sympathy" and found for Pascu. This is a case to emulate in a world where we want to protect the trope of friendship, even if it is obvious in this case that no real friendship actually existed, for it lacked reciprocity.

There is, of course, another valence to these entrapment cases, one that dovetails with the privilege of giving care explored earlier. Perhaps these defendants deserve special consideration not because someone else "abused" a friendship but because friendship is evidence of mitigated culpability. Helping out our friends, perhaps, should earn us goodwill within the criminal law. A bill introduced in the U.S. Senate in 2006 is illustrative: The bill offers sentencing reductions for minor participants in drug conspiracies if they "acted on impulse, fear, friendship, or affection."[75] Notably, the proposed bill also furnishes an enhancement for friendship abuse, when a drug conspirator uses "impulse, fear, friendship, affection, or some combination thereof" to ensnare others into a conspiracy. This indicates that abuse of friendship and being motivated by friendship can be seen by legislators as culpability factors (and courts might take their lead from this insight). This would seem to be an important lens into the Bernie Madoff fraud, too, which infiltrated communities of close friends: sometimes the abuse of a friendship seems a reason to enhance a penalty and sometimes trying to help one's friends seems a reason to relax harsh penalties.

Testimonial privileges, Fourth Amendment jurisprudence, and the entrapment defense are all legal domains where more sensitivity to friendship could be usefully developed to protect a friendship's privilege of privacy. Of course, a regime of complete "non-recognition of the friend"[76] in which we seal off friendship from law entirely might give friends more privacy in a sense, but the form and range of privacy protections enumerated here would arguably pay friendship more respect and do more for its protection in our society.

The Privilege of Vindicating Rights

Finally, there may be an argument for conferring on friends the privilege of "third-party standing" in our federal legal system: giving them the ability to vindicate claims on their friends' behalf. Although no federal court fully recognizes such a form of standing, it may be yet another way to have the legal system give the status of friend more visibility and respect in the law.

It is, of course, a truism of federal standing doctrine that people must seek to vindicate their own rights and must sue only on their own injuries. The constitutional prerequisites to standing that are deemed to flow from Article III of the U.S. Constitution's purported "case or controversy" requirement are "injury, causation, and redressability."[77] But there is also a "prudential" limitation that the Court has imposed: the prohibition against third-party standing.[78] The central ideas in this prudential doctrine are (1) that third parties are not well situated to protect vigorously the interests of the "true" parties to a dispute; (2) that the justice system will work more efficiently if it limits third-party standing; and (3) that third parties may seek to vindicate a right that the real party-in-interest wishes to forgo.

Still, the Court has carved out a set of exceptions to the rule. Two of these exceptions could, perhaps, become the basis of a true third-party "friend" standing. The first exception is that when there are substantial obstacles preventing a party from asserting her rights, a third party—if the third party can prove that she will adequately represent all the interests of the original party—may overcome the presumption against third-party standing.[79] One way to respect friends may be to fit them into this exception, conferring on them a presumption that they will adequately represent their friends' interests.

The second exception is similarly susceptible to recognizing friends' privilege of vindicating their counterparts' rights. This exception "permits an individual to assert the rights of third parties where there is a *close relationship* between the advocate and the third party."[80] This category has been applied to allow third-party standing for doctors to represent the interests of their patients, for lawyers to be named parties on behalf of their clients, for political organizations to represent the interests of their membership, and for vendors to sue on behalf of their customers. To be sure, the Court refused to allow third-party standing in the context of a mother trying to gain standing to challenge the death penalty exacted on her son in the famous Gary Gilmore case.[81] But it may, nevertheless, be possible to develop a jurisprudence that would allow friends to vindicate the rights of their counterparts.

This chapter shows that friends could be more fully embraced by our legal institutions. But it just as clearly shows that friendship *does* make a difference to the law in a number of previously unnoticed ways. Ira Ellman recently argued that "[w]e do not…have a law of close friends."[82] That's not quite right, after all. Although conventional wisdom suggests that the friend does not matter at all to the law and that friendship carries no legally enforceable duties or privileges, doctrinal evidence does not bear out that supposition. The value of friendship is pursued in ad hoc ways, and the law seeks to give some consideration to its value, however latently. The moments where friendship is relevant to the administration of law are not substantial, consistent, or systematic. Yet they are pervasive enough to conclude that the law does not wholly stay out of people's friendships. Thus, those who insist on the law's nonrecognition of the friend (either for the law's sake or for friendship's sake) must probably acknowledge that our current legal regime does occasionally take notice of friendships and, indeed, regulates them.

To be sure, this chapter also shows that the law has no self-conscious, consistent, or well-considered approach to friendships and its role in regulating them. The law neither seeks to support friendships nor leaves them fully alone. There is something haphazard about the law's approach to friendship that invites further study by lawyers, lawmakers, judges, and scholars.[83] At the very least, this chapter begs further exploration of the ways law makes friendship matter, why it makes friendship matter in the ways it does, and whether there are particular areas within the law that are especially appropriate (or inappropriate) for the promotion of friendship. Indeed, it may very well be that friendship-burdening duties could be perceived as undermining friendships and that I may only be able to sell friendship-strengthening privileges as properly tailored to help promote friendship.

Friendship-burdening duties, like the duties of rescue, disclosure, and fair dealing, might ultimately lead people to issue friendship disclaimers: "I like you alright, Ethan, but I do not want to be your friend for legal purposes." Perhaps these duties would lead to fewer friendships rather than more general friendship promotion. I am not sure about that, for reasons I'll explore in chapter 7. But even if people issued such disclaimers from time to time, it isn't clear that would necessarily be a bad result. If people were more honest about how they felt about one another and how close they felt with their group of acquaintances, they might save others from a lot of personal pain. It is not obvious, in any case, whether such a friendship disclaimer should be sufficient to overcome the potential duties of friendship developed here. Perhaps friends should be judged by what they *do* rather than by what they say, trying to reap the benefits of friendships without being subject to their duties.[84] As I noted in chapter 1, we can sometimes find ourselves in friendships without quite intending that result, notwithstanding proclamations we issue to ourselves or to our counterparts.

Ultimately, this chapter seeks to whet the appetite for what a public policy of friendship sensitivity and promotion could look like in a practical way. The next two chapters are more sustained studies on how to make this work and how to make it consonant with large bodies of law and theory that control specific areas of law. We can say abstractly that we want the law to help friends—but we are always going to bump against reasons the law has for its policies that might be decidedly indifferent or even hostile to friendship. That will require us to weigh costs and benefits in particular areas. But from a more abstract standpoint, we must begin to realize that a continued effort to weigh the benefits of friendship-promotion and sensitivity lightly and to overemphasize the costs of these methods of incorporation can take a real toll on friendship. One that is hard to measure, to be sure, but we can't keep ignoring friendship and expecting it to take care of itself.

It should be fairly obvious from the doctrinal explorations offered here of how certain courts have let (or not let) friendship matter that judges and legislators have spent little time thinking about who should qualify for the status of friend when friendship is deemed relevant. Accordingly, any of the more aspirational or purely speculative ways the law could serve friends has little guidance from current cases about how to designate friends. How, for example, could a court or legislature identify who should count as a friend sufficient to allow him or her to vindicate the rights of a party through third-party standing? None of the little jurisprudence there is on friendship within the law furnishes a workable definition of the category. We are back to the very first question with which we began.

This is exactly where chapter 1 should prove useful. If the arguments of chapters 2 and 3 were persuasive, there is good reason to expand the ways the law recognizes, promotes, and facilitates friendship. But the law can only do so if it has a workable concept that it is aiming to promote. That concept will always have to be context-specific and somewhat open-ended. But I hope my discussion thus far has made some progress on these underexplored issues in our legal system. The next two chapters move beyond suggestion and go deeper in thinking about friendship and the law.

CHAPTER 5

The Friend as a Fiduciary

J OHN AND DAVID were both thirty-three years old and had been friends since college. They were not merely casual friends but stayed in touch regularly and were important parts of each other's lives. They shared intimacies, secrets, and confidences and trusted each other with almost everything. If asked, they would surely have said that they loved each other and found each other to be very close to the center of their respective circles of affection.

For some years, both had been looking for a way out of academia and a way to pay for their children's private school tuitions. They had often imagined that they would pursue a business venture together and, given their competencies and interests, had assumed that an environmentally friendly beverage company in China would suit them well. They also both believed that the venture would enrich them professionally and financially. Although they had been chatting casually about the plan for four years, neither had taken any affirmative steps to make the company a reality and neither had suggested to the other that their business idea was confidential.

Last year, David was approached by a wealthy acquaintance, Daniel, who was setting up shop in Beijing. Daniel casually knew David and John from college but knew nothing of their plan to go into business together. David, assuming that his "green" beverage company was unlikely to become a reality with John anytime soon (John was in the middle of researching his next book in South Korea and seemed, for the moment, fulfilled by the academic life), pitched Daniel on the idea. Daniel loved the plan and quickly set up Datong Drinks, a drink company that preached the unity of earth and humanity. Reasonable projections suggested that the company would be hugely profitable over the next five years. Datong gave David a consulting contract (as a finder's fee reward, of sorts) worth $1 million.

John had been traveling in South Korea doing research over the year and stopped in Beijing on his way back to the States. He went to his favorite coffee shop in the hutongs of Beijing and asked for a drink menu. He ordered a Datong "double green" iced tea. When he read the label, he was surprised to learn that someone else had beaten him to the punch on his business idea with David: the label was explicitly environmentalist. Then he noticed that the president of the company was Daniel, someone he had known in college.

He called Daniel in Beijing, and they met up over some duck and beer. Daniel told John the story of Datong and told him of David's role in the development of the idea and his $1 million contract.

John became furious and started thinking of ways he might sue David. John knew David had betrayed their friendship in selling out their idea to Daniel. But he was not sure if he could make out a legal claim against David. He knew they had no explicit contract and did not quite think any theft claim or intellectual property claim could be sustained. But John had just completed reading a biography of Justice Benjamin Cardozo. He remembered the famous case of *Meinhard v. Salmon* and its most famous pronouncement:

> Joint adventurers, like co-partners, owe to one another, while the enterprise continues, the duty of the finest loyalty. Many forms of conduct permissible in a workaday world for those acting at arm's length, are forbidden to those bound by fiduciary ties. A trustee is held to something stricter than the morals of the market place. Not honesty alone, but the punctilio of an honor the most sensitive, is then the standard of behavior. As to this there has developed a tradition that is unbending and inveterate. Uncompromising rigidity has been the attitude of courts of equity when petitioned to undermine the rule of undivided loyalty by the "disintegrating erosion" of particular exceptions. Only thus has the level of conduct for fiduciaries been kept at a level higher than that trodden by the crowd. It will not consciously be lowered by any judgment of this court.[1]

John wondered: Did David violate any fiduciary duties to him as his friend? Was friendship a kind of "joint adventure" such that David's actions could be deemed usurpation of what should have been their joint opportunity? Were not the two of them in something "jointly, for better or for worse," as Cardozo described Meinhard and Salmon's venture? (The allusion to marriage in *Meinhard* is hard to ignore. Indeed, one of the briefs in the case emphasized that Meinhard and Salmon were "on terms of social intimacy. They were warm and personal friends. In 1901 and 1902 they met each other three or four times a week, frequently dining together. In the summer of 1902, and off and on during previous summers, they roomed together.")[2] Did David misappropriate information for his own purposes that could be deemed confidential? If so, what remedy should be available to John? Should David have to share his contract earnings from Datong? Should all profits David receives from Datong be disgorged and placed in a constructive trust for the benefit of both friends? For John exclusively? Should John be compensated from those earnings for his prorated contribution to the idea?

These queries stem neither from a real case nor from some law school exam.[3] But the central issue they raise—whether friends are fiduciaries for some purposes and in some contexts—is not wholly hypothetical either. Courts often need to assess whether the duties of friendship in moral life can be translated into legal duties. When and if courts do transmogrify friendship's duties into legally cognizable ones, they tend to enforce the duties through a set of remedies often considered equitable: disgorgement, the constructive trust, restitution. In short, the body of law that courts consider when presented with fact scenarios like the fictional one just sketched is the law of fiduciary duties. And John was not far off in his channeling of Cardozo's *Meinhard* opinion. In what follows, I defend the use of fiduciary duty law to police the activities of close friends in certain contexts. Although the example of David's behavior illustrates the way a fiduciary duty of friendship might be breached, I hope to provide some guidance here on other ways the law of fiduciary duties could be employed to monitor the actions of usually trustworthy close friends or those who pose as them.

To be sure, the fiduciary concept is still very much contested,[4] and some famously think "there is no subject here."[5] Still, I hope to make the case here that the law of fiduciary duties provides a good framework for friends to understand their duties to one another better, could give courts a useful set of rhetorical and analytical tools to employ when they are forced to entertain disputes that arise between close friends, and, finally, could help direct courts to furnish betrayed friends certain kinds of remedies that are most appropriate for achieving justice within the dispute context of friends suing friends. This is not the first effort to expand the reach of the fiduciary concept into new sorts of relationships that are not always considered within the ambit of fiduciary duty law.[6] But the case for thinking of friends as fiduciaries is exceedingly persuasive and underappreciated, both in the law and in our lives. The attention to detail about remedies and limitations here is absolutely essential, for whereas the previous chapter surveyed and suggested many areas of law where the concerns of friendship might be relevant or might become more relevant, here I want to show that careful attention to a particular policy area can lead to some more determinate results about the proper incorporation of friendship and law.

In short, we should accept close friendship as triggering certain fiduciary duties. Courts have already started to treat friends as fiduciaries and there is much that can be appreciated about friendship itself when friends begin to see their relationships through the lens of the fiduciary principle. In this way, this chapter also begins a process of working backward, too: the law not only has something to learn about friendship, but friends, somewhat unexpectedly, may also improve their relationships by learning a bit about certain areas of law.

THE FIDUCIARY

Before one can ascertain whether calling friends fiduciaries is simply a category mistake, one needs a working understanding of the fiduciary idea in the law. Although there is plenty that scholars and judges can't agree about, there is widespread agreement about much having to do with fiduciaries, and I focus here on those areas of agreement.

The Fiduciary Relationship

Certain categories of relationships are virtually always treated as fiduciary in nature. They include attorney-client, corporate director-shareholder, trustee-beneficiary, managing partner-partner, agent-principal, employee-employer, guardian-ward, and physician-patient. For the most part, I will adopt the convention of calling the first in the dyad a "fiduciary" and the second a "beneficiary." Sometimes other relationships are also deemed fiduciary and, like the paradigmatic examples, are treated as such as a mere function of the relationship's existence rather than on a contextual analysis of the *quality* of the particular relationship. These are called "formal" fiduciary relationships.

But relationships of status are not the only kind of relationships that are treated as fiduciary in the law. There are also "informal" fiduciary relationships, which are identified through more qualitative evaluations. These relationships are sometimes called "confidential relationships" or "fact-based."[7] They are routinely identified when a court finds that a relationship of "trust" exists and that one party dominates, is superior to, or is especially vulnerable to another party. Admittedly, vague standards for confidential relationships abound, but there is no question that courts embrace many types of relationships on the basis of their internal qualities rather than their names. Although this imprecision can be frustrating for fiduciary typologists and those who wish the law of fiduciary duties to provide firmer guidance on the forms of relationships that are susceptible to treatment as fiduciary, no typology of the fiduciary could be complete without recognizing a few central features: the concept is self-consciously open, flexible, and adaptable to new kinds of relationships.[8]

It will only be possible to get more specific about which relationships qualify for treatment as fiduciary once one has a firmer understanding of the concept of the fiduciary itself. But that effort must await more information about what is at stake in calling someone a fiduciary. Therefore, I defer further discussion about identifying fiduciary relationships until after I explore the fiduciary duties and the remedies associated with the breaches thereof.

The Fiduciary Duties

Once a court determines that a fiduciary relationship has formed between parties, courts can be expected to scrutinize the conduct of the parties against the background of a set of duties to which fiduciaries must conform their behavior. Although the list of "true" or "pure" fiduciary duties—duties that are imposed *only* on fiduciaries—can be quite short, the list of duties that are associated with fiduciaries, duties that may also be imposed on other kinds of parties but tend to be discussed in the context of fiduciary relationships, is somewhat longer.[9] Certain fiduciary relationships implicate the majority of the mélange of duties that follow, and some trigger only consideration of a few. Ultimately, there is stunning variety, both in scope and substance, in the set of duties that apply to any given fiduciary relationship. Capturing the set at a level of generality will suffice here.

The core fiduciary duty is the *duty of loyalty*, a duty of unselfishness. This is not quite a requirement of full altruism, but it requires a high degree of taking account of a beneficiary's interest. As Lynn Stout puts it:

> The keystone of the duty of loyalty is the legal obligation that the fiduciary use her powers not for her own benefit but for the exclusive benefit of her beneficiary. It is highly improper—indeed proscribed—for a fiduciary to extract a personal benefit from her fiduciary position without her beneficiary's consent, even when she can do this without harming the beneficiary.[10]

The fiduciary is prohibited from engaging in self-interested transactions and is saddled with the task of pursuing the interests of her beneficiary. So "inflexible" is the duty of loyalty that it requires a fiduciary to be "undivided" and "undiluted" in her fidelity, though, of course, fiduciaries are allowed to attend to their own personal needs, obligations, and activities.

From a practical standpoint, this restrictive duty requires fiduciaries to pursue self-dealing only after getting an informed waiver from their beneficiaries and to avoid conflicts of interest, secret profits, and misappropriation of benefits that should accrue to the beneficiary or the joint relationship. Even with this most central fiduciary duty, however, the strictness with which it will be enforced varies, depending on the type and scope of the fiduciary relationship at issue.

The second duty that is routinely discussed in connection with fiduciaries is the *duty of care*. This duty requires fiduciaries to perform their responsibilities for their beneficiaries with reasonable diligence and prudence. Although the duty resembles a basic requirement to avoid negligence, the duty is flexible and can require more substantial diligence than would be required of nonfiduciaries. In contrast to the predominantly prohibitive nature of the duty of loyalty, the duty of care has an affirmative component occasionally *requiring* affirmative action. In practice, however, the duty of care is relatively weak, at least in the corporate context, and it is rare for a fiduciary to run afoul of it. Courts tend to give fiduciaries substantial discretion in performing their responsibilities; recklessness and gross negligence tend to be the standards as a matter of practice.

Aside from these two central fiduciary duties—or, perhaps, growing out of them—are a set of duties that are routinely associated with fiduciaries. Fiduciaries have a *duty of utmost candor and disclosure*.[11] This may take the form of requiring doctors to reveal their personal financial interests to their patients (even when those interests are not related to a patient's health)[12] or it may take the form of a general "accounting" requirement, necessitating accurate bookkeeping subject to inspection by the beneficiary as well as the disclosure of all relevant information pertaining to the relationship.[13]

The flip side of the disclosure requirement is a *duty of confidentiality*. The professional responsibilities of lawyers and doctors generally prevent them from revealing the confidences of their clients and patients, respectively. But fiduciaries commonly are required to maintain secrets and respect duties of confidentiality. This fiduciary duty is not only the duty not to misappropriate the information for the fiduciary's own use but is also a duty not to communicate the information itself.

Perhaps a more controversial duty associated with fiduciaries is the *duty of good faith*.[14] It is controversial because many have a hard time distinguishing a fiduciary's duty of good faith from a general duty of good faith that pervades all performance of contractual duties (about which more in chapter 6).[15] Moreover, some feel that the duty of good faith is simply a way of expressing duties imposed by other obligations, like the duty of disclosure, the duty of loyalty, or the duty of care.[16] But it is not hard to find courts articulating the idea that fiduciaries owe their beneficiaries a higher standard of good faith than would be required of mere contract partners: "Utmost" good faith is the benchmark, and the breach of that duty in the fiduciary context can lead to more substantial remedies for the injured than might be true in different transactional contexts.

The Fiduciary Remedies

There is a set of remedies that courts routinely impose when they find a breach of fiduciary duty. Indeed, if it were not circular and decidedly unhelpful in guiding courts, one might even be tempted to define the entire field of fiduciary law by the remedies extracted from fiduciaries. Although the remedies, like the fiduciary duties themselves, get enforced with variable degrees of strictness depending on the relationship and the nature of the breach, there are some general commonalities in the remedies used in the fiduciary context. In sum, fiduciaries who breach their duties will likely find themselves needing to disgorge their profits, place their earnings in a constructive trust to share with beneficiaries, restitute their beneficiaries, and/or pay punitive damages.

Disgorgement often follows from the breach of the duty of loyalty: if a fiduciary has betrayed the principle of unselfishness, she will have to disgorge all of her profits. This remedy is demanded of the defaulting fiduciary even if the self-interested transaction caused no harm to the beneficiary. For example, a trustee who self-deals with the assets of a trust beneficiary will be expected to disgorge his profits even if no damage came to the property of the beneficiary. Of course part of the reason for the extreme remedy of disgorgement (no profit for trustee even if beneficiary isn't harmed) is to deter self-interested conduct. But at least part of the rationale for the distinctive disgorgement remedy is that beneficiaries will rarely be capable of formulating precise expectations; they rely on their fiduciaries quite broadly, so measuring damages by the fiduciary's gain can make more sense than an expectation-based remedy, common in contractual breaches. Nevertheless, standard "loss stemming from breach" damages are also routinely available, if not especially distinctive.

The remedy of disgorgement is often accomplished through a "constructive trust" imposed by law. Indeed, *Meinhard v. Salmon* itself is illustrative. In this case, Salmon misappropriated a business opportunity that arose from his real estate venture with Meinhard. Salmon's breach of his fiduciary duties to Meinhard resulted in a court-imposed constructive trust over certain assets that should have been shared: "A constructive trust is, then, the remedial device through which preference of self is made subordinate to loyalty to others."[17]

Restitutionary remedies (of which disgorgement and constructive trusts can be sub-species) have long been identified with the breach of fiduciary duties, and they enable beneficiaries to extract from their fiduciaries potentially supercompensatory remedies. Even in a *contract dispute* between a fiduciary and her beneficiary, for example, the measure of damages might exceed mere "expectancy damages," the standard measure of compensation available in contractual relationships.

A classic example is *Snepp v. United States*.[18] Frank W. Snepp III, was bound by a contractual duty not to publish a book about his activities with the Central Intelligence Agency without submitting it to the agency for prepublication review. Although no confidential information was, in fact, revealed, the courts required Snepp to pay a restitutionary rather than a compensatory remedy (through a constructive trust). The fiduciary relationship between Snepp and the government triggered supercompensatory remediation, even though breach of a contractual term usually results only in "expectancy" damages, not a profits-based recovery.

Still, courts' use of restitution to achieve equity and to reverse the effects of "unjust enrichment" need not be pursued only through a profits-based remedy. Rather, courts may require fiduciaries to pay a fair price in an unfair transaction instead of disgorging their profits. Restitutionary remedies can also be contribution-based: a beneficiary can be compensated in accordance with his contribution to an enterprise. Contribution-based restitutionary remedies undo the effects of unjust enrichment in a retrospective way without focusing on profits or prospective recovery.

Finally, punitive damages may be available in a suit for breach of fiduciary duties even though such damages are not routinely available for breaches of contract. Thus, above and beyond disgorgement and other forms of restitution, punitive damages may be assessed as well when a breach is extreme or a product of malice or fraud.[19]

The Fiduciary Concept

With this introduction to all things fiduciary in place, I can endeavor to say something more general about the concept of the fiduciary. Although I cannot aim to settle the long-standing disputes among those who seek grand unified theories of the fiduciary concept (and those who think no such unified theory is possible),[20] there are a few relatively uncontroversial propositions about the concept on which almost all can agree. My aim here is not to rationalize or justify the bulk of the case law surrounding fiduciaries but only to identify some of its organizing attributes. That will enable me to support my assessment of the concept's applicability to friendship.

It is common to observe that fiduciary relationships are relationships of trust, where one party trusts another more than would be true in a standard commercial transaction. This strong-form trust tends to arise from the fiduciary's greater expertise in the interaction at issue (like a lawyer's knowledge), greater control over assets (whether real property or information), or high degree of influence over a beneficiary's decision-making process. For this reason, when discussing the fiduciary concept, courts often focus on the fiduciary's "discretionary authority" or "power" over something a beneficiary owns (or over the beneficiary himself) and look for resultant dependency or vulnerability in the beneficiary. The *degree* of control, complexity, and dominance or the broad range of the underlying relationship can also help direct courts in figuring out how strictly to enforce fiduciary duties and how to impose a proper remedy.

So what is notable about the fiduciary duties and remedies and how do they help reveal the concept of the fiduciary that guides the finding of a fiduciary relationship, the scrutinizing of the fiduciary's duties, and the imposition of a remedy? Most important, the fiduciary duties and remedies evidence special concern with policing opportunism and discretion in contexts where monitoring costs are very high and bonding is exceedingly important to the functioning of the relationship. The duties are relatively stringent because the fiduciary has easy access to important resources of the beneficiary, and the remedies are supercompensatory in part so as to deter misuse thereof and related misbehavior. The fiduciary relationship is one especially susceptible to abuse because fiduciaries are especially difficult to monitor and because so much must be shared with the fiduciary to get the relationship functioning properly. Because trust itself functions as the only real monitoring and bonding device (aside from back-end lawsuits) in the fiduciary context, courts attempt to protect and promote the trust—and make sure it is not betrayed too often. The remedies are one way courts signal to parties that they should not betray trust; they aim to facilitate beneficiaries' reliance on the trustworthiness of their fiduciaries.

To be sure, in many contexts, trust accomplishes its objective, and courts will try not to intrude on the relationship excessively. For all the talk of stringency in enforcing duties in fiduciary law, courts can be notably passive and deferential to fiduciaries. But this should not be surprising: the entire point of standing in a fiduciary relation to a beneficiary is that the fiduciary is supposed to take on a special role of judgment, representation, and control. Nevertheless, it is just as true that trust will facilitate taking advantage of the beneficiary, and accordingly, fiduciary law is sensitive to the fragility of trust.

Another notable feature of fiduciary law is its unapologetic moralism, which is revealed through the definition of the relevant relationships, the contours of the concomitant obligations, and the imposition of the remedies in any given context. Although parties may usually freely breach their contracts without any sermonizing by the courts, breaches of fiduciary duties routinely meet with tones of explicit opprobrium and disapproval. When considering fiduciary law, courts generally write as if they are importing moral requirements into the law through their policing of fiduciary relationships: fiduciary default is often seen as a moral shortcoming. Writing in moral terms not only leads courts to draw from the moral sphere and to influence a fiduciary's behavior,[21] but it also can help sustain and nourish social norms.[22] Such writing accomplishes the latter task by framing for actors what their conduct should be and by expressing publicly and symbolically the norms of good behavior.

To be sure, Judge Frank Easterbrook and Daniel Fischel have famously argued that fiduciary duties lack a "moral footing," that moralistic language appears in plenty of judicial decisions outside the fiduciary context, and that a sound theory of the fiduciary concept must focus on what courts actually do, not what they say.[23] But it remains hard to ignore the courts' own conception of what they are doing when they are reviewing claims of fiduciary default. Indeed, even if Easterbrook and Fischel are right that a grand unified theory of fiduciary law would need to take stock of the actual practices of courts first and foremost, surely rhetoric is relevant as well. The courts do routinely speak in moralisms in the fiduciary context—an empirical observation Easterbrook and Fischel do not and cannot contest—and that practice furnishes some insight into the legal concept under consideration.

The apparent moralism of fiduciary law is also consistent with the general concept identified here: a regime that seeks to support and promote extralegal trust to police and monitor opportunism that could and does occasionally result from easy access to beneficiary property, information, or resources. The reinforcement of social norms through moralized rhetoric, and haphazard legal intrusion into the moral sphere is of a piece with the entire corpus of fiduciary law. Fiduciary law, in fact, relies on extralegal norms: the law in this area is full of open-ended standards that are not fully enforced by legal sanctions. Still, managers and directors who are bound by the fiduciary laws tend to comply because morally guided behavior is so much the background on which fiduciaries act.[24]

It is widely known that "*Meinhard*'s dictum still seems to be applied broadly"[25] and that it is, as one commentator colorfully put it, "the oldest war-horse in the repertoire of...fiduciary duty" with a potent influence on fiduciary law.[26] But against this background, is it sensible to apply the concept of the fiduciary to the friend?

THE FRIEND'S LIKENESS TO THE FIDUCIARY

Some have suggested that we are living in the age of the fiduciary.[27] Perhaps, then, the concept is ripe for expansion into other areas of life, where it may be appropriately applied to reinforce, sustain, and even create extralegal norms. Although some courts stubbornly treat the fiduciary concept as a mere list to be applied to particular cases, Eileen Scallen has observed that courts have "attempted to formulate rigid definitions of fiduciary relationships and the concomitant obligations as though these concepts were uniform and unchanging. This may result in an ephemeral illusion of certainty and predictability. It also misrepresents fiduciary law."[28]

Given the purposes I just highlighted, I suggest that friends should be more routinely considered fiduciaries for each other. Certain parallels between the friend and the fiduciary are easy to see; others require more elaboration. In what follows, I focus on trust, the difficulty of monitoring friends, and the possibilities for opportunism within friendships, which are all central to the fiduciary concept. Together, these parallels counsel for courts to take seriously claims by close friends that certain types of betrayals should be treated as breaches of fiduciary duties and remediated accordingly. Of course, given the variety of fiduciary relationships, duties, and remedies the law recognizes and provides, recognizing friends as fiduciaries as a general matter will not tell us how, more specifically, the fiduciary relationship of friendship should be policed. I defer those more specific details until later in the chapter, after I show how the law has already started to treat friends as fiduciaries.

Trust and Friendship

In the first place, we tend to trust our friends especially, perhaps even more than we trust our lawyers (whom the law will treat as our fiduciaries!). They are our guardians, our counselors, our therapists, our managers, our directors, our partners. As I suggested in chapter 1, trust is one of the defining attributes of friendship itself.

To be sure, trust undoubtedly occurs between strangers in many transactions as well. Trust at some level is necessary even for arm's length transactions between standard contracting parties, and "fictive" business friendships with some heightened levels of trust are common.[29] Yet true friendship furnishes a paradigmatic case of trust and provides an important benchmark for how trust can operate in an ideal relational context. Without that important model, all relationships of trust might be undermined. Humankind needs trust as a foundational good for societal organization and survival.[30] Trust is an easy good to destroy and once destroyed a very hard injury to heal. It thus behooves an area of law that self-consciously pursues the protection and promotion of trust in society to remain sensitive to trust's paradigmatic case.

Why is trust—and protecting it—so important? Aside from ethical arguments that might stress that trust should not be betrayed as a most basic moral requirement (and an additional argument, of course, that the state must pursue what is moral in the fiduciary context), one can emphasize, along with Francis Fukuyama, that trust is one of the most important of the social virtues that can lead a nation toward economic development and prosperity.[31] If our capitalist economic system is one to which our legal system must remain committed, it would seem inadvisable to disrupt relationships of trust or fail to find a system of preserving, sustaining, and promoting them. Indeed, precisely because every economic transaction trades on trust to some degree, debasing trust in society by failing to uphold the most basic standards of trust in paradigmatic trust relationships would be counterproductive.

Consider Justice Harlan Stone's assessment of the Great Depression:

> I venture to assert that when the history of the financial era which has just drawn to a close comes to be written, most of its mistakes and its major faults will be ascribed to the failure to observe the fiduciary principle....More than a century ago equity gave a hospitable reception to that principle and the common law was not slow to follow in giving it recognition. No thinking man can believe that an economy built upon a business foundation can permanently endure without some loyalty to that principle.[32]

In a more contemporary milieu, Larry Ribstein also identifies the promotion of trust as central to fiduciary law and a prosperous society. He highlights that the "disposition to trust is socially valuable because it reduces the need for externally enforced constraints, and therefore the costs of human interaction. Thus, a society in which trust in this sense prevails may be wealthier than one in which it is absent."[33] Or consider a slightly different argument presented by Robert Gordon: "[E]ncouraging people to deal with one another as strangers progressively erodes the underlying relations of solidarity, reciprocity, and trust upon which capitalist economies essentially depend."[34] Accordingly, a fiduciary law that ignores the exemplary trust that friends share risks undermining the concept of fiduciary law itself, as well as the legal and economic system it is supposed to serve and enrich.

Thus, the argument here is, at one level, simple: Friends, as a category, are paradigmatic exemplars of trust. And because fiduciary law aims to protect and promote trust, fiduciary law should treat friends as fiduciaries.[35] But a bit more can be said in favor of treating friends as fiduciaries from the standpoint of the fiduciary concept's concern with trust.

Another way to think about the concern for trust in the law of fiduciary relations is to put the idea in a slightly different, but related, light. Instead of seeing the fiduciary relationship as merely a relationship of special entrustment, we might focus on the *high costs of distrust* in fiduciary relations. Thus, parties in a fiduciary relationship *require* high degrees of trust and must freely share confidences, secrets, and information for that relationship to serve its purposes well. The doctor-patient and attorney-client contexts are ones where it is obvious that the costs of distrust are very high: doctors and attorneys cannot do their jobs well if patients and clients are not forthcoming and revealing with them. Nor can husbands and wives and partners (either of the domestic or commercial kind) have very good relationships with too much distrust. If we think these relationships have social value—and that the law should contribute to helping produce and sustain that value—the law must help facilitate trust and mitigate the high costs of distrust.

One way to optimize the fiduciary relationship, then, is to allow resort to the legal sanctions associated with fiduciary duties to create a safe environment for trust to flourish. Because the costs of distrust are too high, fiduciaries must be controlled by the law. Potentially more important, however, than the actual enforcement of strong duties to target distrust and betrayed trust directly is fiduciary law's "framing" function, as Margaret Blair and Lynn Stout have called it.[36] The gist of this idea is that "fiduciary duty rules, and the strong language in judicial opinions such as *Meinhard*, arguably help create extralegal norms."[37] In short, fiduciary law is about signaling to fiduciaries that they ought not to be self-interested in transactions with and for their beneficiaries; it is generative of trust where costs of distrust are especially high.

Friendship is clearly a setting where costs of distrust are high. For a friendship to function properly and to achieve the requisite intimacy to enable it to be the source of so much pleasure and dignity, friends must have a reliable trust between them. Friends cannot be friends at all without disclosure, authenticity, and openness. Accordingly, it would be beneficial for fiduciary duty law to signal to friends the standard of conduct appropriate to their setting. To be sure, as Ribstein warns, we "must carefully choose the conduct [we] stigmatize. The law may be ineffective if it tries to develop a norm that is too far removed from existing perceptions of good behavior. Courts squander their moral authority by condemning conduct that people widely regard as being in the ordinary course of business."[38] Yet friendship is certainly a context in which a norm of "good behavior" is reasonably assumed, so stigmatizing the betrayal of close friends hardly seems likely to squander a court's "moral authority." Indeed, quite the reverse may be true: a court may be able to claim its moral authority only by not turning a blind eye when close friends betray one another and demean friendship itself.

The Problems of Monitoring and Opportunism in Friendship

The concept of the fiduciary concerns itself with something other than mere trust. Although trust clearly sits at the center of the concept, fiduciary law also has another related set of preoccupations: trying to minimize monitoring costs in contexts where it is very difficult for a beneficiary to supervise his or her fiduciary and policing the consequent potential for opportunism. As Kenneth Davis once helpfully put it, fiduciary law is in place to avoid having the beneficiary "looking over the fiduciary's shoulder."[39] Friendship, like the classic fiduciary relationships, presents a context where monitoring is difficult, leading to a high potential for opportunism.

Although courts often write as if there is a clear two-part test for finding a confidential relationship—one that requires trust *and* vulnerability, dominance, or influence—a high degree of trust, such as the trust between close friends, necessarily leads to a substantial degree of vulnerability. As Annette Baier argues, "When we trust we accept vulnerability."[40] Indeed, the very concept of trust carries with it some degree of vulnerability from the entrustor to the trustee. Baier goes further, too, foreshadowing my argument here about the friend as a fiduciary: "Trust is an alternative to vigilance and ... trustworthiness is an alternative to constant watching to see what one can and cannot get away with, to recurrent calculations of costs and benefits. Trust is accepted vulnerability to another's power to harm one."[41]

Obviously, this account of trust captures an intimate trust, not the garden-variety trust necessary for parties to a contract. The trust in Baier's account is one that can be shared only by people who genuinely place their welfare into one another's hands. This kind of entrustment is paradigmatically the trust we share with our close friends. Consider this view—also Baier's—that sounds in the tones of fiduciary law quite directly: "[T]o trust is to give discretionary powers to the trusted, to let the trusted decide how ... one's welfare is best advanced, to delay the accounting for a while, to be willing to wait to see how the trusted has advanced one's welfare."[42]

What this form of trust between close friends shows—for this kind of trust is most evident between such intimates—is that the concerns of fiduciary law with monitoring and opportunism are very much relevant between trusting friends. This is especially so because of the broadness of the delegation of discretionary authority between close friends. Baier again: "The assurance typically given (implicitly or explicitly) by the [friend] who invites our trust, unlike that typically given in that peculiar case of... promise or contract, is not assurance of some very specific action or set of actions, but assurance simply that the trusting's welfare is... in good hands."[43] Although contracting parties actually partake of this form of relationship more often than conventionally thought (as we shall see in chapter 6), fiduciary law, unlike traditional contract law, is organized around this mode of interaction: furnishing one party with discretion and very indefinite instructions about how to carry out his or her role.

Thus, Baier connects the core case of trust in a friendship to the concerns of fiduciary law: discretionary authority that is difficult to monitor or supervise that leads to the ability of the fiduciary to harm his or her beneficiary opportunistically. This difficulty of supervision and monitoring stems in some measure from the impossibility of being fully clear about what set of actions a friend must take or refrain from taking in his or her role as a friend.

That this dynamic is typical in friendship cannot be seriously questioned. We cannot always ask our friends if they are betraying our confidences: asking such questions, supervising our intimates regularly, and raising the prospect of distrust does much to degrade trust and to prevent it from forming in the first place. We do not specify detailed contracts with our friends because giving them a wide berth of discretion is itself an act of friendship. Indeed, it is constitutive of friendship not to demand complete preagreement on every detail of friendly performance. But for just that reason, it is difficult to supervise them. We cannot keep too careful tabs with our friends, since that would itself betray intimacy.

Of course, the mere possibility for opportunism is a thin reed on which to hang substantial fiduciary duties with unusual remedies. And, indeed, in the case of friendship, one might think that there would be a very high degree of compliance with the norms of friendship, such that no legally enforceable duties would be necessary. Whether because of reputational harms that bad friends suffer or owing to the mere power of the norms internal to friendship and the personal guilt associated with being a bad friend, one might predict a high degree of compliance with friendship's internal morality. But the case reporters tell a different story: our courts are full of these cases.

Courts could then serve the same function of signaling and framing appropriate conduct in the context of friendship with the rules and moralisms that fiduciary law embraces. Admittedly, this signaling is somewhat easier to communicate to corporate directors, who probably consult lawyers somewhat more often than friends do.[44] But I doubt it is true that people only learn that the law controls their conduct and, accordingly, conform their conduct to the legal norms, through lawyers or legal research. Many of us generally hope the criminal law deters crime, even though an average criminal probably does not consult with a lawyer or law books before committing a crime.[45] Something about the justice system's coercive enforcement mechanisms penetrates into society to help members control their conduct. There is nothing very mysterious about this either: information about coercion trickles down somewhat easily. So even though the signaling Delaware courts can achieve in the corporate context is probably more efficient (because corporate counsel are following the caselaw pretty carefully), there is no reason to think that signaling cannot also function properly, albeit indirectly, in the friendship context.

Indeed, friends probably do consult lawyers in many of the sorts of cases to which fiduciary duties would apply. When we sell our businesses or our homes to our friends, we may very well get lawyers involved. Many of the cases I cite as examples of the friendship-fiduciary contexts below actually resemble ones in which parties would traditionally be represented by counsel. And in the hypothetical with which I begin this chapter, when David sells out John to Daniel for a $1 million consulting agreement, David may very well choose to get representation. In these sorts of cases, lawyers would better know how to instruct their clients to behave if only courts would be consistent about the role of friendship in fiduciary law. David might be getting counsel to transact with Daniel and could learn about his potential liabilities to John in a frank conversation with a lawyer schooled in the friend-as-fiduciary model, especially if the transaction was controlled by a jurisdiction holding friends to be fiduciaries.

The Friend as a Moral Fiduciary

I have made my basic case for why the friend seems to fit comfortably within the legal concept of the fiduciary. But here I pause to make clear a different aspect of my argument about treating friends as fiduciaries. Quite apart from what the law does about our friendships, friendships themselves stand much to gain if friends began thinking of their moral duties to one another through the lens of fiduciary obligation. Much, of course, has been written in our philosophical, literary, and cultural tradition about the relationship of friendship. However, relatively little has been written about the special code of ethics involved in it.[46]

This chapter—by placing fiduciary law and friendship side by side—suggests that we might achieve moral guidance within our friendships by taking seriously the "friend-as-fiduciary" model it defends. Consider some of the prototypical duties the law imposes on fiduciaries: the duty of loyalty, the duty of care, the duty of utmost candor and disclosure, the duty of confidentiality, and the duty of good faith and faith dealing. Taken together, these are excellent rules of thumb in our interactions with our friends. Even if they are relatively nonspecific, they have enough content to guide us to the nature of friends' responsibilities to their counterparts.

We must be unselfish with our close friends, acting in ways that promote their best interests. We must affirmatively and diligently aim to serve their welfare without negligence. We must be straight with our friends and try not to obtain unreasonable advantages at their expense. We should not steal business opportunities that come from within the relationship. We should not unduly influence our friends to act in a way at odds with their interests. We must keep and respect their confidences. We must try to avoid conflicts of interest between our personal gain and our duties to our friends. And we must deal with our friends fairly, often showing them special levels of good faith beyond how we might treat strangers. These are deeply important moral guidelines—and although they are not terribly controversial, seeing friends as fiduciaries puts in clear relief the moral duties we owe our friends. Thinking about our role as friends through the lens of fiduciary duties could help us become better and more reliable friends.

Thus, even supposing the friend-as-legal-fiduciary argument fails, there is much to be gained by thinking of the friend as a moral fiduciary. Friends share a paradigmatic form of trust: trust is reposed in us as friends, resulting in tremendous vulnerability and potential for opportunism.[47] Understanding this exposure—an exposure fiduciary law helps illuminate—might help us be more careful with our friendships in our moral lives. This would be no small accomplishment, even if legally enforceable fiduciary duties prove too unseemly for the friendship context.

THE LAW'S AMBIVALENCE ABOUT FRIENDS AS FIDUCIARIES

Unseemly though it may be in theory, in practice courts *have* considered friendship to trigger certain fiduciary duties. It would be dishonest, however, not to acknowledge that courts are ambivalent and inconsistent about their practices in this regard. Let me first survey the landscape, investigating what courts have said and done about treating friends as fiduciaries. Then I'll offer a few specific recommendations about how, going forward, courts ought to analyze cases in which friends allege a breach of a fiduciary duty based on friendship.

It is not hard to find cases in which courts disclaim the notion that friends are fiduciaries for one another. *Wilson v. Zorb* (from chapter 4)[48] is as clear as any case—and makes the point well because the court went out of its way to be explicit about the parties' "close friend[ship] for many years," noting that they were "intimately associated in social activities." The court detailed how often the parties socialized and the nature of their relationship, indicating that their personal relationship was distinct from their professional one. Nevertheless, the court rejected the claim that the friends stood in a fiduciary relationship to each other. This conclusion is a common one (as we also saw in chapter 4).[49] Perhaps a more radical statement of the principle comes from a 1993 case, *Silvia Moroder Leon y Castillo v. Keck, Mahin & Cate:* a "trusting friendship . . . however strong, does not establish a fiduciary relationship."[50] Or, perhaps with more explanation, from an 1881 Connecticut case, *Hemingway v. Coleman:*

> We have before us a contract of sale, the parties to which are of full mental capacity; the vendor believes the vendee to be her friend, and that the friendship, dating from the time when he served her husband as a laborer, has continued unbroken during the seven years which had elapsed since that service terminated; and she believes him to be honest because of his fidelity. Although friends in fact, in law and equity they were strangers and stood at arms length in the matter of contract; for friendship is unknown to law or equity; in it neither finds any relation involving special confidence. He had not by being a friend become the guardian of her interests in any such sense as to impose upon him a legal duty to sacrifice his own to theirs.[51]

Often courts give even more detail in their refusal to recognize friendships as fiduciary relationships, rather than relying on broad pronouncements about friendship's immunity from the law. They often specify that friendships can exist among the relationships the court will consider fiduciary or confidential but that the friendship itself cannot be the predicate on which a fiduciary relationship can be established. This idea is routinely expressed by a court's looking for additional evidence of "undue influence" or "dominance" within the relationship to trigger the fiduciary duties.[52]

But not all courts would be uncomfortable with my attempt here to defend the idea that the friend deserves to be treated as a fiduciary. For example, *Thompson v. Thompson*, a 1928 California case, held that "[f]iduciary relations are not found solely in those legal relationships, such as guardian and ward, husband and wife, trustee and beneficiary, but are also found where in fact the relation of trust and confidence exists between trusting friends."[53] Other California courts have similarly recognized that "friendship, affection, and a close relationship" are sufficient to trigger fiduciary obligations.[54] Still another California case required of a friend that she prove her utmost good faith to her friend, a standard reserved for those in fiduciary relationships; the friendship itself served as the predicate on which to base the fiduciary obligation.[55] And a California court in 1972 explicitly wrote, "we have no difficulty in finding a fiduciary relationship established…*by virtue of* the long, intimate, personal friendship of" the parties.[56]

California is not alone in recognizing the friend as a legal fiduciary. Courts all over the nation have embraced the idea that a friendship can trigger fiduciary obligations;[57] certainly, friendship is often listed among the relationships that can be considered fiduciary.[58] One court even clearly specified that the fiduciary duty of good faith and fair dealing requires friends to give each other a "fair price" in a transaction between friends.[59] Two other courts imposed constructive trusts—classic fiduciary remedies—over the property of defendants in part because the defendants stood in fiduciary relationships to their "close friends," whose property they misappropriated.[60] And another court found a friendship to support the duty of good faith and the duty to act "with due regard to the interests of the other party."[61] Ultimately, courts will often acknowledge that friendship "is often an important consideration and undoubtedly furnishes a vantage ground for one is not likely to expect a friend to deceive him into a bad bargain. As against a friend no shield is worn nor sword drawn in defense. Friendship tends to disarm."[62]

The latter set of cases basically adopt the perspective of this chapter: our close friends should be considered our legal fiduciaries. But one could go further in treating friends as fiduciaries: one friend's very status as a close friend could implicate the other friend's vulnerability, such that perhaps courts should not need to pursue too carefully a separate second-stage inquiry about dominance, superiority, or influence. Consider *In re Estate of Long*, a case that gestures toward this further step: "Mere friendship can result in a fiduciary relationship. *This position of superiority may arise by reason of friendship.*"[63]

In *Long*, the court makes explicit that "mere" friendship alone can lead to the trust and vulnerability necessary to establish a fiduciary relationship, which can, in turn, trigger all sorts of obligations and special remedies for their breach. Although the determination of a fiduciary relationship between friends will always need to remain a fact-based inquiry (for there are many types of friendships, and only close ones will implicate the sort of trust relationship so central to the fiduciary concept), there is good reason that courts should not hesitate to conclude that close friendships are appropriate contexts in which to enforce fiduciary duties. The friendship itself, as *Long* recognizes, can be the source of the requisite "superiority."

Indeed, some courts, when presented with a transaction that seems to have been based in no small part on friendship, hold friends to fiduciary duties *even if* the parties involved were both sophisticated. Thus, even if it would be hard to say with a straight face that one friend "dominated" another in a given context—a traditional consideration in fiduciary duty cases—friendship itself can give rise to fiduciary duties. Consider in this regard *Gray v. Reeves*:

> A point is made that Mr. Gray was a shrewd and successful business man and ought not to have been misled by promises that, when revealed in the courtroom, seem to be unreasonable. But [this argument] overlook[s] an element which disarms caution; that is, friendship.... The impulse that leads men to trust those in whom they have confidence cannot be ignored by the courts.... Hence, when men deal as friends and the one accepts that as true which, but for the element of friendship, would put a man upon inquiry, the law will protect him in his trust as certainly as it will deny him relief if the personal relations of the parties are such that the dealing is at arm's length.... To say that a man who is moved to part with his money under such circumstances is to be held at arm's length is to deny sustenance to the very root of society; to make friendship a liability instead of an asset.[64]

Bush v. Stone is another instance of a court focusing on a friendship to create fiduciary obligations, notwithstanding a plaintiff's experience and business sophistication. The majority held the defendant to fiduciary standards because the parties "worked together, they had repeated business contacts, and were close family-type friends." The court emphasized that "the plaintiff and defendant became close personal friends . . . and remained as such for . . . 26 years. The plaintiff trusted the defendant the same as if he were a member of his own family [and] [t]hey hunted, visited, and had repeated social contacts together."[65] The friendship supported certain rights for the beneficiary plaintiff, notwithstanding the plaintiff's expertise in the type of transactions at issue.

Thus, courts have embraced the friend-as-fiduciary model in certain contexts and rejected it in others. In some respects, this ambivalence should not be surprising, for there are many ways of being friends. This is clearly a context where the rough cut of chapter 1 reveals itself to be somewhat inadequate because to gain fiduciary treatment in law, friends probably need to be especially "close" friends. Not all modalities of friendship raise all the concerns with which fiduciary law is preoccupied, and the reality of friendship's many forms virtually requires a subtle, fact-based analysis in any given friendship presented to a court. We do have casual friendships, and it would be unreasonable for the law to impose special duties on us when we are little more than acquaintances. Texas courts have gone out of their way to distinguish "business friendships" from close, personal ones that get fiduciary treatment in the law.[66] Ultimately, there will always need to be something ad hoc about a court's determination of whether a friendship rises to the level of a fiduciary relationship in any given context, and it will always be the beneficiary's burden to put forth clear and convincing evidence of the nature of the friendship. That is true to the flexibility of fiduciary law and to friendship's variety.

Notwithstanding the difficulty of making general pronouncements about friendship and fiduciary law, however, there are a few more specific guidelines that are worth considering to aid courts in integrating the friend-as-fiduciary idea promulgated here into fiduciary law. As Justice Frankfurter famously wrote, "[T]o say that a man is a fiduciary only begins analysis; it gives direction to further inquiry."[67] The bag of fiduciary duties actually varies among classes of fiduciaries, so more work is necessary in specifying the how.

HOW TO TREAT FRIENDS AS LEGAL FIDUCIARIES

Here I present five recommendations that, together, paint a fuller picture of my friends-as-fiduciaries proposal. These are attempts to be more concrete about how to implement the friends-as-fiduciary idea that pervades this chapter. They are not exhaustive rules, but they should give a feel for how to move from the basic thought that we should incorporate insights about friendship into our law to actual rules in a particular policy area.

Close Friends Are Vulnerable to One Another

As discussed above, some courts have started to appreciate the "disarming" nature of close friendship. These courts are on the right track and should be emulated. When courts understand that certain types of close friendships depend on vulnerability, they will no longer seek any additional evidence of vulnerability or inferiority in trusting friendships. Because there are many categories of friendship and types of friends, it would be implausible to create a presumption that all friends are fiduciaries for each other—but courts should be very careful before announcing, as so many do, that "mere" friendship cannot serve as a predicate for a fiduciary relationship. Courts are far from consistent on this point, and the survey of the evidence here suggests that friendship *can* serve as predicate for a fiduciary relationship. Further, the normative argument here suggests that friendship of a certain kind should be able to serve as one; indeed, being true to fiduciary law may require it.

To be sure, courts should not lose sight of what they are trying to do through their application of fiduciary law and should not thoughtlessly add a relationship to the list for rote application. But close friends should not be immune from the grip of fiduciary law; their trust in one another should be recognized as a paradigmatic form of trust that leads to vulnerability.

A "Friendship Judgment Rule"

Beyond the guidance the friends-as-fiduciaries idea can offer in identifying fiduciary relationships, it can also help recommend the specific duties that should flow from the relationship. As I highlighted earlier, the panoply of fiduciary duties is implemented variously (in scope and substance) depending on the relational context. In the corporate law context, where the enforcement of fiduciary duties is relatively lax (relative to the trustee-beneficiary context, for example), corporate fiduciaries are presumed to have performed their duties of care with due diligence. This presumption is enshrined in "the business judgment rule," which is, as one famous case puts it, "a presumption that in making a business decision the directors of a corporation acted on an informed basis, in good faith, and in the honest belief that the action taken was in the best interests of the company."[68]

In enforcing a friend's duty of care, it seems that the parallels with the corporate law context warrant an analogous "friendship judgment rule."[69] Friends have extremely complex and broad-ranging relationships: the duties of friendship are always underspecified and can always shift from under our feet. Friendships themselves are always organic, always in motion, and always responsive to shifting realities. It is impossible to be too exacting about what would count as meeting or violating a relevant duty of care; the discretion friends need recommends deferring to the judgment of friends unless departures from good behavior are manifest. Mitchell also finds a rationale for the business judgment rule in a court's difficulty in ever assessing what the "truth" of proper conduct would be in a corporate enterprise.[70] The same may be the case in friendship, too: courts won't know the "truth" about the performance of good friendship, so we should give friends a wide berth.

Obviously, there is a danger that the exception of a friendship judgment rule might swallow the whole range of fiduciary duties that this chapter seeks to have imposed on friends. It might be a hollow victory for my agenda here if the enforcement of fiduciary duties in the context of friendship mirrored the pattern we see in corporate law with very feeble enforcement.[71] But aspects of the duty of candor, the duty of confidentiality, the duty of utmost good faith and fair dealing, and the duty of loyalty would remain enforceable, a friendship-judgment rule notwithstanding. Even the duty of care could be found to be violated. In any case, as one court memorably put it, at "the heart of a...fiduciary's duty is an attitude, not a rule."[72] And fiduciary law needs a reorientation of its set of attitudes to be more sensitive to the fragility of trust within friendships and to do its part to help sustain and promote trust between friends.

Being Loyal to Friends

The duty of loyalty can be enforced very rigorously, allowing courts to void all "interested" transactions and enabling courts to sanction any fiduciary who does not always put his or her beneficiary's welfare as a first priority. But it can be enforced more selectively, too, having courts focus mainly on bad acts or malfeasance of the fiduciary, on whether a fiduciary has misappropriated opportunities that came to him or her on account of having the status of fiduciary, on egregious self-dealing without consent of the principal, and on competition with a principal without his or her consent. The latter set of foci of enforcing the duty of loyalty makes more sense in the context of friendship.

The blurry lines within the morality of friendship that provide people with only schematic guidance about how far they have to go to pursue their friends' best interests—when one is competing with a friend for the same jobs must one give him or her all the market information one has at one's disposal, for example?—suggest that it would be very hard to require friends to be fully altruistic. Indeed, a "despotism of virtue"[73] might draw fiduciary law too far away from the moral standards of conduct that give it its authority. Friends have high expectations of one another, but they can also be more forgiving than they would be of a stranger who wrongs them, whose excuse may trigger indifference. Accordingly, a more flexible and less stringent form of the duty of loyalty to govern friendships is probably warranted.

Giving Friends Their Due

There is at least one area in the law of fiduciaries (introduced in chapter 4) where it seems *inadvisable* to treat the friend as a fiduciary: that of gifts and wills. Indeed, some courts have also recognized this exception to treating friends as fiduciaries.

In the law of gifts and wills, when fiduciaries are named as donees in transactional contexts in which they take part, they are traditionally required to prove that they have not unduly influenced the donor or decedent in her choices about how to dispose of her property.[74] The burden of proof falls immediately on the fiduciary-donee to make a showing of utmost good faith and to prove an absence of undue influence.[75] If the law more broadly embraced the friend-as-fiduciary model, it would likely become much more difficult for donors to gift or bequeath property to their friends. This result may be perverse, so any more systematic effort to recognize the friend as a fiduciary should embrace mindfulness that the fiduciary burden of proof in the gift and will context should probably not apply to friends, where good faith gift giving seems common.

As it turns out, some courts have already recognized that preventing friends from accepting a gift or becoming a donee under a will makes little sense, fiduciary law notwithstanding. Indeed, sometimes courts will allow a friend to take a gift or bequest without a requisite showing of utmost good faith and an absence of undue influence, *even if the donee and donor are in an established formal fiduciary relationship.*[76] For example, consider this pronouncement of a Massachusetts appellate court in *Markell v. Sidney B. Pfeifer Foundation, Inc.:*

> Not infrequently an attorney will draft a will or do estate planning work for a relative or close friend and associate; and in such a case, if the attorney or a member of his immediate family is named as a [donee], a court called upon to examine the transaction, although it may suggest that the better practice would be for an independent attorney to do such work, and although it may state that such a transaction should be viewed with great circumspection, will not apply to such a transaction the presumption of impropriety which is applied when dealing with one whose fiduciary status is uncomplicated by ties of... close friendship.[77]

The court even furnishes a reason for this differential treatment of those in fiduciary relationships (and double fiduciary relationships from the perspective of the friend-as-fiduciary model, to boot):

> The reason for the distinction is that, in the case of an exclusively fiduciary relationship, it can reasonably be presumed that that relationship influenced the transaction; and the policy of the law is to favor the fiduciary's duty of loyalty and to discourage business or donative transactions which inure to the personal benefit of the fiduciary. But where there is also a relationship of... friendship, gifts or other acts of generosity are natural and to be expected; in such a setting the reason for the presumption of impropriety dissolves.[78]

Thus, friendship can provide a reason for generosity, such that gifts and bequests between friends should not be held to the strict standards of other fiduciaries.[79] The latter parties must show utmost good faith and an absence of undue influence. Otherwise, their gifts and bequests will be invalidated as a matter of law.

To be sure, not all courts agree that a close friendship in an otherwise fiduciary relationship is sufficient to shift the burden of proof of undue influence back to the contestant rather than it being laid squarely on the fiduciary to rebut a presumption of undue influence.[80] Indeed, *Cleary v. Cleary,* a more recent decision of the Supreme Judicial Court of Massachusetts, flatly rejects the *Markell* case.[81] Still, even if it remains true (in Massachusetts, anyway) that a formal fiduciary *who is also a friend* will still be subject to the traditional fiduciary burden to rebut the presumption of undue influence, the *Cleary* court simultaneously leaves open the possibility that, at least for the purposes of gifts, trusts, and wills, a "friend is not usually a fiduciary, and therefore the ordinary burden of proof applies."[82]

Although it is likely that courts following *Cleary* would be required to hold the friend to the special burden of the fiduciary if the law more generally recognized the friend as a fiduciary, one could still disaggregate the general demarcation of a fiduciary relationship in friendship and its attendant consequences. As I described earlier, calling a relationship fiduciary does not generally mean that a standard set of duties always applies. Rather, the law should allow friends to receive gifts and bequests in transactions in which they take part without having the burden of proof to show their good faith and to rebut a presumption of undue influence.[83] Giving gifts is so quintessentially central to friendship that it makes little sense to have the law look on such gifts with any special suspicion.

Restituting Friends

Just as in cases of garden-variety breach of fiduciary duty, there can be no singular off-the-rack remedy when it comes to remediating breaches of the fiduciary duties of friendship. "Restitution" is the broad name we give to the equitable remedies for breaches of fiduciary duties. But, as I suggested earlier, restitution comes in many forms and is not the exclusive remedy for breaches of fiduciary duties. Accordingly, it would not be sensible to focus on any particular remedy as *the* remedy appropriate to breaches in the context of friendship.

But there is one form of restitution that might be recommended more broadly, even if it will not fit well with every case. In particular, Hanoch Dagan's discussion about restitution in contexts of informal intimacy helps identify a particularly appealing form of remedy when someone breaches fiduciary duties to a friend: contribution-based restitution. Dagan sees this as an especially useful remedy for the "legal facilitation of relationships of long-term reciprocity" in contexts important to one's identity but driven by neither "sheer pursuit of self-interest" nor by pure "acts of good-samaritanism."[84] Because friendships fit the bill—they are long-term relationships of reciprocity that are neither fully altruistic nor egoistic and are sources of solidarity and identity—Dagan's preferred remedy may be a useful guide in remediating breaches of the fiduciary duties of friendship.

Dagan's particular form of restitutionary remedy that might be useful in adjudicating allegations of breaches in the friendship context arises most clearly in cohabitation cases, one of which also presents as a friendship case of a sort. Dagan's recounting of the tale of *Frambach v. Dunihue*[85] sets the stage. A widower with seven children and a couple with four children became close friends—so close, in fact, that they decided to cohabit with their families over a nineteen-year period. Eventually, one party asked the other to leave their joint home (though there is little indication in the record of why the friendship came to a sudden end). Although the trial court decided that the families and friends should share the property's value down the middle, the appellate court took an approach common to the cohabitation context (when there is no contract between the parties that otherwise controls asset distribution on break-up): contribution-based restitution. That is, each family was awarded a "share" of the joint home in proportion to how much money and effort it had put into creating the value. Dagan warns us that it would be hard to see the contribution-based restitutionary remedy as the majority position—plenty of courts treat cohabitants as essentially married, splitting property down the middle, while many other courts essentially try to deter "living in sin" by refusing to make any equitable distributions. Still, Dagan demonstrates that it is a common and desirable "middle-of-the-road" approach.

Dagan identifies and endorses a set of normative rationales for contribution-based restitution in the cohabitation context that might apply between friends. First, he sees those engaged in informal intimacies as falling somewhere "between spouses and strangers." Accordingly, he believes that the doctrinal structure should support that situation, affording those in informal intimacies more protection than the law would give to strangers, who receive nothing other than their contractual entitlements, and less protection than spouses, who he thinks should receive half of an estate to reflect the altruistic aspirations of marriage. Something about that rings true in the standard case of friendship.

Second, Dagan explains a detail about the administration of the contribution-based restitution remedy: it measures only benefits that fall outside "the ordinary give-and-take of a shared life."[86] This limitation enables those in long-term reciprocal relationships to avoid keeping tabs in the day-to-day services the parties provide for one another and enables courts to stay out of intimacies to some reasonable extent. The focus of contribution-based restitution, then, is on substantial investments of time, energy, or money into a partner's business or assets that fall outside the ordinary give-and-take.

One can easily see here as well why this type of remedy might usefully guide the law in friend-as-fiduciary cases. Certainly, no one wants broken friendships to lead to litigation as a matter of course; the idea of people suing their ex-friends for the value of their ordinary services as friends sounds preposterous. Focusing on substantial benefits that can be restituted through a contribution-based remedy seems appealing to limit the number of suits courts would need to consider and to give effect to the reality that much that we do for our friends is gratuitous—and should remain so (for all the reasons gifts should be encouraged and facilitated between friends). But sometimes we aren't doing things fully gratuitously, and it isn't fair to immunize all exchange between friends from the law just because we sometimes intend to do things gratuitously.[87]

To put this remedy into application, consider the hypothetical with which I began. John might sue David not for a full disgorgement of his $1 million contract on account of his potential bad faith, potential breach of a duty of confidentiality, and a potential misappropriation of a "corporate" opportunity but for a restitutionary remedy based on his contribution to the idea and its development; the recovery would not be offset by any friendship benefits extrinsic to the idea.

Ultimately, even if contribution-based recovery occupies an important place as a default rule of sorts for breaches of friendship's fiduciary duties, surely sometimes it will not be a proper remedy. Even in the John and David hypothetical, it may seem undercompensatory. Indeed, precisely because John and David so much more resemble spouses than strangers, a remedy closer to marriage's presumption of equal division may seem in order: friendship, like marriage, should be, ideally and aspirationally, egalitarian. So sometimes it would make sense to require a friend-defendant to share earnings and award a profits-based remedy rather than a contribution-based remedy. That would be a judgment call that would depend on the intensity of the friendship—and judges have the capacity to differentiate between degrees of friendship for the purpose of constructing an appropriate equitable remedy. Perhaps, however, they should presume an absence of a spouse-like friendship unless there is clear and convincing evidence otherwise.

The fiduciary concept recognized by our law is a flexible one. I have argued here that it is flexible enough to encompass enforcement of certain duties of friendship that people all know well from their moral lives. Friendship—of a certain sort, to be sure—is undoubtedly a relationship of trust and vulnerability, and fiduciary law is set up specifically to give effect to and frame this sort of special relationship. Even if some are ultimately persuaded that the misfit between the friend and the legal fiduciary is too severe or that recognizing the friend as a fiduciary would be too damaging to fiduciary law or the institution of friendship itself, much can be learned from putting fiduciary law and friendship side by side. Indeed, there are lessons of proper conduct that friends would do well to internalize even if they will never carry the force of law. Moreover, whatever one thinks of the normative agenda presented here of trying to get more courts to appreciate the trust and vulnerability constitutive of close friendships, I have shown that the law in many jurisdictions already treats certain types of friends as fiduciaries and that many plaintiffs ask courts to treat defendant-friends (or former friends) as fiduciaries, subject to their special duties and remedial opportunities. This chapter should help guide courts when they are presented with such claims, and should enable them to adjudicate these cases more systematically and with greater sophistication. Nothing I have argued for here suggests that all friends qualify for fiduciary treatment; rather, courts must not fear that there is some category mistake being made by those claiming fiduciary duties from their friends or former friends.

My hope is that this chapter has furnished much more detail about how a recognition and sensitivity to friendship in the law can be implemented. Chapter 4 performed a survey of how the friend is already recognized in law—and made many suggestions about how we might build into it still more sensitivity to friendship. The amount of detail here shows just how much work is necessary to translate my general recommendation in this book into specific policy designs and, ultimately, how much a careful study of certain legal concepts can do to illuminate friendship itself. These tasks are also at the center of chapter 6. And chapter 7 aims to reckon with a central objection that still must be met to convince readers to climb aboard.

CHAPTER 6

Friendships as Contracts—and Contracts as Friendships?

C HAPTER 5 SHOWED just how much work is necessary to flesh out any individual suggestion for how to integrate the study of friendship and the law. Still, the effort does bear fruit: there are ways of thinking about friendship's character that help us see it as amenable to treatment by legal doctrines that are already designed to admit relational considerations. Moreover, thinking about certain legal frameworks helps illuminate something about friendship's demands in people's moral lives. This chapter also pursues this strategy of getting deeply into an area of law and legal theory to see what we might be able to learn about friendship and the law itself.

We know that marriages take the form of contract. But contracts are not generally like marriages. Friendships are also, in part, types of contracts. Yet many contracts are also like friendships. At the least, it is more illuminating to think of contracts as friendships than it is to think of contracts as marriages. Let me explain.

For some time, so-called relational contract theorists (or "relationalists")—those who urge us to focus on "relational" elements in contracts in order to devise a theory and law of contracts—have sought to convince us that the bulk of contracts are types of marriages, particularly the most relational ones where there is some deep relationship matrix between the parties to the contract.[1] More modestly, perhaps, they suggest that marriage is a good analogy for contracting in relational contexts.

The core idea of "relational contract as marriage" is that most contracts, like marriages, share the following properties: (1) they ensnare parties into and control party compliance through a thick set of social norms; (2) they generally give parties autonomy in resolving internal disputes through those social norms; (3) they are very costly to exit; (4) they leave many terms open; (5) they tend to be incomplete, especially on the issue of how the parties will cooperate over time; (6) they establish interdependence, partiality, and solidarity; and (7) contracting parties will tend to presume good faith and best efforts in performance and will implicitly tend to allow for easy modifications for changed circumstances.

The purchase of the analogy for relationalists, however, is tied up with their most general point that discrete one-shot transactions between strangers have occupied the center of "classical" contract law and theory to its detriment. In reality, as relationalists have usefully been showing since 1960s, contracts involve thicker relationships than those among mere strangers. Indeed, they argue that we cannot and should not understand the social practice of contracting as a practice among strangers—and that insight has dramatic implications for how we regulate our entire market economy.

This chapter makes an effort to replace the marriage analogy in relational contract thinking with a story that ties contracts and friendships closer together. I first provide a brief overview of relational contract theory (as it is conceptualized by contracts scholars in law schools). Then I highlight how friendships are very much like relational contracts and how friendship can be illuminated by exposing its morphological similarity to relational contracts. I then turn to argue that friendship *rather than marriage* should be viewed as the paradigmatic relational contract. Finally, I explore some of the legal and theoretical ramifications of my view that friendships are similar to relational contracts.

RELATIONAL CONTRACT THEORY: A SYMPATHETIC RECONSTRUCTION

As many have observed before me, it is a difficult business to summarize relational contract theory. There are many "relationalists"—and some who view themselves as relational contract theory's critics concede that "we are all relationalists now."[2] Still, for my purposes here, a quick sketch should be sufficient.

At the center of relational contract theory are three basic commitments: an empirical observation about the real world of contracting, a related effort to reorient the paradigm under which contract theory is organized and analyzed, and a set of normative and doctrinal prescriptions for how to apply contract law to disputing parties. It is probably fair to say that it is only the empirical observation (and a moderate form of it, at that) that the theory's critics are willing to concede.

The Empirical Claim

The empirical observation around which consensus has formed is that many contracts in the real world involve long-term, complex relationships and are not merely "one-shot" discrete transactions. In these "relational contracts," social norms often seem to play a larger role in controlling the parties' conduct than the threat of legal sanctions do.[3] Trust and social solidarity tend to underwrite and support (and, in turn, tend to be underwritten and supported by) these types of contracts; and informal cooperation, coordination, and collaboration are typical. In these types of relationships, parties expect some form of loyalty (though less loyalty than would be expected of the fiduciaries encountered in chapter 5).

Although contracts between strangers are, of course, possible, relational contract theory emphasizes that many contracts do not show this pattern of strangership. By contrast, relationalists highlight just how often contracts are formed between parties who are otherwise connected in preexisting and ongoing relationships. Business relationships often involve meaningful affective ties—business friendships aren't merely "fictive" but can often involve real affect.[4] More, relationalists observe that when parties find themselves in such ongoing relationships, contractual behavior tends to be driven by informal and implicit dimensions of their mutual understandings rather than by any "paper" deal that exists on account of formalities taken within the relationship, if any.

Just noticing that many contracts show a pattern of ongoing relationships with informality is not terribly controversial anymore, though it took awhile for these insights to be fully understood by and incorporated into mainstream contracts thinking. There are, nevertheless, two significant cleavages between relationalists and nonrelationalists that have emerged from this now widely accepted empirical observation: (1) what follows from this observation as a matter of general contract theory and (2) what follows from it as a normative and prescriptive matter within contract law. At least some of that dispute turns on the meaning and extent of the empirical claim, after all. So we will have to revisit this supposedly consensual part of relational contract theory once we see some more about what is at stake.

The Analytic Claim for a Paradigm
Shift in Contract Theory

Relationalists contend that relational contracts are so prevalent in the real world that the general theory of contract must itself acknowledge this practical reality. That is, contract theory and law must be oriented in such a way as to put relational contracts at their center. This can mean several things.

First, if relationalists are right that many (some would say *most*, if not *all*) contracts are relational,[5] it could be useful to analyze contracts on the basis of some continuum or gradation from the most discrete to the most relational. This method of analysis would enable one to differentiate more easily among types of contracts and apply the policy approach that is appropriate to each contractual context. Second, because relational contracts are so common, relationalists argue that the general theory of contracts needs to respect the nature of real contracts in the world and not operate with a presumption that the law of contracts is to be designed as a law for strangers, in which there is little background trust. Rather, a new paradigm is needed to account for the degree to which relational contracts are central to the enterprise of contracting. This doesn't mean turning every contractual relationship into a fiduciary relationship, but it does mean staying honest to parties' true expectations for one another.

One can easily understand why relational contract theory's analytic claim is more controversial than its underlying empirical claim. Some relationalists might think this analytical claim about reorienting contract theory follows from the empirical claim. But that isn't necessarily true. The empirical claim around which there is little controversy is actually a rather modest one: many contracts are relational. All that follows from this claim, perhaps, is that general contract theory must make room for analyzing and respecting a class of relational contracts. But that hardly requires a paradigm shift. Nonrelationalists' resistance to the analytical claim comes at least in part from their sense that the empirical claim, in its moderate form, can easily be accommodated by slight modifications of reigning contract theories and doctrine. So nonrelationalists can simply reject the more aggressive empirical claim that *most* contracts are meaningfully characterized by relational properties and can be usefully analyzed according to where they fall on the discrete-relational continuum.[6]

This underlying empirical dispute is actually pretty hard to resolve. It is extremely difficult to get a sense of what is happening in "most contracts," and it is very hard to say how pervasive a contract type needs to be to require reorienting the theory of contract. These difficulties are at least part of the reason we are unlikely to see much conciliation between the camps anytime soon.

There has been a recent and useful approximation of the empirical question in some scholars' close look at the 1996 General Social Survey economic sociology module: they find that "people buy and sell goods and services from friends and kin" and that "*substantial percentages of major transactions take place between friends, relatives, or compound ties.*" More specifically, "almost one-half of all used-car purchases from individuals (46.0 percent) and home purchases where no agent is used (46.8 percent) are transactions between relatives, friends, or acquaintances." About one-fourth of purchases of legal services and home maintenance services are similarly within a social network.[7] Does this evidence resolve the dispute about the analytic import of the central empirical claim of relational contract theory? Of course not. But it does at least help the theory get more refined about some of the types of consumer transactions that tend to involve the use of strong social networks.

Even if one isn't overwhelmed by the extant evidence supporting the strong form of the empirical claim, one can nevertheless subscribe to a form of the analytic claim. To wit, one could concede that deeply relational contracts are actually a rather small class of contracts, all things considered, but are so attractive in their foregrounding of cooperation, collaboration, and solidarity that we should want to model other contracts on that particularized, even if somewhat atypical, form. One could argue that modeling contracts on deep relationships of collaboration and solidarity would orient parties better in their transactions—and could even help maximize their surplus.

The opposite is also true, however: one could concede the strong form of the empirical claim and still resist the analytical claim on normative grounds. One could say, along the lines I suggested in chapter 2, that preserving forms of "strangership" is essential to our economy and society and, accordingly, contracts should be modeled on personal distance, as traditional contract theory has been. If we design contracts and orient our contract theory as something categorically different from our personal relationships governed largely by moral and social norms, the argument goes, we are most likely to avoid the juridification or contractualization of intimate personal relations.[8] Although we lose something in the fit of the theory (if the strong empirical claim is, after all, true), we gain some protection of the private sphere from the law. That outcome, it is argued, is normatively desirable (though chapter 7 and much of this book ultimately reject this argument).

There is one more real benefit of relational theory, however: unlike most of its competitors for organizing thinking about contracts, it is highly pluralistic. Many have tired of seeking a fully coherent singular theory of contractual obligation because it is just too hard to find a singular narrative that fits the whole world of contract doctrine. Sometimes promises matter, sometimes reliance matters, sometimes economic efficiency matters, sometimes status matters. So relationalists by and large want a set of doctrines that doesn't promote just one thing but really tries to make sense of the relationships and transactions that the thing called "contract law" controls.[9]

The Normative Claim About Contract Law

Aside from description and theory, there is also a relationalist claim about what the law *should* be. And there is plenty of controversy about relational contract *law*.

No use reinventing the wheel here, so consider Mel Eisenberg's summary of the doctrinal suggestions relationalists embrace:

(1) Rules that, in the case of relational contracts, would soften or reverse the bite of the rigid offer-and-acceptance format of classical contract law, and the corresponding intolerance of classical contract law for indefiniteness, agreements to agree, and agreements to negotiate in good faith. (2) Rules that would impose upon parties to a relational contract a broad obligation to perform in good faith. (3) Rules that would broaden the kinds of changed circumstances (impossibility, impracticability, and frustration) that constitute an excuse for nonperformance of a relational contract. (4) Rules that would give content to particular kinds of contractual provisions that may be found in relational contracts, such as best-efforts clauses or unilateral rights to terminate at will. (5) Rules that would treat relational contracts like partnerships, in the sense that such contracts involve a mutual enterprise and should be construed in that light. (6) Rules that would keep a relational contract together. (7) Rules that would impose upon parties to a relational contract a duty to bargain in good faith to make equitable price adjustments when changed circumstances occur, and would perhaps even impose upon the advantaged party a duty to accept an equitable adjustment proposed in good faith by the disadvantaged party. (8) Rules that

would permit the courts to adapt or revise the terms of ongoing relational contracts in such a way that an unexpected loss that would otherwise fall on one party will be shared by reducing the other party's profits.[10]

We don't need to take each suggestion apart to get the gist: In response to the reality and centrality of relational contracts to understanding contractual practice, relationalists put forward doctrinal suggestions that tend to be a set of loose standards rather than formalistic rules. Most important (and this is not reflected in Eisenberg's list of doctrines), as Ian Macneil has recently emphasized, the relationalists' key recommendation to courts is that when they are faced with disputing parties in relational contracts, they should seek to apply the intrinsic norms of the relationship to settle the dispute—even if an application of classical contract law to the parties' paper deal might lead to a different conclusion. Again, relationalists emphasize the implicit dimension of contractual undertakings and the unfolding nature of the contractual relationship, which develops and gets modified over time, even if the paper deal doesn't reflect such developments. Relationalists direct judges to apply social norms to disputing parties, since the social norms are the real scaffolding for the parties' relationship and must be given respect and effect. This doesn't mean, however, that relationalists reject the application of all external norms; applying legal norms is always, in part, the application of external norms. Relationalists only require heightened sensitivity to calibration with internal norms as well.[11]

In their proposal's most modest form, relationalists urge incorporating trade usages, courses of dealing, courses of performance, and a general good faith obligation. But this urging has largely already been adopted by modern contract law through the Uniform Commercial Code; the common law also already embraces these minimalist relationalist prescriptions.[12] Most adherents of modern relational contract theory, however, believe that these modest incorporation strategies of letting the parties' relational norms control as a legal matter do not go far enough. They recommend a much more substantial effort to mine parties' relationships for implicit understandings and social norms—and to analyze their relational properties to help resolve disputes between them. These implicit understandings can play a role in adjudicating questions of formation (did a contract form?), performance (was this really what the parties expected or is this a breach?), modification (did the parties modify their agreement?), interpretation (what did the parties mean in their agreement?), and remedies (what does the aggrieved party deserve on account of the breaching party's behavior?).

This set of normative claims that relationalists offer about their preferred approach to contract law has met with substantial opposition. In the first place, it is very difficult for some to envision how to operationalize a special set of judicial principles to govern relational contracts. To operationalize the principles successfully, one would seem to need an easily workable definition of the relational contract as a threshold matter. However, it is difficult, nonrelationalists argue, to pin down with any degree of clarity which contracts should count as relational ones.[13] Although duration is often the test used as a shortcut by relationalists, it is clearly an insufficient one: there are short-term transactions that trigger substantial interdependence and long-term transactions that remain "discrete" and controlled primarily by legal documents and formalities. And once the test for what counts as a relational contract becomes so diluted as to encompass every contract (because every contract establishes some relationship), there is not, as Eisenberg has argued, much room for a special relational contract law.

But Eisenberg's critique of relational contract theory misses its mark in several ways. First, it is only one brand of the normative claim that seeks special treatment for a small class of relational contracts. More thoroughgoing relationalists might very well concede that there need not be a special set of standards that would only apply to "relational contracts." These relationalists would have contract law develop a generalized law to apply to all or most contracts, in light of their relational nature. So the operationalized legal definition of the relational contract that Eisenberg considers necessary may not be after all.

Alternatively, if we take Macneil's most recent suggestion for the content of relational contract law—to apply internal relational norms to contractual disputes, whatever the relationship and whatever the contract—no complicated work needs to be done to separate relational and nonrelational contracts. Rather, to the extent that any relational norms exist, the law should remain sensitive to them. That may not be an easy task, but it doesn't implicate Eisenberg's concern about differentiating relational and nonrelational contracts.

More important, perhaps, Eisenberg fails to prove that there is no way to operationalize a law of relational contracts (though it is, admittedly, always tough to prove a negative). Although he seems to think a "spectrum approach" (locating contracts along a discrete-relational continuum) is "acceptable...from a sociological and economic perspective," he concludes that such a continuum cannot be used within contract law because "many or most contracts will have both relational and discrete elements" and because "[r]ules whose applicability depended on where a contract is located in a spectrum—that is, on how many relational indicia the contract has and of what kind—would be rules in name only."[14]

Yet this entire argument hinges on a substantive view about the desirability of rules over standards, something relationalists tend to contest as part of their normative claim. Indeed, Eisenberg offers no *argument* that standards are not capable of being legally operationalized; he simply states that it would be hard to develop clear rules using a spectrum approach, revealing his preference for rules over standards. The multifactor set of inquiries that relationalists prefer are not less law-like than clear formal rules, though it is also clear why "rule of law" rhetoric is routinely invoked against relational contract theory's doctrinal and normative prescriptions, which reflect standards, not rules. When relationalists tell judges to apply the intrinsic norms between parties to a contract dispute, we can debate whether that is a good direction to give judges and whether a judge could ever carry out the direction *well* in light of evidentiary difficulties. But we can't really say with any certainty that such a direction is not capable of being operationalized in the law.

There are two related substantive objections to directing judges to apply such norms to contractual disputes. One is an argument deriving from the pathbreaking work of Lisa Bernstein, which tends to show that the law cannot easily incorporate trade usages and customs: few actually exist and few are generally observed.[15] This skepticism that the law can discover internal norms within relational contracts is quite relevant for relational contract theory: whereas relationalists claim that the law should incorporate and seek such norms, evidence that tends to show that such norms are rarely mutually understood and rarely embraced by parties surely complicates the viability of that claim.

Still, there is reason to believe that Bernstein's work can be read more as a cautionary note about *evidence* than as a decisive proof against relational contract theory as such. In short, Bernstein's empirical studies are obviously limited to a few areas of inquiry. And although they are fascinating windows into certain trade communities, it hardly follows that there are no immanent norms that exist, that can be discovered, that are followed, and that courts can enforce.[16] In any case, another plausible response to Bernstein's findings is to find ways to get courts to send relational disputes into mediation, arbitration, and agency management, since these institutions are likely more capable than courts of discovering such norms anyway, if and when they exist.

Eric Posner offers a second and related concern about the possibility for and likelihood of "radical judicial error."[17] He thinks judges would not be competent to discover or apply intrinsic norms. He is quite clear that this assumption of radical judicial incompetence is just an assumption, though he offers a bit of empirical evidence to prove the incompetence in at least one area, consumer credit contracts.[18] The gist of his argument is that judges are going to resolve disputes essentially at random if they are instructed that they must consider parties' internal norms because of their incompetence. However, he thinks it is within judges' competence to engage in formalistic decision-making—and that they should stick to that task. Posner's argument—and the argument from judicial incompetence more generally—supports a formalistic approach to contract law, which sits in substantial tension with relationalists' normative claim about how contract law should be administered. To be sure, formalism may be attractive for other reasons, too—perhaps nonrelational norms in contract law support the underlying relationships best, and judicializing relational norms might interfere with the informality that makes them successful in the first place—but judicial incompetence seems to be central to the nonrelationalist view that implicit social norms ought not govern contractual disputes in court.

This is clearly not the place to attempt to settle the age-old debates between formalists and nonformalists and between objectivists with respect to contract law on the one hand, who favor outward signals of agreement and meaning, and subjectivists on the other, for whom parties' intentions should always prevail. But a few observations seem appropriate in light of the recent effort to rejuvenate formalism in response to the relationalist challenge.

First, the assumption of *radical* judicial error is quite difficult to swallow.[19] Admittedly, the empirical evidence available to settle the question of the error-proneness of judicial decision-making is remarkably thin. Yet the claim that judges would do *no better than random* at using their common sense to understand the underlying deals in contractual contexts, it would seem, should bear the burden of proof.[20] Posner has not met that burden yet, and until and unless he or someone does, to presume that properly instructed judges and juries can get it right much of the time (or at least on average better than random) is far from outlandish. Indeed, even if there is the possibility for radical judicial error in a class of cases, those are the cases in which formalism might be appropriate; relational norms can still be applied in other cases where the parties' intentions can be made relatively clear through context and common sense.

Second, if judges are in fact so incompetent at divining business deals, there is reason to suspect they would be similarly incompetent at the rigors of formalism. After all, formalism's contributions to contract law—consideration, the statute of frauds, the parol evidence rule, the plain meaning rule, offer-and-acceptance principles, indefiniteness rules—are hardly uniformly applied and can be unpredictable for parties and lawyers alike. Maybe it is somewhat easier to enforce a paper deal than it is to enforce a real deal, which is hard to discover— especially when parties have incentives to lie when the relationship breaks down. But it is still altogether plausible that judges wouldn't be very good at formalism either. They like their discretion and aren't any better at potentially undesirable acontextual rule application than they are at hard questions of discovering immanent norms. And if they aren't very good at formalism, formalism isn't a great alternative to the complexity of discovering relational norms. Consider Judge Richard Posner (yes, Eric's father) on the matter:

> There has never been a time when the courts of the United States, state or federal, behaved consistently in accordance with [legal formalism]. Nor could they, for reasons rooted in the nature of law and legal institutions, in the limitations of human knowledge, and in the character of the political systems.[21]

Third, formalism's premise that parties will be properly chastened and, in anticipatory response to formalistic courts, put all their important matters into formal arrangements, is not obviously viable. It is ultimately an empirical question whether formalism as a judicial strategy can actually succeed in getting parties to do so, since the choice parties face about whether to use formalities is a complex one. Parties choose not to do so for many reasons. For example, contracting with forms is very costly, and since few contracts actually result in legal disputes, this cost is often not worth incurring. Moreover, in many cases, a long-term relationship will be presumed to require accommodation over time that cannot easily be anticipated at some moment of formal contracting. Finally, in many cases contractual relationships are premised on social and interpersonal ties (even though parties will want legal sanctions once the relationship ends), such that getting formalistic about the paper deal up front would lead parties not to cooperate at all, costing both parties the surplus they otherwise could have achieved from the relationship.

Given these factors that contribute to the sort of incomplete and gap-ridden contracts we see in relational contracting, formalism might actually serve not to chasten parties at all but only to prevent these forms of cooperation altogether.[22] Relational contractors are already the ones most allergic to formal planning, so it is an odd fit to insist on formalism in these contractual contexts. Alternatively, formalism might succeed in part—but then the parties might be risking getting stuck in their formalities and might not be able to rely on the flexibility and good faith that make relational contracts so successful in the first place. Moreover, legal norms, when they are formalistically applied, risk eroding the underlying relationship, which does so much of the work in keeping parties in line.

There is a related argument against formalism from within relational contract theory. Relationalists' normative claims are underwritten in some measure by an orientation toward using contract law to support "organic solidarity." This means that the law must be made resonant with people's affinities and symbolize to people their general sense of obligations—or risk illegitimacy.[23] It is an open empirical question whether formalism interferes with the ultimate legitimacy of contract law, whether people might feel that a formalistic approach to contract does not resonate with their aspirations for relational contracts. But relationalists argue that we are more likely to achieve contractual justice—however defined—and contractual legitimacy by tailoring contract law's application in light of the real relationships between parties, not the fictitious and incomplete ones on paper. Of course, formalists understand that there are real costs associated with formalism, but relationalists see those costs as so deeply undermining contract law's purpose and legitimacy that they can't stomach them. More practically, although formalists emphasize all the gains in predictability and "rule of law" that might result from a commitment to enforcing only clear paper deals that are bargained-for promises (the technical requirement of "consideration" for a classical contract), relationalists focus on a different kind of "calculability": the ability of the parties themselves, rather than their lawyers, to predict the eventualities. The capitalist system—if that is one's point of departure for designing contract—can work better, relationalists argue, if parties can bank on their real deals, not idiosyncratic paper deals that their adversarial lawyers draw up with little sensitivity to the underlying relationship between the parties.[24]

I don't expect to resolve all of these central debates in contract theory here. I only hope to give a flavor of the status of the debate for the time being. My ultimate intervention, laid out below, supports the relational theory of contract by highlighting how relational contracts are like friendships—and how that analogy can illuminate ongoing debates within contract law and theory.

FRIENDSHIP AS RELATIONAL CONTRACT

To argue that friendships can be illuminated by relational contract theory is not to argue that the entirety of the social institution of friendship can be understood in contractualized terms. Nonetheless, I must repeat here, perhaps belaboring the obvious, that friendship is something more than a "mere" contract, even a relational one—to make sure I do not alienate readers from my argumentative endeavor here with what could look like a category mistake. With the appropriate caveats in place (and I shall put some more in place later), I assert that thinking of friendship as a relational contract can be an illuminating window into the interpersonal relationship of friendship. Fiduciary law, as shown in chapter 5, captures some of the basic rules we expect of our very close friends. But a somewhat weaker tie than the ones people have with their closest friends can be illuminated by the idea of the relational contract.

Friendships and relational contracts have several basic structural features in common. In both types of relationships, there is an understanding that parties contemplate a long-term endeavor to fulfill shared goals that will enhance their welfare.[25] Although parties are never fully expected to engage in complete selflessness in fulfilling their mutual commitment to one another in either friendships or relational contracts, they are generally supposed to be taking their counterparts' interests as independent reasons for action.

In pursuing their relationships in the cases of both friendships and relational contracts, parties will often furnish gifts and favors to one another at least in part to signal that they are not "merely" commercial partners. But the nature of the gift-giving is rarely a matter of pure altruism. To be fair, in some contractual settings gifts are refused precisely so as not to muddy the waters with a commercial exchange. Consider this letter that gets sent to businesspeople in Korea who try to give gifts to Motorola executives there:

> I hereby wish to thank you for your kindness in sending a gift. While I
> know that your intentions were positive, in order to avoid even the

appearance of anything but a business relationship built on the business value offered by our respective organizations, Motorola's Code of Business Conduct requires that we not accept gifts from our business partners, other than low cost promotional items. Therefore, I am respectfully returning your gift. I would like to take this opportunity to emphasize that it is really unnecessary to send gifts and thank you once again for your gesture of friendship.[26]

This is a fascinating but quite unusual business practice. This strategy forces Motorola Korea to lose business, since it is de rigueur in Korea to accept and give such gifts.

So, too, are there examples of friendships where we really try to stop the gift-giving. Such giving is often irrational—the money is more valuable than the gift in most cases, but we feel awkward giving cash—and sometimes signals that we aren't really all that intimate, for true friends go to each other's houses often enough that they probably don't need the bottle of wine to even out the dinner invitation. But the standard cases of both relational contracts and friendships generally partake of gift exchange and reciprocity.

These reciprocated gifts and favors signal commitment and consideration of one another's interests over and above the commitment and consideration that result from "mere" commercial exchange in one-shot discrete transactions. And there is a deliberate effort in both types of relationships to show partiality: we prefer our friends for all sorts of things (whether for companionship or for continued relational efforts)—and those with whom we have long-term contractual dealings often are presumed to get our business when contract renewal time or a need for a new product approaches.

In both types of relationship, the requirements for behavior are rarely well-specified. Indeed, the high degree of interdependence between the parties results in complexity, with a set of rather varied duties within the relationship. We enter these relationships without fully knowing what we shall be called on to do. Uncertainty in our basic responsibilities is *constitutive* of these relationships—and they rely heavily on implicit and tacit understandings.[27]

When it does become necessary to specify particular conduct, parties tend to do so in very general, broad, or vague terms. Most often, parties simply can't allocate risks of their mutual endeavor at the start of a relationship because so much is uncertain. Indeed, the very incompleteness of the deal between parties is central in defining what counts as a relational contract—and friendship shares this incompleteness in the specification of parties' rights and duties.[28]

Yet there *are* some general principles of conduct that can be presumed in both types of relationships: First, there is an assumption that parties will behave in "good faith" throughout the often uncertain term of the relationship (or risk destroying it). This is a lighter duty than the good faith requirement in fiduciary relations discussed in chapter 5—but is more stringent than the rules about how one may treat strangers. Second, both parties will expect "best efforts" in producing joint value from the relationship. And, finally, both parties will expect parties to adjust their assumed responsibilities reasonably if underlying circumstances change.

In light of the nature of the obligations that arise from within these relationships, parties generally do not seek legal enforcement of the entitlements that flow from them. As Bob Gordon has written of relational contracts, "In bad times the parties are expected to lend one another mutual support rather than standing on their rights; each will treat the other's insistence on literal performance as willful obstructionism."[29] So long as the relationship is still in place, meddling by the law is generally disfavored—and most parties to these relationships would think it bizarre and "countercultural" to seek legal enforcement. That said, on the dissolution of the relationship or on a substantial breach of an agreement evidencing betrayal or opportunism, seeking remedies at law is not altogether uncommon, and the law will have to find a way to resolve such disputes. Even though friendships and relational contracts will not generally seem to the parties like legal relationships when the parties are in them, whether because they are successful or because resorting to the law seems unpleasant and counterindicated by the nature of the relationship itself (its culture, so to speak), legal enforcement of duties is reserved as a rare remedy for certain types of defections from the parties' good faith, best efforts, and reasonable adjustment duties. Sometimes parties will seek to formalize some portion of the deal between them and sometimes they won't, but the threat of legal sanctions is rarely the motivating factor for compliancein.[30]

The mere fact that resort to the law is rare does not mean that friends and those in relational contracts lack mechanisms for enforcing relational obligations. Social norms internal to the relationship and reputational networks outside it play a strong role in keeping the parties in line. These social norms can be enforced through practical concerns about keeping the relationship alive or about reputational costs a defecting party may incur in the future with another party, and general stigmatic concerns about being a good friend and a good business partner.

In sum, many aspects of friendship can be clarified when viewed through the lens of relational contract theory. When we think of friendship as a relational contract, we can get a better feel for why obligations within friendship are so hard to specify, why people tend to do so—when they do—rather generally and vaguely, what these obligations amount to, why people don't seek to use the law to control conduct within friendships, and how people are successful in maintaining compliance anyway though social norms. Although this window into describing friendship can't be exhaustive, it nevertheless proves to be a useful perspective on implicit dimensions of friendship, revealing its underlying structure. We have numerous portraits of friendship from sociology, psychology, literary studies, religious studies, political theory, anthropology, and philosophy—but the structure of the relationship and its attendant obligations can be further illuminated by understanding its morphological similarity to relational contracts in the law. Just as fiduciary law, as we saw in chapter 5, has some useful insights to offer those who try to understand friendship, so does legal thinking about contracts.

SOME COGNITIVE DISSONANCE MANAGED

That friendships can usefully be thought of as relational contracts doesn't, of course, mean that one can make a clean one-to-one correlation between the two practices. There are many different sorts of friendships and many kinds of contracts. Here I pursue a few discontinuities between the two types of relationship. But I don't think these discontinuities undermine the basic arguments of the chapter for reasons I will explain.

Value

From the perspective of practices of human valuing, the two surely occupy different places in people's lives. Although most people, if asked, would say they consider both relational contracts and friendships "valuable," they would also likely concede that they are operating with a different conception of value for each. In the case of relational contracts, people would say that they are valuing them in a financial or instrumental sense (for wealth generation or capital-formation); in the case of friendships, by contrast, people would say they are valuing them *in themselves*.

But what does it mean for something to be valued in itself? Philosophers are helping us to answer this question. In his recent account of valuing, Sam Scheffler offers the following sketch (though he self-consciously refrains from explaining whether his account can be linked with instrumental valuing):

> [V]aluing any X involves at least the following elements: (1) A belief that X is good or valuable or worthy, (2) A susceptibility to experience a range of context-dependent emotions regarding X, (3) A disposition to experience these emotions as being merited or appropriate, and (4) A disposition to treat certain kinds of X-related considerations as reasons for action in relevant deliberative contexts.[31]

Central to Scheffler's picture of valuing is a form of emotional susceptibility and a requirement that the subject doing the valuing tends to regard the emotions that follow from that susceptibility as merited. Under this definition, it is relatively easy to see how friendship routinely meets the requirements of human valuing: we are emotionally susceptible to our friends and feel fairly comfortable with our emotional posture to them. It is likewise plain how relational contracts are not obviously of the same character: we don't tend to be as emotionally invested in our long-term contracts, though they surely provoke rage from time to time when we feel we are being treated unfairly. Although parties to relational contracts tend to believe that their counterparts are valuable or worthy and will have a disposition to treat relationship-based considerations as reasons for action, their emotional susceptibility to the relationship—its formation, maintenance, and success—is much more attenuated in the standard case of contracts than the emotional susceptibility in the standard case of friendship is.

The degree of attenuation of emotional vulnerability within relational contracting highlights how different it is from friendship. Although *some* relational contract partners might display emotional susceptibility, *all* friendships must display this feature in substantial measure to qualify as an instance of friendship and an instance of participation in the value of friendship. Moreover, without the disposition to experience the emotional vulnerability as being merited or appropriate, parties also would have a hard time understanding themselves to be in a friendship. Not so with relational contracting partners as a general matter: Although some such partners may have a similar attitude toward their emotional vulnerability, too much emotional investment seems inappropriate in a commercial context. At the very least, we expect those who exhibit such susceptibility (and those who endorse their susceptibility) to have had a preexisting interpersonal relationship on which a relational contract was built.

Thus, from the perspective of valuation, there are clear differences between friendships and parties to relational contracts as a general matter: friendships are essentially connected with people's emotional lives (and only sometimes connected to our financial lives), and relational contracts are essentially connected with people's financial lives (and only sometimes connected affectively to their emotional lives). Nevertheless, this doesn't prevent us from seeing friendships as relational contracts, so long as we keep the analogy in perspective. That each type of relationship is valued differently doesn't render it useless to think about them side by side. And although the type of value that each creates seems different in a fundamental way, they are both value-generating relationships that those within them tend to value, however attenuated emotional vulnerability may be in the instrumental form of valuing prevalent in relational contracting.[32]

There is, however, another point worth considering. For some, it would seem that the particular valuing process within friendship consists in its not being thought of as contractual in any way.[33] Generally, friends don't self-consciously think in terms of contract, and it might be thought to debase the relationship itself to model it thereon. If the moral value of friendship consists in complete voluntariness,[34] exploring its morphological similarity with the domain of contract—which seems to be about compliance backed by legal sanction—can risk undermining what is so special about friendship. In some measure, this is a riff on a similar argument we confronted earlier that gets launched against relational contract theory more generally.

But relationalists take the position—which I hope can be more clearly understood at this point (and I will amplify this in chapter 7)— that it is only a crude caricature to see contracts as solely backed by legal sanction and interpersonal relationships as backed only by something else: both contracts and interpersonal relationships mix legal and nonlegal forms of sanctions to maintain compliance in the real world. Real obligations flow from each type of relationship and real freedoms exist within each to defy the norms that control them. Neither of these relationships is enforced specifically by the law all the time. The law rarely requires specific performance in any contract (relational or otherwise) and would likely dismiss any case of a friend trying to enforce a "mere" social duty of friendship (like a dinner date).[35] All the same, both relationships can be legally enforced to some extent, under certain conditions. It is hard to see how we debase personal relationships by revealing that there is an implicit contractual structure in them, especially when that contractual structure is thoroughly relational: in both cases, special internal norms of heightened duties and care pervade and control the relationships. And in both cases, the parties share a complex and uncertain range of responsibilities that emerge from the relationship itself.

Exchange

A related concern is that contract is principally about exchange and friendship is not. Contracts are surely premised on mutual benefit and a thin form of reciprocity, but treating friendship as a form of transactional exchange, implied by thinking of it in terms of contract, is crass and inappropriate. Indeed, the visceral emotional reaction of taboo that some are likely to feel at the very thought of friendships being "reduced" to contractual or market relationships commands some response.[36]

Although, again, there may be something to the idea that different sorts of exchange are at work in relational contracts and friendships, there is also by now a respectable window into interpersonal relations that shows them to be meaningful forms of exchange. To be sure, it would defy common sense to see friendship as *only* exchange.[37] Friendship "is not really supposed to be a relationship in which each side carefully weighs up the costs and rewards of their interaction before proceeding, in the way that happens with, say, business contracts."[38] But of course we keep accounts, even if just approximately. We are generally generous with one another in these relationships and hope for reciprocation over a long time horizon, since we are confident in a future with our friends. But if things get out of hand and one friend is doing a lot more than the other to keep the relationship going and intimate, no one should be surprised by a confrontation for an accounting—or a termination of the relationship.

Indeed, the very dichotomous way that those who draw on this distinction put it relies on a too simplified picture of business and commercial relationships. That is, very often business relationships are forged on the backs of friendships, where it is not easy to disentangle what is motivated by the commercial part of the relationship and what is by the friendship part; the confusion may exist not only for outside observers but for the parties as well.[39]

More significantly for my purpose here, friends' purported desires to prove that their relationships are different from "mere" commercial or business enterprises do not vitiate the claim that there is an undeniable element of exchange embedded in every friendship. As I suggested earlier and introduced in chapter 1, much of what looks like "altruism" can be modeled as exchange. Friendships generate a sense of debt, since our friends routinely help us out of pickles. Although we may say, when we are feeling romantic, that acts of friendships are never undertaken out of a sense of obligation, friendship's very foundation in reciprocity, equality, and warmth virtually requires some evenness in exchange. If one takes more than one gives, if one fails to reciprocate one's friend's effort over time, if gifts and favors stop going back and forth, a friendship cannot continue. Friendship is not exhausted by peering at it through the lens of exchange, but it is a central feature of the relationship—and seeing friendships as relational contracts helps reveal that dimension of them. This dynamic is no less true of parties to relational contracts, who are also eager to make displays of friendship within a larger network of exchange.

Unity of Interests

Some might suggest that the interpersonal relationship of friendship rests on a unity of interests that could never be mirrored in relational contracts. Ultimately, friends engage in reciprocity because they wish their counterparts well for their own sake—and they share so many interests that they can treat one another as "second selves." No commercial relationship, the presumptive domain of contract, can unify the interests of the parties in the way friendship can.

There is a kernel of truth to this differentiation between friendship and relational contracts. Indeed, the closer friends are, the more unified their interests—and the less their relationship looks like a contract (this is why, perhaps, as friends get closer and closer, it makes more and more sense to treat them as *fiduciaries* for one another, not as "mere" relational contractors), assuming for the moment that relational contracts in the standard case do not create unified interests.

Yet there are some qualifications to issue about this differentiation. First, this, too, is an overly romantic conception of friendship. In the average case of friendship (even if not its paradigmatic form, perhaps), friends rarely have unified interests. They have many priorities and several friends, all competing for attention. Even in our most intimate relationships, we have to juggle too much to impute any perfectly unified interests to friends. It just isn't possible for parties to a friendship to always have unified interests, especially when a friend's lover, parent, employer, professor, or child is also competing for attention. Indeed, as we saw in chapter 1, conflict and conflict resolution techniques are constitutive of friendship, too.

Moreover, we only rarely own property in common with friends—and even if we don't find ourselves literally competing for property in our friendships,[40] we are bound to have disparate interests on a number of fronts, both personal and professional. Although we are undoubtedly expected to be generous with our friends and treat them with good faith, few of us expect our friends to put our interests on equal footing with their own. In a rare case (of a "best" friend or an emergency), we might expect such loyalty. But it is not the general case at all.

There is a bit of underromanticization of the institution of contract here as well. Relational contract theory highlights just how much interdependence and unity of interest can be created through the relational contract itself (and the underlying relationships that are part of the contractual matrix). Accordingly, it might be more fair than it seems at first to put friendship and relational contract side by side on the dimension of the unity of interests. Neither establishes a perfect unity of interest in the standard cases of each—and both establish some unity, limited in scope, as well.

Natural Persons, Friendship, and Organizations

We might appreciate that something is amiss in thinking about friendships as relational contracts when we realize that friendships must be limited to natural persons but relational contracts have no such limitation. Corporations and organizations can be friends only by analogy; and only natural individuals can be friends. Yet, as I have argued in other work, it is more than likely that contracts between organizations ("Type 3" contracts) and contracts between organizations and natural persons ("Type 2" contracts) are just as much at the core of contract as are contracts between natural persons ("Type 1" contracts).[41] So how can a practice, friendship, that reasonably comes only in the shape of a Type 1 contract be illuminated by a practice, relational contract, that has many other shapes, of which friendship may not partake by its very nature?

It turns out this isn't much of a challenge for this part of my argument. Perhaps this challenge shows some limits of my argument:

there are real differences between contract and friendship as social practices. But analogical arguments do not require perfect correspondence of the concepts being compared. In any case, nothing about this failure of perfect isomorphism vitiates the usefulness of thinking about friendship as, in certain respects, a prototypical Type 1 relational contract. I am not arguing here that all relational contracts are friendships, only that all friendships display central properties of relational contracts—and that this observation is a useful way to understand the dynamics within and requirements of friendship.

But perhaps I am throwing in the towel too quickly here. We do have groups of friends to whom we relate qua group (think of C.S. Lewis's friends Ronald and Charles from chapter 1)—and we have relationships with couples, whether as couples ourselves or as individuals. These sorts of friendships might, after all, serve as plausible analogies for Type 2 and Type 3 contracts. I haven't worked out how that might play out through the rest of my analysis, but it is a provocative suggestion. Indeed, much economic sociology clearly assumes that friendships among organizations can be meaningful. And a recent article about friendships between countries similarly suggests that organizational friendship is a meaningful concept.[42]

RELATIONAL CONTRACT AS FRIENDSHIP

I observed at the outset that relational contract theorists tend to want to treat relational contracts as types of marriages—and my hope here is to expose the benefits of instead treating relational contracts as types of friendships. There are several benefits to reorienting the paradigmatic relational contract to being a friendship rather than a marriage. And this reorientation should furnish several lessons for relational contract theory and relational contract law.

Decentering Marriage

In the first place, there are very good reasons to decenter marriage quite generally from the various roles it already plays in our legal system. Consider some of these reasons recently suggested by scholars with quite different points of view: (1) privileging marriage discriminatorily excludes those who cannot partake in marriage in a way that privileging equal-opportunity friendship does not;[43] (2) privileging marriage contributes to gender inequality in our society in a way the promotion of friendship need not;[44] and (3) decentering marriage could "enable[] new forms of commitment, responsibility, love, care, and relatedness other than those of idealized 'mother' and 'father,'" and "husband" and "wife."[45] In short, to the extent that we model the ideal form of a relational contract on marriage rather than friendship, we are unnecessarily reinforcing marriage's centrality in our private and public law to our detriment. Friendships can serve as the model relational contract all the same, without needing to buy into the normative agenda that props up marriage's centrality to our lives and law. In addition, unlike many other ways we might center friendship so as to decenter marriage, it is hard to see marriage enthusiasts getting too exercised about this modest method of undermining marriage.

Exit Costs

Relationalists seek to highlight the similarity between relational contracts and marriages in some measure because exit costs from both are quite high. Getting divorced is usually a quite elaborate affair and is a decision rarely taken casually. Parties grow interdependent throughout a marriage, and that interdependence is just the feature that relationalists claim is also present within relational contracts. As David Friedman writes,

> [o]nce a couple has been married for a while, they have made a lot of relationship-specific investments, borne costs that will produce a return only if they remain together. Each has become, at considerable cost, an expert on how to get along with the other. Both have invested, materially and emotionally, in their joint children.... [T]hey are now locked into a bilateral monopoly with associated bargaining costs.[46]

But friendship is actually the better analogy here: friends also display the relevant sort of interdependence with relatively high exit costs (relative to the exit costs generally associated with associations with strangers). But marriage's exit costs are too high to serve as a baseline for relational contracts. Friendship's exit costs are also substantial, to be sure, and there are real prices to pay for extricating oneself from one. Indeed, unlike marriage, there is rarely a moment of divorce in friendship. In the standard case, friends don't really break up; growing apart tends to be a slow process of developing new, more intimate ties elsewhere. Unless there is a massive betrayal, it is hard to say when things have turned irrevocably against the relationship's durability.

Ultimately, the exit costs in friendship are usually lower (though hardly nonexistent) and much closer to what we might tend to think is common in the relational contract sphere. Parties to a friendship and parties to relational contracts are generally free to terminate in a way that marriage partners are not. For marriage partners to agree to terminate, they must turn to law—and pay for it. Divorce is never free; even when it is done online, amicably and without child or pet custody issues, for mere hundreds of dollars, it usually exacts substantial emotional costs. And, in any case, it usually triggers a much bigger transaction cost than an agreement to terminate a friendship or a relational contract, which parties are generally free to do without the help of the law. To be sure, they may have to turn to lawyers and may be prevented from free exit because they have to pay damages first—in both relational contracts and friendships. But the analogy with marriage doesn't hold: no one *needs* the state's permission to terminate in the other types of relationships.

Exclusivity

Marriages, for the time being, can only be valid between two individuals and must be exclusive. That just isn't the case with friendships. Even if friendships are essentially dyadic,[47] one can certainly have more than one friend. Since the realm of contract clearly does not limit parties to one partner (this wasn't the type of exclusivity discussed in chapter 1), friendships are again here the better analogy than marriages.

There is something more here, too—and it relates to an earlier point about interdependence. Although relational contracts tend to breed and feed off of interdependence, the degree of that interdependence is not commensurate with that within purely exclusive relationships and bilateral monopolies. To be sure, some relational contracts are bilateral monopolies, but they needn't be at their core. Friendship is more true to the nature of the relational contract because it is not a betrayal to have other partners, so long as one deals with one's counterparts in good faith. This point also relates back to the discussion about the lack of the unity of interests in relational contracts and friendships: marriages command a type of internal egalitarianism[48] that friendships simply do not (even though they are predicated on a certain form of equality, too).

Common Ownership

In marriage, common ownership of property is a very common arrangement. It is often a default rule the law will supply, and at a relationship's dissolution, most states will enforce some version of common ownership of all marital property between parties to a marriage. Yet in neither relational contracts nor friendships would we generally assume that parties intend to share their property in joint ownership. There are, to be sure, some very close friendships and business partnerships that do have such an arrangement. But friendships and relational contracts do not generally display this ownership pattern, which is quite typical within marriages. This difference between marriages and relational contracts is instructive for how we might set up a law to regulate relational contracts on the one hand and marriages on the other, so it is best to model the relational contract on the type of property assumptions that prevail instead within friendships. To treat all relational contracts as marriage partnerships would not be true to the prevailing ethic within relational contracts, which are closer to friendships.

Default Rules

There is a more general point to make about default rules and marriage. For the most part, marriage law is full of *mandatory* rules, not default rules that parties may circumvent by agreement if they choose. By contrast, relationalists have argued for relatively few mandatory rules (like robust good faith and best efforts requirements); there is an assumption that parties may still contract around whatever other default rules the law will exact from them. Friendship would seem to work this way, too: there are precious few mandatory rules (though robust good faith and best efforts in performance may very well be two of them, for without them, it is hard to call the relationship a friendship in the first instance). But other than a small list of mandatory duties, most friendships, like relational contracts and unlike marriages, admit a wide range of choice about how to structure and perform the relationship. As friendships get closer and closer to marriages in intimacy and interdependence, they get closer and closer to fiduciary relationships, with their attendant set of more elaborate mandatory duties, as discussed in chapter 5. But the general case of relational contract seems much more analogous to the general case of friendship than to that of marriage.

Formalities

There is an important difference between marriages and relational contracts from the standpoint of relational contract theory—and the difference is so central that it is rather surprising that relational contract theorists so often talk about contracts as marriages. Marriages (other than rare "common law marriages") require formal entry and formal exit; they generally cannot be entered or exited without clear formalities that are extremely easy for outsiders to spot. Yet relationalists generally argue that although those who enter relational contracts sometimes use formalities, they do not rely on them exclusively. For relationalists, there need not always be clear formalities between parties to establish contractual obligation, and courts should be lax about requiring formalities to find contractual liability. Indeed, this element of relational contract theory is the one most opposed by formalists, who certainly don't want courts finding contracts to have formed without establishing that the parties have engaged in relevant formalities. Perhaps unsurprisingly, then, the law-and-economics scholars who have embraced the idea of relational contract as marriage and marriage as relational contract have veered toward formalism: marriage is very formalistic at both formation and break-up.

Yet friendship seems like the better analogy to relational contracts here, at least from the perspective of relational contract theory. The relationship of friendship tends to be fluid (there is rarely a magic moment of formation); it does not rely on formalities for entry or exit; it does not get regulated by law only on entry and exit (as marriage does); and it can create obligations in nonformalistic ways. Formal entry and exit does not reflect the reality of practice in relational contracting; accordingly, friendship is the better paradigm.

Although, of course, contracts can be formalized, what is distinctive about relational contracts is that even when some part of the relationship is formalized, there is much more to the deal besides. One could say the same of friends, too: although surely friends can enter formal contracts (and unquestionably legally enforceable [relational!] contracts, too), relational contract theory would emphasize the underlying social relationship that is also a source of obligation. In any case, in relational contracts as in friendship, formalities are the rare case, whereas in marriage, formality is the standard case and is a prerequisite to getting the relationship off the ground in the first place.

Enforceability of Intra-relational Promises

Finally, if we model relational contracts on marriages, we are threatened with a potentially perverse result: that virtually all promises within commercial relationships—even ones that are written down and bargained for—could be rendered unenforceable. The governing law surrounding contracting spouses is that only in rare cases will courts enforce their agreements, *even if they are accompanied by formalities like writings and consideration.*[49] Whether owing to a failure to find that the parties intend to create legal relations or owing to some more general public policy argument, courts tend to refuse to adjudicate contractual disputes between spouses within a marriage. This is at odds with the normative dimension of relational contract theory that recommends the enforceability of internal norms and promises from within relational contracts. Accordingly, it is potentially bizarre to model the relational contract on a type of relationship that cannot get the law involved no matter how hard it tries. Despite some underdeveloped enthusiasm for the view that friends should be wholly immune from law,[50] few would really argue that contractual obligation between friends should be held unenforceable as a categorical matter. Friendship is the better analogy because like relational contracting partners, friends can make enforceable agreements without the difficulty we see in the marriage context.

A Caveat

I hope I have shown here why friendship rather than marriage ought to serve as the paradigmatic relational contract. Does this really mean that all contracts are friendships? I am not committed to that view. Instead, I hope to have shown that relational contracts partake in the morphology of friendship (and vice versa) and can usefully be analyzed through their similarities to the structures of friendships. Analogical and morphological reasoning doesn't commit me to the full-scale identity of relational contracts and friendship, only to the idea that they have relevant similarities that can help us understand each concept better.

Still, and quite important, many relational contracts are built on the edifice of a friendship, and the preexisting friendship itself is the predicate that creates the relationality to the contract in the first place. Consider Eric Posner's observation: "what appears to be an arm's length contract between two anonymous firms is often the result of negotiation of two friends who belong to the same social club or sit on the board of the same charitable organization.... Contracting parties are often friends."[51] And sometimes friendship is not the predicate for the relational contract but a *result* of the relationship triggered under the contract. Posner again: "Friendships arise not as the natural byproduct of time spent together and mutual interest; on the contrary parties spend a great deal of effort, time and money trying to make friends" to further the business arrangement.[52] In short, there are certainly some business relationships that seem to come short of "real" friendships, but it is not so neat a division that we can ignore all the similarities in the structure of these modes of interacting. These *overlaps* between friendships (whether "fictive" or real) and relational contracts are interesting in their own right and are often overlooked by commentators and courts.[53] The arguments offered thus far might very well help guide thinking about how to handle such overlaps.

Yet some parties to relational contracts do not have preexisting or consequent friendships attendant to their contractual relationship. And this is where my thesis seems most attenuated, for it suggests that the contractual relationship itself is a type of friendship, if only a thin one, and should be treated as such. In what follows, I hope to furnish some of the intellectual payoffs of thinking of the world of relational contracting this way—both for relational contract theory and for the law of contracts.

But first I must say something about the seed of doubt I planted earlier in this chapter. If I am serious about the morphological similarities between friendships and relational contracts, it should give me some pause that relational contracts are often between organizations and between natural persons and organizations, whereas the moral seriousness of friendship makes sense only between natural persons.[54] Friendship is a special case of partiality, such that we adopt our friends' ends as our own; an economic organization should be treated only as a means. Although we can have an emotional susceptibility to an organization and value it—alumni contributions to educational institutions seem to reflect this relationship—it would be very bizarre to call our ongoing relationships with these organizations friendships. Certainly, firms as entities barely can be thought to have emotions at all. To say they do isn't as much a moral error as it is bewildering.

Although I concede that this difference between "types" of contracts is important in developing a general theory of contract, I'm a little less worried about the distinction for my much more modest ambitions here. After all, I'm not building a general theory of contract. I am simply observing some counterintuitive similarities and overlaps between the concepts, hoping to suggest that these analogies and overlaps can teach us something about friendship, contract law, and contract theory. Since I don't find the *value* of the practice of contract in friendship, I do not need to worry that many core cases of contract will not share in the moral value of friendships. That comparing relational contracts to friendships might prove useful in analyzing the practice of contract is sufficient for my purposes here.

FRIENDSHIP, LEGALITY, AND FORMALITY

In the final analysis, an analogical argument is only as powerful as what it can illuminate. One can point out thirty-five similarities between two concepts, but if there aren't relevant similarities that illuminate important questions, the comparison is hard to justify writing about. Revealing the analogies between relational contracts and friendships does, however, shed new light on old problems.

The Legal Enforceability of Friendship?

Counterintuitive as it may seem, viewing relational contracts as friendships (and friendships as relational contracts) supports the idea that some duties that emerge from within friendship are legally enforceable. Friends can generate legal obligations through what seem to be acts of friendship and private promises. Because the perspectives of relational contract as friendship and friendship as relational contract reveal the substantial verisimilitude and overlapping of the concepts, we cannot neatly reserve friendship for outside the boundaries of law. This does not mean, however, that all such duties are legally enforceable. Figuring out which promises or duties are enforceable is no easy task for the law, but the law cannot and does not embrace an oversimplified exclusion of all legal enforceability between friends.

Let's consider several examples. The easiest case for enforceability seems to be a deal between good friends that meets all of contract law's classical requirements: definite offer, acceptance, consideration, and the like. Only very few would suggest that the law must stay out of friendship completely to protect friends from the law. It would certainly surprise many friends in the business world who have transacted on the assumption that the law would enforce their deals to learn that the law will leave them to their social norms because the law is supposed to stay out of friendships. Even if the underlying friendship is explicit and serves as the trust predicate for the deal itself (that is, without the friendship, no deal would have been reached in the first place), legal enforceability is not likely to be denied, whatever was true in Aristotle's time. Recognizing that many relational contracts overlap with friendships helps us see how necessary some degree of enforceability is, even in relational contracts that are purportedly more reliant on social norms than the law. That the parties see their obligations (subjectively) as relying on friendship is no bar: if the friends meet legal requirements, the law will enforce their agreements when they fail, whatever they think the source of their obligations is (unless it is a self-consciously sham transaction).

But change the case slightly. Imagine that two friends transact with all of contract law's requirements but one says to the other prior to formation: "Buddy, I need you to sign this form contract because my boss requires it. The form claims to be our total deal on all points. But you know full well that I'm going to ignore those provisions that don't really sum up the deal we've been talking about. We're old friends and I'm not going to screw you." Formal application of what contract law calls the "parol evidence" rule would render the side deal unenforceable; the writing is clear that it controls.[55] Yet from the perspective of relational contract theory, at least some of the internal norms of the relationship should be given legal effect. Accordingly, the implicit deal should prevail: friendship's duty of good faith becomes enforceable against a form contract.[56] Quite generally, the more relational a contract—the more it involves or is like a "real" friendship—the more justifiable it is to give legal effect to friendship's duties of good faith, best efforts, and reasonable adjustments, and the more the failure to abide by these standards might constitute an independent breach. Rigorous application of the law's formal requirements in this class of cases seems less appropriate because of the underlying relationship.

Or consider a friend who gives her counterpart a good deal on renting a house she owns.[57] Because of the friendship, the owner gives the renter a very good deal—a much cheaper rent than the renter could get on the open market. Because of the friendship and not wanting to risk awkwardness, the owner doesn't bother with a formal lease agreement. Still, the friends exchange a few e-mails with basic terms about price, duration, and general expectations. Imagine that although the e-mails are sufficient to meet the writing requirements associated with land transactions, nothing is said in the e-mails about subletting—and that the default rule in the jurisdiction is that all leases may be transferred. Can the renter sublease the property to a third party at market rate and keep the windfall? If the owner sues because she feels her trust has been violated, what will result?

From one perspective, a court might say that the default rule should prevail: one of the risks of dealing as friends is that one can be taken advantage of. That, after all, is the fragility and risk of friendship. Without that fragility and risk, there may not be a way to forge a friendship. Indeed, friendship norms require forgiveness, and the owner's forgiveness might be imputed by a court stuck with the task of intervening in the relationship (or fashioning a remedy on rupture).

But from another perspective, the renter is clearly being unjustly enriched and taking advantage of a friendship. Why shouldn't a contract law seeking to be true to the real deal rather than the paper deal between the parties try to police this opportunistic conduct of the renter?

Notice that whichever perspective one takes here, however, it is ultimately relational—and either approach vindicates a relational approach to contract law. Does this mean relational contract as friendship and friendship as relational contract produces no answer about what a court should do, since it could do either and still be relationalist? I don't think so: that both considerations should be within the sensitivity of the court does not put the court in equipoise. Rather, more detail about the motivations of the owner's "good deal" and the renter's opportunism and dealings could ultimately decide the dispute. If the renter had to go to another state to take care of an ailing family member or friend and needed the sublease's windfall to cover costs in the other state, it might make more sense to require the friend-owner to take the loss and adhere to the default rule. By contrast, if it is a simple case of opportunism and preying on a friend, it is much easier to force the "friend"-renter to hand over her ill-gotten profits as a violation of the implied contractual terms. Obviously, there are lots of other variables here; for example, in today's day and age, it is the failure to ask the owner that seems most strange in the hypothetical and seems to suggest malfeasance on the part of the renter. But put aside these complicating dimensions (imagine the owner was out of contact camping in Yosemite without internet access) to think through the basic principles themselves.

What about the realm of *private* promise, favor, gift, or duty, when friends don't seem to be self-consciously entering the legal or economic sphere, as perhaps they do in the previous cases? Here, too, the twin perspectives of relational contract as friendship and friendship as relational contract prove illuminating—and recommend legal enforceability some of the time. But that these perspectives recommend enforceability some of the time is itself an innovation, given the propensity of the scholarship surrounding "gratuitous promises" to counsel for a general policy of unenforceability in this class of cases.[58]

When I casually promise a friend to take in her paper when she is away, my friend and I rarely contemplate legal enforceability. Indeed, it doesn't even look like a transaction. One would think a friend absurd or not much of a friend for demanding legal enforcement of such favors; most would probably think a judge absurd for granting it. But one of the lessons of relational contract theory more generally is that parties to relational contracts will only rarely contemplate legal enforceability themselves. That is not the threshold for legal enforceability in our law. Thus, something other than mere "contemplation" on "formation" must serve as the relevant test for legal enforceability: it simply doesn't really matter to the law whether any "intent to form legal relations" materializes. Notice, though, that the relationalists' preference for the incorporation of social norms by the law still provides interesting guidance: the social norm itself counsels against legal enforceability some of the time—but not all the time.

Does the analysis change when we enter the realm of the financial?[59] Can a "commercial purpose" test work? Maybe. Think about a simple informal loan to a friend. Suppose a friend loans you $25,000 because you've loaned her about that much when she was in financial trouble. You've ignored Shakespeare's (or Antonio's) advice in *The Merchant of Venice*: "If thou wilt lend this money, lend it not / As to thy friends, for when did friendship take / A breed for barren metal of his friend? / But lend it rather to thine enemy, / Who if he break, thou mayst with better face / Exact the penalty." No formal papers are drawn up—and she'd never have loaned that much to a stranger without collateral of some kind. Can she enforce the debt when you delay repayment beyond a reasonable amount of time? Or was the loan a mere "act of friendship" that should be shielded from legal enforceability and treated as a gift? The perspectives of friendship as relational contract and relational contract as friendship help us see this outlay as part of an overall exchange relationship, allowing parts of contract law to make it enforceable. To be sure, you might have longer than usual to pay back—and might even get a favorable "friendship" interest rate (if you hadn't already agreed on one). Perhaps you'd also get an easy discharge in a bankruptcy situation. But most generally, it would be quite hard to argue that the loan shouldn't be enforceable at all.

But there is reason for equivocation about using the realm of the financial as the sine qua non for enforceability, highlighting that friendship duties do not become enforceable merely by entering the financial sphere. For it is not the case that anything that counts as a commercial activity would qualify for enforcement. When friends buy each other rounds of drinks at a local bar for several years and then one skips out on his responsibility before leaving town for good, does the stiffed friend have a legal cause of action? There is undoubtedly a commercial dimension to the relationship, but it seems reasonable here to think a friend odd for considering such a lawsuit. Yet why is the friend odd?

Not quite because a duty never developed in the first place. On the contrary, the reciprocation of the gifts over years triggered an implicit promise and reasonable reliance for reciprocation. But we would still think the friend crazy to sue, mostly because the lawsuit would cost more than the drink. The law shouldn't be used to enforce this duty at least in part because the law is designed to be too expensive a remedy for such minor derelictions of duties.[60] It isn't that we can rely on a simple test of what the parties contemplated (though perhaps here parties did contemplate the risk of being stiffed; that is constitutive of friendship, too). Nor can we rely on a test of commercial or financial activity, for even though that test is met here, no legal enforceability should follow.

But when we up the ante in the reciprocal gift exchange, it starts seeming harder to deny enforceability. If every year friends took turns buying each other season tickets for the local ballet company—a layout of several thousand dollars—a stiffed friend might well pursue legal sanctions without being deemed absurd.[61] Moreover, a court would have good cause to force a friend to make good on an implied promise to provide such season tickets so long as there was an inequity without enforcement.[62] If the stiffed friend had already received as many tickets from his friend as he had purchased for his friend, no cause of action should lie. The court's job is not to keep the friendship going—that is, after all, quite clearly the realm of the nonlegal social sanction. It is only to prevent and remediate serious opportunism that results in a substantial injury. What this example reveals is that "intention to form legal relations" and tests for enforceability having to do with "commercial activity" only get us so far when it comes to determining the legal enforceability of acts and promises predicated on friendship. Context and common sense must prevail, as relationalists generally urge.

One could reasonably ask, however, whether the duties discussed here, when enforced, are really *contractual* ones. How can we simply convert relational obligations into obligations of contract? One answer comes from relational contract theory: nothing prevents those "status-based" duties from being thought of and captured by contract law. One of the benefits of relational contract theory (to those who embrace it) is precisely its willingness to admit multifarious modalities of obligation into its overall structure. To be sure, a relational contract theory will account for the possibility that some gifts and promises to make gifts ought to be treated as purely gratuitous, that that is really their intention. But not all gifts work this way, and a pattern of reciprocal gift-giving is a signal that exchange can be enforced without degrading the value of the gift or the relationship. Even old-fashioned contract law can reach this result of enforcing what look like gifts through what is known as "promissory estoppel": a doctrine that disables a gift-giver from refusing to give their promised gift if the other party has relied on the gift promise and that reliance was reasonably foreseeable by the gift-giver. But relational contract theory refuses to treat this as a mere marginal case. And it provides a framework to evaluate reasons for enforcement and a careful method for weighing the equities.

Contractual obligations emerge from a multiplicity of sources, whether from consent, promise, reliance, benefits-conferred, or status. The twin models here (friendship as relational contract and relational contract as friendship) help us see this in salient relief—and further support those who would build a contract theory around several loci of obligation. In any given context, "contract law" may prefer to focus liability on one of these sources of obligation, but there is no singular organizing principle that accounts for all contracts. We do contract law no great service by building the edifice of contract around only one of these sources of liability, suggesting that the others are merely exceptional cases. Relational contract theory highlights just how mis-leading such models are.

Ultimately, friendship can play numerous roles in establishing legal liabilities. A friendship can serve an evidentiary function (friendship proves there is a best efforts clause, which doesn't otherwise appear in the paper deal); it can sometimes create the obligation itself through implication and conduct (the friendship underwrites a finding of breach); and it can sometimes be relevant in fashioning a remedy (because it was friends who came to blows in the litigation, a specific performance order is especially unlikely to result in successful repair). Being open to seeing contracts as friendships and friendships as con-tracts helps us see how relationships matter in the application of contract law.

Revisiting Relational Contract Law

The window into relational contract theory developed here also sup-ports many of the theory's normative prescriptions for standard relational contracting in business. The model supports the relational-ists' case to relax rigid requirements of offer, acceptance, definiteness, and consideration within relational contracts. One of the most illumi-nating features of putting relational contracts and friendships side by side is seeing how absolutely central informality is in the constitution of these relationships. Just as we might degrade or deter friendship by *requiring* parties to engage in formalities (thus turning all friendships into mini-marriages), so, too, would we risk undermining relational contracts and their internal efficiency by refusing to recognize their needs for informality, reciprocated gift-giving as exchange, and incompleteness. By requiring formalities so as to get enforceability, we are clipping the wings of relational contracts. Formalism about formation would increase contracting costs so substantially that we might never get these contracts off the ground in the first place.[63] The model here only further supports the arguments of those relationalists who argue against adherence to contract's "classical" restrictions in the case of relational contracts.

As with formation, so with interpretation. The relational contract as friendship model also supports the relationalists' commitment to deeply contextual interpretation over formalistic modes of interpretation that would only give effect to a paper deal. Where friendship is concerned, there are equitable reasons to enable judges to look behind paper deals to the real deals. Relational contracts, like friendships, are complex relationships that need to keep some obligations incomplete to function properly; those agreements adjust over time. Courts need the freedom to enforce those implicit dimensions of contracts to keep those relationships from being abused.

Ultimately, formalism just doesn't make sense for relational contracts, as it doesn't for friendship. There is a coherentist argument that we ought to have a law that reasonably tracks how people actually do business. There is an economic argument that we ought not to force people into contracting costs that they needn't undertake; after all, most contracts succeed, and parties rarely have to worry about court intervention. There is the further economic argument that forcing ex ante bargaining risks rupturing the trust and solidarity the relationship already establishes. And there is the normative standpoint that the cost of formalism is injustice and there is no sufficient benefit to outweigh it. Even if formalism is possible and desirable in discrete transactions where there is no friendship or relationship to speak of (or where such a description is plainly too attenuated to take seriously), such a technique cannot and should not be used to marginalize the real deals that parties enter into and rely on in complex relational agreements. Thus, the model here further confirms relationalists' lack of sympathy for formalism.

Yet not all of the relationalists' normative prescriptions withstand scrutiny when viewed from within the models explored here. For example, to the extent that some relationalists have urged that relational contracts should be treated like partnerships and that courts should "adapt or revise the terms of ongoing relational contracts in such a way that an unexpected loss that would otherwise fall on one party will be shared by reducing the other party's profits,"[64] these prescriptions are supported by the relational contract as *marriage* model much better than by the relational contract as *friendship* model. Although friendship has a basis in equality, to be sure, nothing about friendship tends to suggest that people in it are only selfless and other-regarding. Although I argued in chapter 5 that very close friends might be required to serve as fiduciaries for one another with attendant duties of loyalty or unself-ishness, the average case of friendship does not require full-scale loyalty and a lack of self-interest. Although marriage is generally such a partnership, where egalitarian sharing is a worthy aspiration, friendship does not present the same case for legally enforced equality. Accordingly, the model of relational contract as friendship is a basis for revising this normative dimension of relational contract theory.

Furthermore, the relational contract as friendship model suggests a reason to be skeptical about some relationalists' desire to use the law to keep relationships and relational contracts together.[65] The fixation on relationship preservation that is evident in much relational theory does not resonate as well with the relational contract as friendship model and may very well be traceable to the relational contract as marriage model, where a relationship-preservation posture is not uncommon. In friend-ships, by contrast, we tend to make exit easier than in marriages—and a relational contract law that is animated by an account of relational contract as friendship would likely focus more on enabling exit than on preserving a relationship. This doesn't mean that parties should be free to shirk a vested obligation—like the hypothetical party who gets free season tickets under the assumption that he will pay for the round of season tickets next year but exits the relationship before his turn to pay comes due. But once the vested obligation is discharged, the law should not waste any resources disabling free exit.[66] This is a lesson we can take by embracing the relational contract as friendship model urged in this chapter. There is a lesson about friendship here, too, perhaps: exit is allowed when the relationship is no longer functioning, and we shouldn't be squeamish about ending relationships clearly and through negotia-tion when the reason for the friendship itself evaporates.

Little in this chapter is likely to have convinced a nonrelationalist to jump aboard the relationalist bandwagon—or minivan, really—in contract theory. Indeed, my arguments for and from within relational contract theory may confirm that relationalists tend to go astray in just the ways opponents most fear: toward the judicialization of intimate relations. Still, my ambitions here have been relatively modest. I have only tried to give relational theory some new life, sharpening some of its claims against its competitors by refracting its theory of contract through an analogy to friendship. I have also offered a provocation about friendship's contractual structure that should be less threatening, once it is seen as a relational contract of sorts. Finally, I have argued that the relational contract as marriage model, which has currency among relationalists, should be replaced with a model of relational contract as friendship. The new models developed here are more honest to relational contract theory, to marriage, and to friendship—and help relational contract theory produce some new insights, support old ones, and revise some of its normative agenda.

The next chapter develops some general insights suggested by the models in this chapter and chapter 5—and serves as an important rejoinder to certain possible objections to the strategies taken in them.

CHAPTER 7

The Trust Problem

I WANT TO use the last chapter of this book both to respond briefly to one of the core objections I tend to hear about some of the suggestions offered in this book (an objection already introduced in chapter 2), as well as to extend some of the insights from chapters 5 and 6, which, I think, help illuminate my strategy of response to this objection. In short, people tend to oppose the "friendship and the law" agenda because they worry that bringing the law to bear on friendship would risk threatening the very foundation and value of friendships themselves. To give legal effect to social norms, these opponents suggest, debases them because they are intended to and should remain always outside the sphere of law. Here is how one scholar puts it:

> Introducing…fiduciary duties [or contractual obligation] into close-knit relationships…requires the parties to negotiate over future litigation, hire lawyers, and draft formal documents, as if they were in an arms' length relationship. This encourages them to behave in other respects as parties in such a relationship. Planning for litigation becomes a self-fulfilling prophecy.[1]

From one perspective, the worry about law undermining strong forms of trust in society sounds academic. Indeed, the worry that I will address in this chapter has become quite central to many different debates among academics who are trying to solve thorny problems about how to corral the law to reinforce trust without undermining it by confusing people into thinking that they can only trust when there is law in the background. But this is not an academic debate only: it speaks to a deep suspicion about mingling the law and friendships and has real ramifications for our policy design. Won't the law ruin intimacy? Won't allowing the law into our friendship space turn a beautiful thing into a litigious affair? Won't involving the law deter friendships?

CROWDING AND DETERRENCE

This objection cannot be taken lightly, and it cannot be definitively resolved here. It is, however, a version of the so-called "crowding out" thesis about which much ink has been spilled:[2] that law crowds out trust relationships. If law *replaces* trust by intervening and enforcing social norms, a regime of trust enforcement through incorporation of social norms will actually undermine the very important brand of trust it is seeking to protect through fiduciary law and contract law. All this effort to protect friendships would have the perverse effect of discouraging them.

The previous chapters, however, make a modest contribution to the ongoing debate about these issues. Chapters 5 and 6 in particular reveal the *supplementary* rather than *substitutional* nature of law to social norms. Because the domains of relational contract law, fiduciary law, and friendship so often overlap and because they are so similarly structured, it is much easier to see that the admixture of these spheres in actual practical terms and in morphological similarity disables us from treating trust and intimate relations as being divorced from law completely. Quite the opposite turns out to be true: friendship, and the trust afforded therein, is a routine predicate for entering legal relations, and legal relations serve to develop trust on the foundation of which intimate relations can develop.[3] Accordingly, it is altogether too simple to assume that the law's occasional incorporation of friendship's social norms will leave them unable to do their work in promoting voluntary cooperation. As the discussion within this book has revealed, whether the relevant model is friendship as relational contract or friend as fiduciary, voluntary cooperation relies on a complex mix of legal and social norms, and the occasional incorporation of some social norms into legal ones will not serve to undermine them altogether. Indeed, occasionally friendships will need the support of legal institutions to develop the social trust necessary to enter personal relationships of complexity in the first place. Friendships help build productive economic relationships, and they also result from them as well.

Those who would press the crowding thesis might very well suggest that legal enforcement of friendship's duties (such as this book recommends in certain circumstances) would *deter* people from entering friendships. And we would be much less enriched as people in a world with fewer and more attenuated friendships. But can we really conclude that treating friends as fiduciaries or exacting legal duties from friends in rare cases of litigation is likely to deter friendship?

This particular claim is probably testable empirically with some rough measurements. One could try to test the level and intensity of friendship networks in different jurisdictions and then attempt to observe if there is any correlation between a given jurisdiction's fiduciary law with respect to friendship and the levels and intensity of friendship in the jurisdiction, controlling for as many variables as possible. Since many of my suggestions for how the law ought to treat friends are based on ways many courts in many jurisdictions actually do treat friends, it should be possible to isolate those jurisdictions to see if the law has done anything to deter friendship in those places (though, to be fair, there are many intrajurisdictional inconsistencies in this area of the law, which almost no one has bothered to try to organize and explore before this book's effort to expose and analyze them). Until that study is done (one that would be quite difficult to design), we are left with only educated conjecture.

But there is, perhaps, an important analogy that might be the basis of sound prognostication, an analogy that did a lot of work in early sections of the book: marriage. Marriage carries with it substantial duties that can extend very far into the future even if it dissolves. Yet it would be hard to believe that these substantial duties do much to deter people from choosing to get married. Perhaps such incidental deterrence—incidental because it is clearly not the law's aim to provide incentives against marriage—functions at the margins among those who are particularly rationalistic in intimate affairs. Surely, that doesn't account for most of us. Yet, generally speaking, the potential incidental deterrence at the margins is not a serious reason to prevent the law's enforcement of special duties within marriage relationships. We might want the state to be neutral with respect to marriage for other reasons—for example, neutrality might help us not to discriminate against those who cannot or do not want to marry for one reason or another—but worrying about deterrence doesn't really make the list.

Friendship, like marriage, provides so many of its own incentives for entry (and it is relatively easier to exit when its costs grow too great) that it is hard to imagine legal regulations actually deterring people from establishing and developing friendships. To be fair, friendship does not carry quite as many legal perquisites as marriage does (nor is it as hard to exit), so the analogy fails in an important way, too: friendship has fewer legal advantages to counterbalance the extra duties proposed here. But I have also in this book recommended plenty of legal benefits we could imagine extending to friendships; these could help avoid this deterrence effect from taking root, if one is really still worried about it. I think it is fair to conclude that the law will do little to prevent people from enjoying the very real, albeit thus far nonlegal, advantages of friendship through, for example, the uncommon enforcement of a fiduciary duty in an extreme case of disloyalty.

It may be that people don't often take their lead from law when they are planning their conduct, especially in intimate affairs, so it is, perhaps, unlikely that these duties could do any good anyway. But we should not too easily count on the irrelevance of law: it holds a sway over our lives because it can coerce us, and it powerfully interacts with the social norms that surely program our behavior at least as much as law does. Indeed, the more "relationalist" law becomes—the more it actually expresses the community's sense of justice in its institutions—the more it can genuinely be called our own, enhancing its resonance, which can increase our own likelihood of compliance with it. We can certainly strengthen friendship by not emboldening imposters who pose as friends and then hide behind friendship when they are called to account for having abused the relationship. And we can help friends plan their transactions better: leaving too much up in the air might not be a very good way to preserve a friendship, when friends do find themselves transacting in various ways. Of course, many people avoid transacting with friends too; it can be awkward to ask our friends to execute their promises when they are having a hard time. As friends, we are supposed to be understanding and we might feel that transactions with strangers (buying their used cars, say) might cause us less stress. But, as decades of research has shown, we don't actually avoid friends in our transactions all the time. So either the law can stick its head in the sand or it can develop some sensitivity to what is going on in the real world.

Ultimately, just because the law can do little to undermine the benefits of friendship does not mean that the law can do little to support the institution through legally enforced duties. I do not think that saying that friendship can survive an occasional legal incursion actually undermines the idea that legal protection can usefully help friendship as an institution. Family and marriage strikes me as a useful analogy here, too: burdening family members with special duties (as we saw the law does in chapter 3) does not, as a general matter, make us think that family is being deterred and left unsupported. Rather, part of the reason we burden families is to protect them and to support the special vulnerabilities prevalent within them. So, too, in friendship: we should protect friends and those who get screwed by those who pose as friends because we value the institution and law can help support the institution, just as it does with families, where special vulnerabilities leave members especially exposed to risk.

Still, it is probably true that a legal regime that does exact special duties from friends would likely result in people being much more clear with one another about their relationship's status, in more than just marginal cases. Your used car salesman might not pretend to be your friend anymore if she is going to be held to have special responsibilities to negotiate in good faith, say, and be required to disclose certain things she might otherwise be able to keep to herself. Some vendors who pretend to be your friend might act slightly more professionally to avoid special duties. But in this way, friendship duties and their potential enforcement will serve an "information-forcing" function, helping parties organize their intimate affairs and enabling them to have a better sense of the identities of their real friends. It is certainly true that false friendships smooth some market transactions— and some false friendships will be deterred as a matter of company policy to avoid extra costs. In a world where friendship carries legal consequences, some people may try to disclaim that they are friends with the people with whom they are transacting.

Sometimes, such disclaimers would be hard for courts to take seriously (because denials of reality don't change reality). Other times, disclaimers would helpfully prevent someone from thinking a party is a friend. Clear signals, which might be incentivized by a legal rule creating default duties for friend, will help the vulnerable know when not to rely. But remember also another overwhelming theme of chapter 4: friends should get benefits, too—and plenty of people might want to shore up their friendships and be clear that they are in friendships so as to make sure they can get the benefits as well.

There is, I think, a real benefit associated with people getting clearer about their relationships, in any case. As Aristotle well understood (and as I reported in chapter 1), much tension within friendships develops because people are not clear about their relational intent and tend to lead other people on.[4] Of course, some friendships are constitutively uncertain. We assume a future with our friends but cannot always guarantee it in light of changing patterns in our own lives; some people we want to keep at just the right distance but not lose as "friends." So, in some cases, being clear isn't really an option. But nudging people to be more honest about how close they feel to the people with whom they interact might not be a bad way to avoid uncomfortable awkwardness in more consequential settings. Thus, although certain types of false friendships may be deterred (or not, as participants try to transition into a real one to get the legal benefits), real ones might be intensified, and parties would be able to send more credible signals about their intent to be trustworthy, since legal sanctions would attach to those who betray trust. When parties draw on the trope of friendship in their transactions and interactions, justice may just demand differential treatment if the transaction goes sour. Or so I have argued throughout this book.

The "enforcement" of friendship will be only rare, in any case, because both social norms and legal costs will keep litigants out of court most of the time. It is unusual that a duty has sufficient value to make it worth suing up on in the first place. And given the limitations developed in this book—in particular, that the law should only enforce a substantial default from a social norm in which legal enforcement isn't specifically or impliedly negated (though courts might need to make sure negations aren't fraudulent or otherwise counter-indicated by the actual relationship of the parties)—it is fair to conclude that the law will do little to prevent people from forming and enjoying friendships. They are likely to come to court only rarely to enforce quite radical departures from acceptable conduct.

There is yet a further reason to be skeptical of the crowding thesis. Crowding is most likely to result—and most likely to serve as a substitute rather than a complement—only when there is an environment of perfect enforcement, where legal norms perfectly incorporate all social norms. That doesn't happen, for several reasons: only some social norms are appropriate for the law to enforce; the law is costly to employ so won't be used to enforce day-to-day legal norms; and there is stigma associated with suing one's friends and relational contract partners, so people are very unlikely to use the law even when legal options are presumably available. This is as true in the context of friendship as in our relationships with our doctors, cell phone companies, cable companies, meat producers, baby toy producers, and virtually every person with whom we contract on an ongoing basis.[5] We may have to resort to legal sanctions in a rare episode of betrayal or fury (whether stemming from contract law, tort law, property law, consumer protection law, employment law, etc.), but this possibility does not crowd out fully the need for trust and some elevated level of vulnerability. I know I can sue my doctor or the hospital if something untoward happens to me when I am under anesthesia. But that sort of trust in sanctions does not help me choose a doctor or hospital, nor does it enable me to develop a good relationship central to my well-being. Indeed, even the perfectly rational calculators among us know that our legal remedies will tend to be undercompensatory when they are available at all: we might lose our remedies because of technicalities, bad lawyers, unreliable juries, statutes of limitations, or other unrelated legal difficulties, all of which we can anticipate as a real risk from the outset. And even if the law punishes really bad babysitters, that punishment will rarely make parents feel whole when a babysitter has killed their child through her negligence. Money damages cannot always fully recompense betrayed trust. Thus, the crowding thesis, even if it is defensible at some level, leaves plenty of room for developing the important kind of trust that makes the world go round, even if the law intervenes in some cases. In the legal landscape of very imperfect enforcement and regulation, trust is far from crowded out. Thus, to the extent that there is any crowding, law will always only make small incursions into our friendships' basis in trust. The law will help police only major defections without intruding too heavily into the social norms, which will continue to function.

DEBASEMENT

There are others who focus on a variation of the "crowding" thesis and insist that any legal ramifications for an intimate relationship, whether a duty or a privilege, just debases the value of friendship. Often, the "debasement" instinct is predicated on a conception of legal enforcement that includes only contracts between strangers and a conception of intimate relations that is altogether too pure or Pollyannaish. I hope I have shown throughout this book that that picture of the legal world is not especially true to reality. We contract and transact with intimates all the time, our friendships and our transactions intersect often, and the law makes friendship matter in a whole host of ways in a range of cases throughout the fabric of the law.

The debasement thesis also seems predicated on the assumption that one can have either "real" trust that operates outside the law *or* legally policed trust, and that in a given context they are mutually exclusive. But that assumption virtually guarantees the conclusion. In any case, the premise is flawed. It simply isn't true that, as Annette Baier put it, "the fact that there is some reliance on the threat of sanctions mean[s] that there will be no room for trust."[6] This book's arguments help show why that assumption is false: trust relationships and legal relationships are mutually reinforcing in many cases. Indeed, as Larry Mitchell has argued, "certain preconditions, like a legal system sustaining the values of trust, are necessary for trust to flourish."[7] Law makes trust possible, in part—even the strong form necessary for open-ended relationships like relational contracts, fiduciary relations, and friendships. The law doesn't only matter when it comes to lawsuits; it structures much about how we interact in our private lives and can help forge and sustain trust.

A related observation: Those who write about social and legal norms routinely fail to recognize that they cannot be divided into separate spheres as neatly as these writers assume. Consider, for example, when we can say that "the law" and "legal norms" intervene in a relationship: it is often only vaguely there in the background and only very infrequently comes to resolve a dispute. When you get into an argument with your phone company, is "the law" your first pass at solving your problems? Surely, we know there is a contract and set of regulations somewhere controlling our relationship with the phone company. But the likelihood of our feeling completely governed by the form contract we were sent when we started the relationship and the web of laws that might be relevant to the transaction is not the first thing we tend to think should govern our dispute: we know we can switch providers, blog about bad customer service, threaten the company with reprisals, and other self-help remedies outside the scope of the "legal" relationship. In such cases, do the legal norms vitiate the possibility of acting on social norms? Even when a dispute arises that seems to be addressed through nonlegal sanctions, an implicit calculation not to use more legal options may be in the background, structuring parties' behavior in disputes. When the phone company addresses your concern, which, imagine, the contract does not require it to do, is it doing because it likes to be known for good customer service? Or is it worried that a mass of discontented customers could lead to a legal challenge of the validity of its form contract?

Or what about when a dispute arises and one party tells the other that she thinks she has some legal rights in play during early negotiations? Is a decision by the threatened party to relent and reach a negotiated settlement obviously a legal one, traceable to the use of legal rhetoric? Or do social norms supplement this situation, proving, again, that the social and the legal work in tandem all the time? What about when one party sends a lawyer's letter to the other? Is that a "legal" sanction, even though the law is not being applied directly and coercively? When a dispute is arbitrated after such a missive, can we say for certain which norm accomplished the compliance and settlement? Does the mere whiff of law, mentioned in a letter, replace all the work social norms do to structure the parties' negotiations? Or what about after a complaint is filed but before either party spends money on discovery? Is a settlement triggered by the filing of a law-suit—rather than a disposition of law itself by a black-robed individu-al—a clear case of settling merely a legal dispute? Or were social norms of settlement and reputational concerns also in play? In short, to the extent that some people fear that social norms will be degraded once the law has taken an interest in them, they would do well to remember how porous the boundaries of the legal and the social are and how often the two types of norms mix to produce compliance in any given context. The arguments developed throughout this book also help make this salient; the mixture is especially likely to reveal itself early and often in relational contracts and friendships, as chapter 6 made clear.

Finally, there is, perhaps, a more philosophical rendering of the debasement thesis that can also be shown to be erroneous though the arguments developed in this book. This form of the argument empha-sizes that the very value of friendship's duties inheres in their lack of enforceability. Once those duties get backed by legal sanctions and the law becomes available to enforce them, perhaps a friend can no longer *communicate* exactly why she is complying with her duty. If you lose the ability to credibly signal to your friend that you are attending to her *because of the friendship* and not because of any other calculation, the relationship itself gets eroded.[8] The concern seems to be that friend-ship itself ceases to be an *independent* reason for compliance once legal enforceability enters the picture.

But there are several reasons to reject this line of argumentation as well. First, as I've emphasized throughout, particularly in chapters 1 and 2, it is too simplistic to assume that the value of friendship inheres in "voluntary" compliance. People comply with their friendship duties for all sorts of reasons: a sense of obligation in friendship is common, whether that sense comes from a fear of being sued at the extreme or, more usually, a fear of a nonlegal sanction. In short, although it is true that the type of sanction may have some quantum of effect on the com-municative potential of compliance (and I just endeavored to show that the line between social and legal sanctions is probably overdrawn, in any case), sanctions are available even if the law doesn't show its hand.

That means that if we insist that the value of friendship comes only from "voluntary" compliance, we are prone to find that friendship isn't valuable very often at all. Not a likely conclusion.

Second, no matter what your contractual theory or your theory of friendship, many contracts between friends will have to be enforceable. Chapter 6 showed that a great deal of contracting is transacted among friends—and almost all would agree that formal contracts between friends will generally be legally enforceable. Can you imagine a world where business deals between friends were suddenly considered unenforceable because of the friendship? That would be quite a bizarre result and would tend to undermine so many business transactions that much of our economic system might very well collapse under the pressure. Yet the "debasement" view, taken to its logical conclusion, is committed to the idea that any enforceable contract that exists between friends will kill the friendship, unless we insist on a policy of nonenforcement for all these contracts. Even those who embrace the debasement thesis must reject this conclusion, notwithstanding the reality that friends will never know if compliance was achieved through the threat of legal sanctions or because of the independent reason of friendship.

Third, many portions of this book suggest that parties to friendships routinely engage in both altruistic and selfish reasoning all the time; friends don't expect any differently and only hope for generosity when it most matters. Friendship as a possible motivation for action is not any less an *independent* reason when other instrumental factors are considered side by side. For example: say you choose to attend the funeral of your friend's mother across the country. You have essentially two clusters of reasons for your action, both of which are independent. First, you do it because your friend asks you to come and you love him. That is your "friendship reason." But you also do it because your friend came to your father's deathbed when you asked, you feel slightly indebted, and you need to go see your sister in the city of the funeral anyway. Imagine that this is your cluster of "instrumental reasons." Does the possibility of there being two independent clusters of reasons for your attending the funeral "debase" friendship? Or is this scenario so typical that it is easy to see how reasoning this way is consistent with the way friendship is actually practiced in the real world? It is reasonable to create a regulative ideal of the perfect friendship in our minds; it is unreasonable to deny the reality of how very close friendships are actually lived and practiced.

Of course, acting principally upon certain instrumental reasons as motivations can risk diluting a friendship, but it doesn't challenge the realm of friendship to acknowledge that "friendship reasons" will sometimes compete with and sometimes complement other reasons. Moreover, in light of the undercompensatory nature of the possible legal sanctions (which I just explored with respect to "crowding"), there is plenty of room for the "independent reason" of friendship to prove itself as the prime motivation for undertaking compliance with friendship's demands in most cases, even if there is also an "instrumental reason" that involves an interest in avoiding a legal claim.

Contract law is actually especially useful to make the point. Generally speaking, one cannot recover in a contract suit for emotional distress, for punitive damages, on "penalty" clauses, for uncertain or speculative damages, for unforeseeable damages, or for attorney's fees. Indeed, it is generally quite difficult to get specific performance: the performance you are actually owed.[9] In short, in almost no case is an aggrieved party to a contract case made whole, irrespective of the measure of damages the law decides to award. Even an award of specific performance does not really make the aggrieved party whole, since she had to sue to get it and can't usually get her attorney's costs.[10]

Multiple theories have, of course, been offered to explain this pervasive policy within contract law, which generations of law students have struggled with over time. How can we say that contract law is supposed to get injured parties what they were promised and put them in the position they would have been in had the contract been performed if we virtually never accomplish its "expectancy" goal? Indeed, most relationalists concede that the law as it is hardly well explained by relational theory, which self-consciously highlights how much the law is driven by an assumption of contracts between strangers.[11] Yet the perspective developed in chapter 6 contributes to understanding this dimension of contract law nevertheless.

To wit, contract law may be undercompensatory in part because it is structured to minimize incursions into private ordering, especially when a thick set of social norms is likely to govern transactions. The law doesn't crowd out trust or debase friendship precisely because its interventions leave plenty of room for nonlegal sanctions to do their work. That is, even if the "crowding" or "debasement" theses were true—a point not conceded here—it is substantially mitigated when the legal norms are themselves largely undercompensatory. This underscores their supplementary rather than substitutional nature. Perhaps if the law perfectly tracked "moral" nonlegal obligations, it is possible that people would stop being able to distinguish their friendship motivations from their business ones (though even there having two motivations hardly kills the possibility for being a good friend). By leaving room open for social norms to function even when a party invokes the law, parties can continue to operate within the domain of social norms.

This point does highlight the need to explore a potential ambiguity about relational contract theory from chapter 6. Relationalists' command to "incorporate" social norms is actually doubly misleading and leads to many mistaken characterizations of the theory. I am hopeful that my discussions here help clarify these confusions, as follows.

First, sometimes the prevailing social norm is precisely to preclude legal enforcement altogether. This doesn't undermine relational theory's incorporation thesis—but it can be missed when it is, as it is so often, caricatured. Much of what we do for friends *is* meant to be gratuitous and has no implicit exchange in view—but not all of it is this way, and we can have no clear rule to separate law and friendship categorically. We may have no obligation to lend a friend money when he asks, but once we do, we should be able to rely on being paid back, assuming it was intended as a loan, informal though it may have been. This is, I suppose, an answer to an early challenge by Adam Smith in *The Theory of Moral Sentiments*:

> If your friend lent you money in your distress, ought you to lend him money in his? How much ought you to lend him? When ought you lend him? Now, or tomorrow, or next month? And for how long a time? It is evident that no general rule can be laid down by which a precise answer can, in all cases, be given to any of these questions. The difference between his character and yours, between his circumstances and yours, may be such, that you may be perfectly grateful, and justly refuse to lend him a halfpenny; and, on the contrary, you may be willing to lend, or even give him ten times the sum which he lent you, and yet justly be accused of the blackest ingratitude.[12]

The relationalist answer to this issue is simply to say: Yes, Adam, we can't force the friend to make the reciprocal loan. But once that loan is made—or once a promise to make that loan is made—we can't use "friendship" as a cover to disable its being enforced. Indeed, the friendship would trigger the borrower's reasonable reliance that the promise to make the loan would be fulfilled in good faith (barring unforeseen forgivable circumstances) and the loaner's reasonable reliance that the loan would be repaid. Those dispositions of reliance should have legal ramifications.

Second, although a relational contract law would tell us that social norms are meant to be translated into contracts in a variety of ways, we can't forget that when it comes to remedies, the law will remain under-compensatory, whatever the social norms. That is for good reason, too: to leave some room for the nonlegal sanctions and the predication of the relationship outside the law to have some force. Punitive damages are awarded appropriately from time to time, but they are clearly the outlier case in contracts disputes. Ultimately, contract law's divergence from social norms is a good thing, in order to provide for social norms a realm of freedom. The undercompensatory nature of contractual remedies makes that possible, without forcing the vulnerable and the taken-advan-tage-of to be wholly without recourse in the event that they suffer because of another parties' opportunism. Indeed, this divergence may, after all, be just what a relational theory would predict: internal social norms would enforce substantial breaches with relatively modest remedies so breached parties aren't left too badly off but would leave to nonlegal sanctions a substantial portion of the enforcement of the deal. Even if that balance of legal and nonlegal sanctions is not contemplated by every relational contract, it is a decent approximation of most, helps explain in part why the law is the way it is, and puts to rest some of the bite of the "crowding" and "debasement" theses for those that tend to be persuaded by them.

I have furnished several methods of rejoinder to the concerns about trust likely to arise within the camp who oppose most of the policy suggestions of this book, as follows:

(1) This book offers legal privileges for friendships that might counteract the concern that friendship will be deterred if we enforce legal duties in them.

(2) There are ultimately larger social benefits from friendship for individuals—worth a modest cost—so few laws could realistically crowd out the trust within friendships. Moreover, the value of friendship just can't be debased by the modest proposals here; friends will still be able to communicate their love and their commitment to the relationship, even if they have instrumental reasons for meeting friendship's moral demands some of the time.

(3) This book exposes the reality that the worlds of friendship and the worlds of law collide all the time, which undermines the idea that law and friendship exist in hermetically sealed environments. Worlds colliding is always threatening—but

realizing it is happening is important for reorienting ourselves. The collision is not creating a Brave New World; but a better world may well be in store if we can adjust and see that there is the possibility for mutual reinforcement and support.

(4) There is always going to be imperfect legal enforcement anyway, leaving social norms room to do their thing. In the friendship context, imperfect enforcement is likely to be even more widespread: unlike the thought of suing our trustees, corporate officers, and lawyers, there is surely substantial stigma associated with suing our friends. No amount of legal regulation will remove that stigma because, for the most part, suing our friends is a way of ending a friendship. Indeed, the suit is pretty strong evidence that the friendship is beyond repair.

What all this means is that there is good reason not to worry too much about our friendships becoming litigious affairs. The agenda of this book—allowing the law to grow more sensitive to friendship and to enable the scaffolding of law to provide some nudges to support the important social institution of friendship—is not likely to destroy what we hold so dear about friendships. The law will not "crowd" out trust or "debase" our friendships.

Conclusion

THIS BOOK IS really the first sustained effort to issue a clear call that we ought to be using our public institutions to help the personal relationship that helps us so centrally: intimate friendship. For a long while, we have been content to believe that friendship neither—in the words of a central figure in the critical legal studies movement—"need[s] much law nor [is] capable of tolerating it."[1] As another legal scholar has put it, we "mark the dignity and specialness of intimate relations" by denying the legal enforceability of promises and economic transactions made in the intimate sphere.[2] But by now I hope to have convinced the reader that this is an altogether too simplified picture of what the law can do for friendship, what the law actually does with friendship, what friendship might illuminate about the law, and what the law might illuminate about friendship's commands. They are not separate and hostile worlds, after all: intimacy within friendship and law collide in many ways. And that is the first recognition necessary to make plausible the rest of my arguments throughout this book about how the law can furnish a scaffolding for friendship, how the law can calibrate itself better to the society it governs, and how friends might learn about how they should behave by looking to legal cues.

To be sure, we will always need to keep in mind Viviana Zelizer's very helpful caution about the *purchase* of intimacy (in her book of the same title),[3] where she elegantly shows just how much intimacy is for sale, purchased, and commodified. Showing that the separate spheres story is too simple doesn't end the analysis, because one still has to find a way to show respect for the deep ways people are committed to the intimate sphere. Even if it turns out that our institutions never quite protect intimacy in the way people expect, careful policy design does require some calibration to people's intuitions about intimacy. Although I hope that by now readers are disabused of the neat story that friendship can and should be hermetically sealed off from the law, it certainly takes at least a book to get there. It isn't easy to counter the strong intuitions many of us have about these matters, but I hope I have made a dent, while being respectful of the purchase the "separate spheres" story will probably continue to inspire, careful arguments to the contrary notwithstanding. Indeed, keeping that purchase in sight also enables a measured and sophisticated approach to the overlaps of and interactions between the law and friendship.

Instead of summarizing what the reader should know by now having read the book, I want to highlight here three paths I *haven't* taken in my effort to explore friendship and the law. That should, by way of conclusion, make salient how much and how little I am truly advocating on behalf of the regulation of friendship.

NO GENERALIZED LEGAL DUTY TO BE A GOOD FRIEND

I am not advocating for a generalized legal duty to be a good friend. I don't imagine a separate cause of action available for the dereliction of abstract friendship duties, asking a court to make sure you get your friends to move your stuff if you helped them move their stuff in the past (and are now stuck paying for movers). I don't ever let my friend live that one down, but my enthusiasm for friendship's legal duties notwithstanding, I'm not suing. Friendship can tolerate ongoing needling about a prior failure to live up to the ethical duties within a friendship, but ongoing friendships also require fundamental forgiveness for small slights. I suspect that even if such a cause of action existed, few would ever come to court to get theirs.

It is nevertheless important not to caricature the sorts of cases where I see friendship making a difference in law. I have generally proposed in my catalogue of friendship's legal duties that friendship be a consideration, a thumb on the scales, embedded within an already existing legal edifice of recognizing the importance of relational variables or relational causes of action, not that friendship furnish a freestanding legal duty that has never before existed. To say that friendship might qualify as a special relationship for the purposes of the duty to rescue or that betrayals of confidences might be actionable between friends or ex-friends only acknowledges that we have a broad system of relational obligation in many areas of the law and that friendship routinely seems to fit the preexisting mold. To say that the internal norms within friendship should help illuminate whether a contract formed and what the contract means is to highlight that a properly designed relational contract law would be able easily to admit considerations of friendship just as it easily admits the incorporation of commercial norms in business contracts.

I highlight this path not taken here to ensure both that I don't get caricatured and that readers see the limits of my arguments in this book. The privileges tend to find a readier reception, despite their not having been more robustly granted thus far. The duties are the ones that draw catcalls and snickering. I want to make sure they get criticized only on their own terms. Those still feeling the purchase of the idea that the realm of intimacy in friendship must be kept apart from the law may be able to take some comfort in the care with which I have tried to urge the incorporation of friendship into law: I haven't done it wholesale, and friendship will always remain, in part, outside law because I do not propose a generalized legal duty to be a good friend.

LITTLE FOCUS ON WEAK TIES
OR CIVIC FRIENDSHIP

Within this book, I have focused here and there on relationships with presumptively less affect than deep friendships. I've explored business friendships and touched on general regard for co-citizens. I've endeavored from time to time to specify some of the advantages that might be credited to weak ties—and strategies to bolster them. But my real interest in this book, ultimately, is finding a way to help and support relations of close intimacy. More could definitely be said about how friendships among co-citizens could contribute to sustaining an attractive and democratic politics—and about how a democratic politics could contribute to sustaining this more attenuated idea of citizen friendship.[4] Yet my primary focus has really been the sort of friendship I described in chapter 1. This isn't the "pure" virtue friendship of Aristotle's imagination, but I do have in mind the sort of friends with whom we discuss important matters of real consequence: our close friends. This suggests that my concept of friendship may be decently tracked by the sociologists who have charted a substantial decline in our society in how often people have nonkin associates with whom they discuss important matters. Thus, their findings are more alarming to me than they may be to others who think "important matters" friendship, as it were, drastically undercounts our friends and companions of deep significance (though, to be fair, the surveys that test "important matters" friendship routinely require associates to have had an "important matters" conversation within the last six months to count as such a friend; I take it we can have close "important matters" friendships with people we don't speak to for six months at a time). It is true that "important matters" friends are a mere subset of the people we might call friends in everyday usage. But the social institution that is really at the core of this book is a deeper sort of friendship than mere "networks" entail. My working definition of friend also coheres with a common usage, too.

RELATIVELY LITTLE USE OF A LAW OF FRIENDSHIP TO FIGHT FOR WOMEN'S OR GAY RIGHTS

One can count on a few fingers those who are already thinking about friendship and the law—and the majority of them are in the feminist and queer law community. Yet this book urges that we focus on friendship for friendship's sake, not on friendship in the service of some supervening goal, however noble such goals may be. I am, I confess (or believe), a feminist and a strong believer in gay rights. I also happen to think we prioritize marriage and child-rearing more than we should, marginalizing those who do not marry or procreate. But ultimately, my interest in friendship is primary in this book—and I want to focus the reader principally on this central institution.

To be sure, there are ways the arguments of this book can be deployed in service of feminist and gay policy concerns. They can also be used by single and unmarried people (of any sexual orientation)—they, too, are a group particularly attuned to concerns about friendship in public policy.[5] Indeed, I have certainly embraced a few of these applications throughout the book: some modes of promoting friendship can help destabilize patriarchy, heteronormativity, and discrimination against women, single people, the childless, and gays. But these results are not the only reasons—or my central reasons—to pursue the legal support of friendship in our society. I see them as additional benefits of pursuing a legal framework for friendship, not the motivation for doing so. And I see feminism, gay rights advocacy, and other progressive movements as informing a way to implement a legal sensitivity to friendship in better and more equitable ways than those in which we have designed our legal regulation of the family. But I'm wary—for all the reasons I've catalogued throughout—of hitching my friendship agenda to other movements that have their hearts elsewhere.

I suspect that gay rights advocates, feminists, and those looking for a more serious rethinking of marriage's place in our legal culture will be disappointed by this book, in the final analysis, because it does not put their concerns at the very center of its argument and plan for friendship promotion. But that is a path I have deliberately chosen. I haven't ignored the concerns of feminists and gay rights advocates, and I have tried to guide the development of thinking about law and friendship in ways that are nondiscriminatory and promote equality on many dimensions. Of course, I welcome further efforts by others to extend the law and public policy arguments and strategies for friendship promotion that I have introduced here.

As public policy designers and lawyers try to apply the suggestions and theories presented in this book, they should keep in mind that many of these proposals do not include a full assessment of costs and benefits. Chapters 5, 6 and 7 were meant to model how lawyers might move forward thinking about costs and benefits with their particular tools, but policy-makers will have to use their tools, too, within their areas of control and expertise. Weighing costs and benefits is absolutely essential before signing on to any of the particular provocations about design tactics that I have presented. But just as surely, lawyers and public policy designers have had an unfortunate tendency to discount benefits and overestimate costs because of a misguided desire to keep law and friendship in separate worlds and a misguided sense that the law can do no good. Armed with the foundation laid in this book, public policy-makers might do better in making more honest calculations in the future. Our poverty amelioration programs, our family law, our health care regulation, our property, contract, and tort laws, our criminal justice system, our conflict-of-interest rules, our judicial recusal protocols could usefully be supplemented with more sensitivity to friendship than we have heretofore permitted or considered systematically. I hope to have inspired a desire to study these issues more carefully in the near future and an interest in starting pilot programs to help friendship along.

When all is said and done, should we, say, extend immigration benefits or employer-based health plans to friends as we do to spouses? That is doubtful, in part because the costs do seem very large indeed. In particular, the number of friends who could qualify for special perquisites suggests that, perhaps, policy-makers ought not seek to protect friends in this max-imalist way. But maybe there would be real benefits to society at large if we allowed people to designate one best friend to collect these immigration and heath insurance benefits to contain the problem of large numbers; as sociologists have been telling us, people actually don't have all that many close friends anyway. To be sure, I have some skepticism about registries, especially ones the state administers, for reasons I've already discussed. But creativity in policy design is urgent—and we need to be thinking about costs and benefits to friendship sensitivity and promotion not only in particular policy areas but systemically as well. I suspect we will see that there are returns on our investments to be had if we support the institu-tion of friendship within the polity. I'm looking forward to friendship's brighter future in a public world where our private friendships really mat-ter—where kin isn't the only legally respected personal affiliation.

One final word: In an age of "law and" proliferation in the academic study of law—"law and the emotions," "law and economics," "law and literature," "law and science"—it is important for lawyers and law teachers to show their bona fides and focus on how they are training the next gen-eration of lawyers. Law professors, I think most would agree, have an ethical duty to teach their students law, not literature. Yet those engaged in these "interdisciplinary" enterprises surely must master areas of research outside law. But they also need to establish that the law tells us something distinctive about the other area of study and to communicate why lawyers of the future should care about these external disciplines. To execute the agenda in this book, I have had to study widely and deeply in multiple scholarly approaches to friendship. But my hope, in the final analysis, is not to found a new school of "law and friendship" scholars. Instead, I hope to have shown that there is actually a distinctively legal approach to friendship. The friend-as-fiduciary and friendship-as-rela-tional-contract models, as presented in this book, really do, I think, illu-minate the personal relationship of friendship in ways only lawyers can.

More important, perhaps, I am calling for public policy designers and lawyers to give more attention to friendship in whatever they are doing. What is more, revealing all the ways friendship can matter to our legal institutions is a task lawyers are particularly well suited to perform. Some might be turned off by lawyers on the friendship scene—a place some of us think of as a refuge from the state. But—romance and prissiness aside—the law is often already there. Averting our gaze is not an option. Let's focus on ways to improve both friend-ship and the resonance of the law by bringing the two social practices and institutions into closer communication.

Acknowledgments

OVER SEVERAL YEARS, many people have read many drafts of many of the chapters in this book and given me their thoughts and comments; I want to thank them all. But here are the readers and commentators I can remember, in no particular order: Peter Goodrich, Christine Hurt, David Arkush, Matt Bodie, Stuart Buck, Jen Collins, Mary Coombs, Bob Ellickson, Ira Ellman, Carissa Byrne Hessick, Fred Lambert, Sarah Lawsky, Orly Lobel, Dan Markel, Jonathan Masur, Laura Rosenbury, Allan Silver, Corey Rayburn Yung, Curtis Bridgeman, Hanoch Dagan, Deborah DeMott, Scott FitzGibbon, Rob Flannigan, Tamar Frankel, Eric Goldman, Jeff Gordon, Brett McDonnell, Larry Mitchell, Hadar Aviram, Doug Moll, Gordon Smith, Lynn Stout, W. Jay Wallace, Verity Winship, Manuel Vargas, Chris Kutz, Steve Vladeck, Bob Scott, Buffy Scott, Alice Ristroph, Eric Posner, Michael Pratt, Michael O'Hear, Stewart Macaulay, Julian Ku, Katy Kuh, Adam Kolber, Paul Ingram, Adil Haque, Jay Feinman, Bill Dodge, Reza Dibadj, Bill Wang, I. Bennett Capers, Dave Campbell, and Mike Cahill.

I had too many conversations about the themes in these pages to count or recount. But some notable ones with David Ponet and Myron Schonfeld tend to be the ones that play in loops in my head. Eddan Katz helped me navigate the world of online friendships, though he failed to get me to join Facebook. Rudy Delson helped with the title; it was just awful before his useful interventions. Sanjukta Paul has always been totally dismissive but challenging and unconsciously supportive in her own way. Allan Silver has been a mensch and mentor ever since I cold-called him one fall in New York. Peter Goodrich treated me to a ridiculously good lunch at a critical juncture; thanks also to him for reading most of the old stuff that no one else can without dying of boredom. Viviana Zelizer reminded me about the double entendre of her important title, which got me to think about my own book differently.

There was an odd moment in the writing of this book when I became aware that the hours I spent thinking about friendship outpaced the hours I spent participating in my friendships. That was a disturbing realization. But my friendship with David Ponet helps remind me on a nearly daily basis that I really do have expertise about the practice, not just the theory, of friendship. Thanks to David for his unmatched availability, emotionally and otherwise. I love you, David.

My library liaison at UC-Hastings, Linda Weir, has always gone above and beyond to get me what I need—and quickly. She is a lifeline and I am grateful for her tireless efforts on my behalf. I also thank my research assistants over the years—Susan Biggins, Fatima Khan, Kassandra Kuehl, Elaine Nyguen, and Doug Ecks. UC-Hastings has always given me the room to write what I want to write and it never breeds its young to conform. I will always be grateful to the institution for its intellectual openness and for its totally sound recent tenure decision.

Friendly faculty workshops at Brooklyn Law School, UC-Hastings, UC-Berkeley, and Hofstra University Law School provided collegial environments to try out some of the ideas presented here. The 1066 Foundation and the Roger Traynor Scholarly Publication Award provided financial support. And Columbia Law School graciously hosted me in the spring and summer of 2009, when much of the work on the book was completed. That school is just a stunning place to do one's work; thanks to Buffy Scott especially for bringing me in.

Editors at the *UCLA Law Review*, the *Washington University Law Review*, the *Emory Law Journal*, and *Policy Review* contributed to the final product here by offering their editorial help on previously published versions of some of the arguments brought together in this book.

My father and one-time coauthor—*Neurilemmoma of the Anterior Ethmoidal Nerve Encroaching upon the Nasolacrimal Duct* remains one of my favorite publications though it has fallen off my CV for obvious reasons—very early on instilled in me the confidence and ethic to write, write, write. Thanks for that. And many thanks to my mother, who read *Billy Budd* aloud to me in the days when I simply refused to do any reading for school. Things have changed—I read a lot these days, of course—but my mother never gave up hope that I'd be interested in school one day. She probably wishes now that I liked school less so I could make more money. But this is a very fulfilling life and I thank her for pushing that one agenda (and only that agenda) as hard as she could.

Linda Schonfeld is the best mother-in-law one could ever hope for. Thanks to the Schonfelds for supporting me so thoroughly these last six years, for giving me a roof over my head while I was completing this book, and for not leaving me to fend for their daughter alone.

Thanks to my agent, Lisa Adams, for seeing the potential this book had to reach a wide audience, to Stephen Dubner at the *Freakonomics* blog for giving me a platform to try out the ideas with their impressive readers, and to Dave McBride at Oxford University Press for helping to make this book a reality and much more readable. Several anonymous evaluators for Oxford University Press also helped me make this book better, though certain pages have grown more defensive than I really feel.

My children did nothing to make this book better and tried to stop me from working on it at every turn. But I'm sure I'll interfere with their life goals in the coming years without really knowing it, so we're even. My partner, Zoe Schonfeld, really tried to create space for me to work on this book, especially during the last push; dedicating the book to her really doesn't get us even. But I'll try in the coming years to pay it back. I love you, Zoe.

Notes

Introduction

1. Miller McPherson et al., *Social Isolation in America: Changes in Core Discussion Networks over Two Decades*, 71 Am. Soc. Rev. 353 (2006). For the most recent challenge to these findings, see Claude S. Fischer, *The 2004 GSS Finding of Shrunken Social Networks: An Artifact*, 74 Am. Soc. Rev. 657 (2009).

2. *See generally* J. Donath & d. boyd, *Public Displays of Connection*, 22 BT Tech. J. 71 (2004).

3. *See* Anthony Giddens, The Transformation of Intimacy: Sexuality, Love and Eroticism in Modern Societies (Stanford University Press 1992).

4. *See* Joseph Epstein, Friendship: An Exposé (Houghton Mifflin 2006); Norman Podhoretz, Ex-Friends: Falling Out with Allen Ginsberg, Lionel and Diana Trilling, Lillian Hellman, Hannah Arendt, and Norman Mailer (San Francisco: Encounter Books 2000); Allan Bloom, Love and Friendship (Simon & Schuster 1993); Andrew Sullivan, Love Undetectable: Notes on Friendship, Sex, and Survival (Knopf 1998). Why are conservatives especially attracted to this subject? Sullivan suggests that conservatives are committed to a "politics of *philia*," whereas "liberals" "are suspicious of particular loyalties and seek to embrace universal values and egalitarian politics." *Id.* at 244. That said, it is fair to say that a conservative taste for friendship notwithstanding, none of these authors translates his interest in friendship into a political or legal program of any kind.

5. Sociologist Sasha Roseneil has done extraordinary work on the class of people who choose to center their lives and their circles of care around friendship rather than sexual partners or kin. *See* Sasha Roseneil, *Why We Should Care About Friends: An Argument for Queering the Care Imaginary in Social Policy*, 3 Soc. Pol'y & Soc'y 409, 411 (2004); Sasha Roseneil, *Care, Values, and the Future of Welfare*, www.leeds.ac.uk/cava/research/strand3d.htm.

6. For example, the U.S. Department of Housing and Urban Development (HUD) launched the "Moving to Opportunity" experiment, which provided the

vouchers discussed in the text. The results of the experiment are analyzed in, e.g., Claudine Gay, *Moving Out, Moving Up: Housing Mobility and the Political Participation of the Poor* (Harvard Working Paper 2009). In July 2008, the *American Journal of Sociology* ran a symposium on the experiment and its related outcomes; it has been thoroughly analyzed elsewhere as well. A recent book on the experiment specifically analyzes what might be learned about the potential communities lost, found, and liberated by the opportunity to move out of high-poverty neighborhoods. *See* XAVIER DE SOUZA BRIGGS, SUSAN J. POPKIN & JOHN GOERING, MOVING TO OPPORTUNITY: THE STORY OF AN AMERICAN EXPERIMENT TO FIGHT GHETTO POVERTY ch. 6 (Oxford University Press 2010).

7. MICHEL DE MONTAIGNE, *Of Friendship*, *in* THE COMPLETE ESSAYS OF MONTAIGNE 140 (Donald M. Frame trans., Stanford University Press 1958). This aphorism is attributed to Aristotle and is the source of a long set of reflections by Jacques Derrida. *See* JACQUES DERRIDA, POLITICS OF FRIENDSHIP (George Collins trans., Verso 1997) (1994). My own take on Aristotle and Montaigne's theories of friendship can be found in Ethan J. Leib, *The Politics of Family and Friends in Aristotle and Montaigne*, 31 INTERPRETATION 165 (2004).

8. *See* Charles Fried, *The Lawyer as Friend: The Moral Foundations of the Lawyer-Client Relation*, 85 YALE L.J. 1060 (1976). But Fried acknowledges that "the ordinary concept of friendship provides only an analogy." *Id.* at 1071.

9. A popular statement of this view comes from Philip K. Howard. *See* PHILIP K. HOWARD, LIFE WITHOUT LAWYERS: LIBERATING AMERICANS FROM TOO MUCH LAW (Norton 2009); PHILIP K. HOWARD, THE COLLAPSE OF THE COMMON GOOD: HOW AMERICA'S LAWSUIT CULTURE UNDERMINES OUR FREEDOM (Ballantine Books 2002); PHILIP K. HOWARD, THE DEATH OF COMMON SENSE: HOW LAW IS SUFFOCATING AMERICA (Warner Books 1994).

10. For some excellent work on world collision and its inevitability, see VIVIANA ZELIZER, THE PURCHASE OF INTIMACY (Princeton University Press 2005).

Chapter 1

1. David L. Chambers, *For the Best of Friends and for Lovers of All Sorts, A Status Other Than Marriage*, 76 NOTRE DAME L. REV. 1347 (2001).

2. BEVERLEY FEHR, FRIENDSHIP PROCESSES 4 (Sage 1996).

3. RAY PAHL, ON FRIENDSHIP 36, 38–39 (Polity Press 2000).

4. *See* Claude S. Fischer, *What Do We Mean by "Friend"? An Inductive Study*, 3 SOC. NETWORKS 287, 288, 295, 298, 300 (1982).

5. *See, e.g.*, ROBERT BRAIN, FRIENDS AND LOVERS 222, 264 (Basic Books 1976). C.S. Lewis wrote that "[i]t has actually become necessary in our time to rebut the theory that every firm and serious friendship is really homosexual." C.S. LEWIS, THE FOUR LOVES 72 (Harcourt Brace 1960).

6. *See, e.g.*, Rebecca G. Adams & Graham Allan, *Contextualising Friendship*, *in* PLACING FRIENDSHIP IN CONTEXT 1, 8 (Rebecca G. Adams & Graham Allan eds., Cambridge University Press 1998).

7. Stacey J. Oliker, *The Modernisation of Friendship: Individualism, Intimacy, and Gender in the Nineteenth Century*, in PLACING FRIENDSHIP IN CONTEXT, *supra* note 6 at 18, 27.

8. *See, e.g.*, Elizabeth Belfiore, *Family Friendship in Aristotle's "Ethics,"* 21 ANCIENT PHIL. 113, 113–18, 126–31 (2001).

9. Sasha Roseneil, *Why We Should Care About Friends: An Argument for Queering the Care Imaginary in Social Policy*, 3 SOC. POL'Y & SOC'Y 409, 411 (2004).

10. *Id.*

11. *See* Sasha Roseneil, *Care, Values, and the Future of Welfare*, www.leeds.ac.uk/cava/research/strand3d.htm ("Across a range of lifestyles, ages and sexualities, and across all of the localities, friendship occupied a central place in the personal lives of the interviewees. There was a high degree of reliance on friends, *as opposed to biological kin and sexual partners*, particularly for the provision of care and support in everyday life.... There was a strong tendency amongst the interviewees to emphasize the emotional and practical significance of friends *over* lovers/sexual partners.") (emphasis added).

12. Roseneil, *supra* note 9.

13. There is a movement under way (outside the United States, for the most part) to protect all intimacy without any consideration or special privileges for conjugal relationships; in theory this movement would be more sensitive to unmarried and unattached singles than most current regimes that privilege certain types of private ordering in intimate life over others. *See, e.g.*, LAW COMM'N OF CAN., BEYOND CONJUGALITY: RECOGNIZING AND SUPPORTING CLOSE PERSONAL ADULT RELATIONSHIPS (2001), http://epe.lac-bac.gc.ca/100/200/301/lcc-cdc/beyond_conjugality-e/pdf/37152-e.pdf; Nancy D. Polikoff, *Ending Marriage as We Know It*, 32 HOFSTRA L. REV. 201 (2003); Brenda Cossman & Bruce Ryder, *What Is Marriage-Like Like? The Irrelevance of Conjugality*, 18 CAN. J. FAM. L. 269 (2001). Ultimately, if friends received the same treatment under the law as married couples, we could get "beyond conjugality." But this radical agenda is not very likely to be adopted anytime soon, and nonconjugal friendship is especially underprotected under current legal regimes, justifying special attention to it here without taking on marriage issues specifically, which raise a whole host of other difficulties.

14. An argument that family and friends are best viewed as non-mutually exclusive can be found in LIZ SPENCER & RAY PAHL, RETHINKING FRIENDSHIP: HIDDEN SOLIDARITIES TODAY 108–27 (Princeton University Press 2006). Their argument is from a sociological perspective, however, not a legal one.

15. *See, e.g.*, MARILYN FRIEDMAN, WHAT ARE FRIENDS FOR? 207 (Cornell University Press 1993) (contrasting the equality of friendship with the unequal power relations in families).

16. *See* Allan Silver, *Friendship and Trust as Moral Ideals: An Historical Approach*, 30 EURO. J. SOC. 274 (1989).

17. *See* JOSEPH EPSTEIN, FRIENDSHIP: AN EXPOSÉ 69 (Houghton Mifflin 2006).

18. ANDREW SULLIVAN, LOVE UNDETECTABLE: NOTES ON FRIENDSHIP, SEX, AND SURVIVAL 204 (Knopf 1998).

19. *See, e.g.*, Aristotle, Nicomachean Ethics, 9.6.1167a22–b15 (Terence Irwin trans., Hackett 1985); Epstein, *supra* note 17, at 60 (citing Cicero's suggestion that friendship requires "agreement over all things divine and human"). Some even use more legally familiar expressions, describing friendships as between those who have achieved a "meeting of the minds." *See* Pahl, *supra* note 3, at 42. Friendship as concord plays a substantial role in theories of "civic friendship," a form of friendship only peripheral to my concerns here. *See* Adam Smith, The Theory of Moral Sentiments 22 (D.D. Raphael & A.L. Macfie eds., Clarendon Press 1976) (1759) (arguing that "concord," understood as friendship among citizens, is required for "the harmony of society").

20. *See* Epstein, *supra* note 17, at 54 (drawing on Georg Simmel's conception of "differentiated friendships"); Norman Podhoretz, Ex-Friends: Falling Out with Allen Ginsberg, Lionel and Diana Trilling, Lillian Hellman, Hannah Arendt, and Norman Mailer 4 (Encounter Books 2000).

21. Lewis, *supra* note 4, at 73–74. The next Lewis quotation in the text comes from page 72. For other discussions of whether friendship is essentially dyadic, see Graham Allan, Friendship: Developing a Sociological Perspective 10, 27 (Westview Press 1989). Perhaps "couple friendships"—the phenomenon of married couples becoming friends—is a counterexample to the prevalence of dyads.

22. Robert C. Ellickson, Order Without Law: How Neighbors Settle Disputes 235 (Harvard University Press 1991). For some evidence that we seem to view gifts quite differently depending on whether we think the giver is giving out of affect, role-responsibility, or cost-benefit calculations, see Daniel R. Ames, Francis J. Flynn, & Elke U. Weber, *It's the Thought That Counts: On Perceiving How Helpers Decide to Lend a Hand*, 30 Personality & Soc. Psych. Bull. 461 (2004). But that we may have differential responses based on our own perceptions of *why* someone gives us something doesn't vitiate the reality that we are engaged in mutual exchange all the time, for whatever reasons—and I would tend to doubt that it is especially easy to tell why a giver *really* does something.

23. *See* Richard Lempert, *Norm-Making in Social Exchange: A Contract Law Model*, 7 Law & Soc'y Rev. 1, 2 (1972) ("[A] number of quite prominent sociologists and social psychologists are prepared to argue that almost all social interaction [including friendship] may profitably be viewed as exchange transactions.") (citing exchange theory classics Peter M. Blau, Exchange and Power in Social Life (Wiley 1964); George Caspar Homans, Social Behavior: Its Elementary Forms (Routledge & Kegan Paul 1961)). As Lempert recognizes, it would defy "common sense" to see friendship as *only* exchange. Lempert, *supra*, at 2–3.

24. This passage is discussed in Allan Silver, *The Lawyer and the Scrivener*, 3 Partisan Rev. 409, 417 (1981). Allan likes to set the record straight that he would have preferred the title of his essay to be "Melville's Story of Wall Street."

25. Epstein, *supra* note 17, at 2.

26. Spencer & Pahl, *supra* note 14, at 50.

27. *See* Michel de Montaigne, *Of the Art of Discussion, in* The Complete Essays of Montaigne 705 (Donald M. Frame trans., Stanford University Press 1958). *See*

also BERNARD YACK, THE PROBLEMS OF A POLITICAL ANIMAL: COMMUNITY, JUSTICE, AND CONFLICT IN ARISTOTELIAN POLITICAL THOUGHT 110 (University of California Press 1993) (contending that, for Aristotle, friendship is "a source of conflict as well as a means of promoting greater cooperation").

28. For some feminists, adding the dimension of conflict and disruptiveness to a portrait of friendship helps mitigate some of the male-centered ideals of equality and similarity. *See* FRIEDMAN, *supra* note 15, at 196. I'm not sure I see how equality and similarity are particularly male values within friendship that exclude women, but I do think conflict and modes of conflict resolution are central, whether they are quintessentially female virtues or not.

29. Some of the most recent research on social networking sites is reported in Pew Internet and American Life Project, Memorandum of January 14, 2009, by Amanda Lenhart, Re: Adults and Social Network Websites, http://www.pewInternet. org/~/media//Files/Reports/2009/PIP_Adult_social_networking_data_memo_ FINAL.pdf.pdf. I rely on this memo in what follows.

30. Some of this work, written by "ethnographers" of the various online communities, is very interesting. *See* David Fono & Kaie Raynes-Goldie, *Hyperfriends and Beyond: Friendship and Social Norms on LiveJournal*, in INTERNET RESEARCH ANNUAL VOLUME 4: SELECTED PAPERS (M. Consalvo & C. Haythornthwaite eds., Association of Internet Researchers Conference. Peter Lang, 2006); danah boyd, *Friendship*, in HANGING OUT, MESSING AROUND, GEEKING OUT: LIVING AND LEARNING WITH NEW MEDIA (Mizuko Ito et al., MIT Press, forthcoming); danah boyd, *Friends, Friendsters, and MySpace Top 8: Writing Community into Being on Social Network Sites*, 11 FIRST MONDAY 12 (2006), http:// firstmonday.org/htbin/cgiwrap/bin/ojs/index.php/fm/article/view/1418/1336; danah boyd, *Friendster and Publicly Articulated Social Networking*, CONFERENCE ON HUMAN FACTORS AND COMPUTING SYSTEMS (ACM CHI 2004), http://www.danah.org/ papers/CHI2004Friendster.pdf. I rely on this work heavily in what follows. *See also* Rebecca G. Adams, *The Demise of Territorial Determinism: Online Friendships*, in PLACING FRIENDSHIP IN CONTEXT, *supra* note 6 at 153. There is also a genre of cultural criticism that takes aim at social networking. It makes for provocative and stimulating reading—but it rarely engages with the relevant research on the subject. For a recent exemplar, see William Deresiewicz, *Faux Friendship*, THE CHRONICLE REVIEW (Dec. 6, 2009), http://chronicle.com/article/Faux-Friendship/49308/. Journalists sometimes do take a look at some of the research but give us very narrow windows into understanding what is really happening and the limitations of the current research. *See* Charles M. Blow, *Friends, Neighbors, and Facebook*, New York Times, June 11, 2010, at A21.

31. ROBIN DUNBAR, GROOMING, GOSSIP, AND THE EVOLUTION OF LANGUAGE (Harvard University Press 1998).

32. *See, e.g.*, Michael Argyle & Monika Henderson, *The Rules of Friendship*, 1 J. SOC. & PERSONAL RELATIONSHIPS 211 (1984).

33. *See generally* Pew Internet and American Life Project, Memorandum of January 3, 2007 by Amanda Lenhart & Mary Madden, Re: Social Networking Sites

and Teens: An Overview, www.pewInternet.org/~/media//Files/Reports/2007/PIP_
SNS_Data_Memo_Jan_2007.pdf. There is some evidence suggesting that people who
develop online "friendships" tend to have less homogenous connections than those
who do not. *See* Gustavo S. Mesch and Ilan Talmud, *Similarity and the Quality of Online
and Offline Social Relationships Among Adolescents in Israel*, 17 J. Res. in Adolescence
455 (2007). But it is too early to know how this will all shake out over time.

34. Quigley Corp. v. Karkus, 2009 WL 1383280 (E.D.Pa.), at *5 n.3. Thanks to
Eric Goldman for the pointer.

35. *See* John Schwartz, *For Judges on Facebook, Friendship Has Limits*, N.Y. Times,
Dec. 11, 2009, at A25. The Committee's recommendation can be found here:
Judicial Ethics Advisory Committee, Florida Supreme Court, *Opinion Number
2009–20*, Nov. 17, 2009, http://www.jud6.org/LegalCommunity/LegalPractice/
opinions/jeacopinions/2009/2009–20.html.

36. For examples, see Jeffrey Boase et al., The Strength of Internet Ties
(Pew Internet and American Life Project 2006); Jeffrey Boase & Barry Wellman,
Personal Relationships: On and off the Internet, in The Cambridge Handbook of
Personal Relations 709 (Anita L. Vangelisti & Daniel Perlman eds., Cambridge
University Press 2006); Anabel Quan-Haase & Barry Wellman, *Capitalizing on the
Net: Social Contact, Civic Engagement, and Sense of Community, in* The Internet in
Everyday Life 291 (Barry Wellman & Caroline Haythornthwaite eds., Blackwell
2002). I rely on this work in these paragraphs.

37. Robert Putnam, Bowling Alone (Simon & Schuster 2000). For critique, see
Claude S. Fischer, *Bowling Alone: What's the Score?* 27 Soc. Networks 155 (2005);
and Boase et al., *supra* note 36, at 3.

38. *See* Aristotle, *supra* note 19, at 8.11.1155a1–9.11.1172a20 (the rest of the
quotations from Aristotle in this section come from books 8 and 9). There is
also much to be learned from Aristotle's slightly different discussion of friendship in
his *Eudemian Ethics* (as well as his discussions in *The Politics* and *The Art of Rhetoric*).
See A.W. Price, Love and Friendship in Plato and Aristotle 121 (Oxford
University Press 1989); Michael Pakaluk, *Friendship and the Comparison of Goods*, 37
Phronesis 111, 129 (1992). Still, because the *Nicomachean Ethics* is the version most
often read and discussed, I focus my treatment here virtually exclusively on the
theory elaborated there.

39. Heather Devere traces the cultural heritage (suggesting that perhaps even
Plato may be a latecomer) in Heraclitus, Xenophon, Herodotus, Lucretius, Lysias,
Plotinus, Epicurus, Euripides, Plutarch, Homer, Sappho, Ovid, Virgil, and Seneca.
See Heather Devere, *Reviving Greco-Roman Friendship: A Bibliographical Review, in*
The Challenge to Friendship in Modernity 149 (Preston King & Heather Devere
eds., Frank Cass 2000). Peter Goodrich also performs a nice genealogy, focusing on
lawyers' contribution to the tradition in particular. *See* Peter Goodrich, *The Immense
Rumor*, 16 Yale J.L. & Human. 199, 206 (2004). Goodrich believes that "it was
lawyers who wrote about friendship because it is what they most lacked and hence
what they most desired." *Id.* at 228. I'm hoping to show here that lawyers have been
dealing with friendships all the time.

40. Etienne de La Boétie, *On Voluntary Servitude, in* FREEDOM OVER SERVITUDE: MONTAIGNE, LA BOÉTIE, AND *On Voluntary Servitude* 189, 220 (David Lewis Schaefer ed. & trans., Greenwood 1998). I have argued elsewhere, however, that La Boétie's account here may be less than fully honest. *See* Ethan J. Leib, *The Politics of Family and Friends in Aristotle and Montaigne*, 31 INTERPRETATION 165, 168, 180–82 (2004).

41. John Cooper provides a substantial defense for the claim that character friendships may have elements of the other, incomplete forms. *See* John M. Cooper, *Aristotle on Friendship, in* ESSAYS ON ARISTOTLE'S ETHICS 301, 309 (Amélie Oksenberg Rorty ed., University of California Press 1980).

42. This last view continues to gain some adherents; some people seem to believe that friends never ask each other to tell lies to cover for them and the like. But, as Dean Cocking and Jeanette Kennett recognize, "[A] good friendship might well include a focus on certain vices." Dean Cocking & Jeanette Kennett, *Friendship and Moral Danger*, 97 J. PHIL. 278, 286 (2000). They go even further: "Heinrich Himmler organized the mass slaughter of Jewish people, but he may well have been a conscientious and loving...friend." *Id.* at 288.

43. *See* Susan Bickford, *Beyond Friendship: Aristotle on Conflict, Deliberation, and Attention*, 58 J. POL. 398, 407 (1996) ("[T]he Greeks used *philia* to denote a wider range of relationships than does our ordinary understanding of 'friendship': relations between business partners, family members, citizens, fellow travelers, and personal friends, among others."). *But see* David Konstan, *Greek Friendship*, 117 AM. J. PHILOLOGY 71, 92 (1996) (arguing that "the Greeks themselves were, like us, quite clear about the difference between friends, relatives, and countrymen"); Jonathan Powell, *Friendship and Its Problems in Greek and Roman Thought, in* ETHICS AND RHETORIC: CLASSICAL ESSAYS FOR DONALD RUSSELL ON HIS 75TH BIRTHDAY 31, 45 (Doreen Innes, Harry Hine & Christopher Pelling eds., Oxford University Press 1995) ("[F]riendship in its essence is much the same for human beings in all societies."). Some see focusing on an enlarged conception of *philia* to be useful in the feminist quest to change how we think about friendship and wish to include within the category all sorts of relationships that I exclude here, like mother-daughter, father-son, etc. *See* Sibyl A. Schwarzenbach, *Democracy and Friendship*, 36 J. SOC. PHIL. 233 (2005). Ultimately, Schwarzenbach is interested in a much thinner version of friendship—civic friendship—than the thickly emotional version that is my principal concern in this book. A similar debate structures the interpretation of the Roman *amicitia*. *Compare* EPSTEIN, *supra* note 17, at 60–61 (explaining that the term "is said to have had its origin in party politics" and "much of it seems to turn on what we today call networking") *with* Powell, *supra*, at 45 (maintaining that the Roman term, like the Greek term, is similar to our own concept of friendship) and David Konstan, *Patrons and Friends*, 90 CLASSICAL PHILOLOGY 328 (1995) (same).

44. It might also mean that once one shows oneself capable of having friends, one is assured of being a good and just person such that friends have no need to cultivate the virtue of justice in addition to cultivating friendship. Or it could mean that since a friend is a "second self," a friend never needs to worry about just

distribution: Self-preservation and self-love will lead to proper distribution, even without an external norm of justice. Somewhat inexplicably, this discussion of friendship and the law in Aristotle remains virtually unnoticed by the generations of extensive commentary on Aristotle's lectures.

Chapter 2

1. LAURENCE THOMAS, LIVING MORALLY: A PSYCHOLOGY OF MORAL CHARACTER 153 (Temple University Press 1989).

2. Robert E. Lane, *The Road Not Taken: Friendship, Consumerism, and Happiness*, 8 CRITICAL REV. 521, 530 (1994).

3. *Id.* at 527. *See also* Joshua Wolf Shenk, *What Makes Us Happy?*, THE ATLANTIC MONTHLY, June 2009, http://www.theatlantic.com/doc/200906/happiness.

4. GRAHAM ALLAN, FRIENDSHIP: DEVELOPING A SOCIOLOGICAL PERSPECTIVE 110 (Westview Press 1989).

5. Nicholas Bakalar, *Bonds of Friendship, Not Family, May Add Years*, N.Y. TIMES, June 28, 2005, at F6. To be fair, kin may still be providing most of the care; it is just that survival from that care is facilitated by friendship, and having close family ties has no effect on the care leading to survival.

6. For the most recent journalistic account, see Tara Parker-Pope, *What Are Friends For? A Longer Life*, N.Y. TIMES, Apr. 21, 2009. The studies can be found as follows: Kristina Orth-Gomer et al., *Lack of Social Support and Incidence of Coronary Heart Disease in Middle-Aged Swedish Men*, 55 PSYCHOSOMATIC MED. 37 (1993); Lynne C. Giles et al., *Effect of Social Networks on 10 Year Survival in Very Old Australians: The Australian Longitudinal Study of Aging*, 59 J. OF EPIDEMIOLOGY & COMMUNITY HEALTH 574 (2005); Candyce H. Kroenke et al., *Social Networks, Social Support, and Survival After Breast Cancer Diagnosis*, 24 J. OF CLINICAL ONCOLOGY 1105 (2006); Nicholas A. Christakis & James H. Fowler, *The Spread of Obesity in a Large Social Network over 32 Years*, 357 NEW ENG. J. OF MED. 370 (2007); Karen Ertel et al., *Effects of Social Integration on Preserving Memory Function in a Nationally Representative US Elderly Population*, 98 AM. J. OF PUB. HEALTH 1215 (2008).

7. Miller McPherson et al., *Social Isolation in America: Changes in Core Discussion Networks over Two Decades*, 71 AM. SOC. REV. 353, 355 (2006) (citing Barry Wellman & Scot Wortley, *Different Strokes from Different Folks: Community Ties and Social Support*, 96 AM. J. SOC. 558 (1990); Jeanne S. Hurlbert et al., *Core Networks and Tie Activation: What Kinds of Routine Networks Allocate Resources in Nonroutine Situations?*, 65 AM. SOC. REV. 598 (2000)). This sociological observation is true of both kin and nonkin ties, but for reasons already adumbrated, I am focusing on nonkin ties here.

8. *See* C.S. LEWIS, THE FOUR LOVES 81 (Harcourt Brace 1960). For book-length treatments of this very theme, see MICHAEL P. FARRELL, COLLABORATIVE CIRCLES: FRIENDSHIP DYNAMICS AND CREATIVE WORK (University of Chicago Press 2001); ANDREW EPSTEIN, BEAUTIFUL ENEMIES: FRIENDSHIP AND POSTWAR AMERICAN POETRY (Oxford University Press 2006); and RICHARD GODBEER, THE OVERFLOWING OF FRIENDSHIP: LOVE BETWEEN MEN AND THE CREATION OF THE AMERICAN REPUBLIC (Johns Hopkins University Press 2009).

9. For some studies confirming these perquisites, see John F. Helliwell, *Well-Being, Social Capital and Public Policy: What's New?* 116 ECON. J. 34–45 (2006); David Krackhardt, *The Strength of Strong Ties: The Importance of Philos in Organizations*, *in* NETWORKS AND ORGANIZATIONS: STRUCTURE, FORM, AND ACTION (Nitin Nohria & Robert G. Eccles eds., Harvard Business School Press 1992); Kyoung-Ok Park, Mark G. Wilson, & Myung Sun Lee, *Effects of Social Support at Work on Depression and Organizational Productivity*, 28 AM. J. OF HEALTH BEHAVIOR 444 (2004); Lori J. Ducharme & Jack K. Martin, *Unrewarding Work, Coworker Support, and Job Satisfaction: A Test of the Buffering Hypothesis*, 27 WORK & OCCUPATIONS 223 (2000); Jeanne S. Hurlbert, *Social Networks, Social Circles, and Job Satisfaction*, 18 WORK & OCCUPATIONS 415 (1991); Gail M. McGuire, *Intimate Work: A Typology of the Social Support That Workers Provide to Their Network Members*, 34 WORK & OCCUPATIONS 125 (2007); Emilio J. Castilla, *Social Networks and Employee Performance in a Call Center*, 110 AM. J. OF SOC. 1243 (2005); Patricia M. Sias & Daniel J. Cahill, *From Coworkers to Friends: The Development of Peer Friendships in the Workplace*, 62 W.J. OF COMM. 273 (1998); MARK GRANOVETTER, GETTING A JOB: A STUDY OF CONTACTS AND CAREERS (2nd ed., Harvard University Press 1995); W.K. RAWLINS, FRIENDSHIP MATTERS: COMMUNICATION, DIALECTICS, AND THE LIFE COURSE (de Gruyter 1992); K.E. Kram & L.A. Isabella, *Mentoring Alternatives: The Role of Peer Relationships in Career Development*, 28 ACAD. MANAG. J. 110 (1985); JAN YAGER, FRIENDSHIFTS: THE POWER OF FRIENDSHIP AND HOW IT SHAPES OUR LIVES (Hannacroix Creek Books 1997).

10. *See* Paul DiMaggio & Hugh Louch, *Socially Embedded Consumer Transactions: For What Kinds of Purchases Do People Most Often Use Networks?*, 63 AM. SOC. REV. 619, 633–34 (1998).

11. *See* Evan M. Berman, Jonathan P. West, & Maurice N. Richter, Jr., *Workplace Relations: Friendship Patterns and Consequences (According to Managers)*, 62 PUB. ADMIN. REV. 217 (2002).

12. *See* David Krackhardt & Robert Stern, *Informal Networks and Organizational Crisis: An Experimental Simulation*, 51 SOC. PSY. Q. 123 (1988).

13. For a discussion of some of these concerns, see K. Bridge & L.A. Baxter, *Blended Relationships: Friends as Work Associates*, 56 W.J. OF COMM. 200 (1992); G.A. Fine, *Friendships in the Workplace*, *in* FRIENDSHIP AND SOCIAL INTERACTION (V.J. Derlega & B.A. Winstead eds., Springer-Verlag 1986); Laura Rosenbury, *Friends at Work*, 30 WASH. U. J. L. & POL'Y (forthcoming 2011); and Paul Ingram & Xi Zou, *Business Friendships*, 28 RES. IN ORG. BEHAVIOR 167 (2008). *See also* Sally Falk Moore, *Law and Social Change: The Semi-Autonomous Social Field as an Appropriate Object of Study*, 7 LAW & SOC'Y REV. 719 (1973) (arguing that "fictive friendships" undergird most American business transactions, in which parties routinely use informal modes of address, exchange favors and gifts, and act "chummy"); *see also* 1 STEWART MACAULAY ET AL., CONTRACTS: LAW IN ACTION 230 n.3 (2nd ed., LexisNexis Matthew Bender 2003) ("A lawyer who deals with contracts and fails to understand the power and the limits of trust and the social sanctions flowing from 'fictive friendships' is incompetent.").

14. For a useful survey, see Viviana A. Zelizer, *Intimacy in Economic Organizations, in* 19 Research in the Sociology of Work: Economic Sociology of Work (Nina Bandelj ed., Emerald 2009).

15. *See* Paul Ingram & Peter W. Roberts, *Friendships Among Competitors in the Sydney Hotel Industry*, 106 Am. J. of Soc. 387, 417 (2000).

16. Paul Ingram & Arik Lifschitz, *Kinship in the Shadow of the Corporation: The Interbuilder Network in Clyde River Shipbuilding, 1711–1990*, 71 Am. Soc. Rev. 334 (2006).

17. *See* Brian Uzzi, *The Sources and Consequences of Embeddedness for the Economic Performance of Organizations: The Network Effect*, 61 Am. Soc. Rev. 674 (1996); Brian Uzzi, *Social Structure and Competition in Interfirm Networks: The Paradox of Embeddedness*, 42 Admin. Sci. Q. 35 (1997).

18. *See* Ely Portillo, *Feeling Alone? You're Not the Only One*, Houston Chron., June 22, 2006, at A1.

19. *See* Lane, *supra* note 2, at 521.

20. Lisa Hill & Peter McCarthy, *Hume, Smith and Ferguson: Friendship in Commercial Society, in* The Challenge to Friendship in Modernity 33, 35 (Preston King & Heather Devere eds., Frank Cass 2000). This is in some tension, of course, with the old adage that we only contract with those whom we *do not* trust.

21. Robert Brain, Friends and Lovers 37 (Basic Books 1976).

22. *Id.* at 110.

23. One of the law-and-society movement's most robust and famous findings is that extrinsic norms outside the law bring civility to business relations. *See* Stewart Macaulay, *Non-Contractual Relations in Business: A Preliminary Study*, 28 Am. Soc. Rev. 55 (1963) (concluding that norms of fair dealing are as relevant as legal rules in Wisconsin business firm transactions); James J. White, *Contract Law in Modern Commercial Transactions, An Artifact of Twentieth Century Business Life?*, 22 Washburn L.J. 1 (1982) (describing how chemical companies allocate supply during shortages according to extrinsic norms, not the law); *see also* Robert C. Ellickson, Order without Law: How Neighbors Settle Disputes 235 (Harvard University Press 1991). The contract law surrounding the sale of goods, at least, is able to make use of background extrinsic norms through its recognition of and deference to "usage of trade." *See* U.C.C. § 1–303 (2004). In so doing, it saves enforcement costs by recognizing a prior not-necessarily-legal relationship.

Yet it only makes sense to allow extrinsic norms to penetrate the legal system and gain legal recognition if the norms themselves (as a general matter) are consistent with the law's normative framework. Since the Uniform Commercial Code is explicitly designed "to permit the continued expansion of commercial practices through custom [and] usage," U.C.C. § 1–103(a)(2), the law welcomes extrinsic norms in this context. Perhaps there is an assumption that certain customs are efficient, and that the law is more efficient when it temporarily makes use of extrinsic norms to police behavior. *But see* Lisa Bernstein, *The Questionable Empirical Basis of Article 2's Incorporation Strategy: A Preliminary Study*, 66 U. Chi. L. Rev. 710 (1999) (arguing that customs and usages of trade cannot be easily identified and do not arise frequently). I come back to these issues again in chapter 6.

24. *See generally* Janice Nadler, *Flouting the Law*, 83 Tex. L. Rev. 1399 (2005) (arguing that harmonizing law and social norms can help to breed compliance—and the opposite can breed noncompliance); Paul H. Robinson & John M. Darley, *The Utility of Desert*, 91 Nw. U. L. Rev. 453 (1997) (same).

25. Peter Goodrich, *The Immense Rumor*, 16 Yale J.L. & Human. 199, 213 (2004).

26. *See* Seymour Martin Lipset et al., Union Democracy: The Internal Politics of the International Typographical Union 67 (Free Press 1956) (finding that patterns of friendship contribute to political integration, "democratic unionism," and a broad sense of community).

27. Aristotle, Nicomachean Ethics 8.1.1155a23 (Terence Irwin trans., Hackett 1985). *See generally* Ronald Beiner, Political Judgment 79 (University of Chicago Press 1983) (emphasizing the centrality of friendship to Aristotle's conception of politics); Anthony Kronman, *Aristotle's Idea of Political Fraternity*, 24 Am. J. Juris. 114 (1979) (explaining how, for Aristotle, friendship can hold cities together).

28. Kronman, *supra* note 27, at 126. Although Kronman is ultimately interested in a generalized civic friendship, this idea holds true for the promotion of deep friendship ties within the polity as well.

29. For a taste of the "neighborhood effects" literature, see Robert J. Sampson, Jeffrey D. Morenoff & Thomas Gannon-Rowley, *Assessing "Neighborhood Effects": Social Processes and New Directions in Research*, 28 Ann. Rev. Soc. 443 (2002); Robert J. Sampson, *Moving to Inequality: Neighborhood Effects and Experiments Meet Social Structure*, 114 Am. J. Soc. 189 (2008).

30. *See* McPherson et al., *supra* note 7, at 358–59 (comparing the results of General Social Surveys between 1985 and 2004 and noting that the percentage of people who talk to at least one person who is not connected to them through kinship declined from 80.1 to 57.2 percent during this period). To be fair, it is not obvious that this study's subject is friendship as defined in the previous chapter. But it makes an effort to measure something outside merely casual friendship and family members.

31. Jeffrey Boase et al., The Strength of Internet Ties (Pew Internet and American Life Project 2006) Further reason to be skeptical of the decline of friendship based on the McPherson et al. study comes from Claude S. Fischer, *The 2004 GSS Finding of Shrunken Social Networks: An Artifact*, 74 Am. Soc. Rev. 657 (2009). In a forthcoming book, Fischer estimates that people have, on average, 11 friends.

32. *See* Peter Bearman & Paolo Parigi, *Cloning Headless Frogs and Other Important Matters: Conversation Topics and Network Structure*, 83 Soc. Forces 535, 547 (2004) (finding that 20 percent of respondents have no one with whom they can discuss important matters); Pamela Paxton, *Is Social Capital Declining in the United States? A Multiple Indicator Assessment*, 105 Am. J. Soc. 88 (1999) (confirming that socializing with friends and neighbors is on the decline). *But see* McPherson et al., *supra* note 7, at 366 ("In 1990, for example, the Gallup Poll found that only 3 percent of their sample reported no close friends; only 16 percent had less than three friends. While there are many differences between the Gallup and [General Social Surveys that

form the basis of the McPherson et al., *supra* note 7, conclusions], this raises the interesting question of whether the important-matters question gets at closer, core ties than the concept of close friend. Another recent telephone survey by [the Pew Internet and American Life Project] also found much larger numbers of core or close friends, when it asked about a combination of types of contact.").

33. Portillo, *supra* note 18.

34. Goodrich, *supra* note 25, at 203.

35. *See* Allan Silver, *Friendship in Commercial Society: Eighteenth-Century Social Theory and Modern Sociology*, 95 AM. J. SOC. 1474, 1476 (1990) ("[F]riendship in modern society is a quintessentially private relationship, not normatively constituted by public roles and obligations—[and] indeed often in distinction from them.").

36. *See, e.g.*, Hill & McCarthy, *supra* note 20 (arguing that Adam Smith and David Hume share this view but that Adam Ferguson does not); Silver, *supra* note 35 (presenting a unified account of these thinkers without distinguishing among their individual views); Allan Silver, *"Two Different Sorts of Commerce"—Friendship and Strangership in Civil Society*, *in* PUBLIC AND PRIVATE IN THOUGHT AND PRACTICE: PERSPECTIVES ON A GRAND DICHOTOMY 43 (Jeff Weintraub & Krishan Kumar eds., University of Chicago Press 1997). These essays are the sources for the paragraphs that follow.

37. *See* ADAM SMITH, THE THEORY OF MORAL SENTIMENTS 220, 223–25 (D.D. Raphael & A.L. Macfie eds., Clarendon Press 1976) (1759); *see also* ALAN WOLFE, WHOSE KEEPER? SOCIAL SCIENCE AND MORAL OBLIGATION 29 (University of California Press 1989).

38. Silver, *supra* note 35, at 1482–83.

39. As Liz Spencer and Ray Pahl show, we too easily assume friendship to be a chosen relationship and family to be a given one. We actually can view friends as given and family as chosen, too. *See* LIZ SPENCER & RAY PAHL, RETHINKING FRIENDSHIP: HIDDEN SOLIDARITIES TODAY chs. 2, 5 (Princeton: Princeton University Press 2006).

40. This point is discussed in David Owens, "Obligation and Involvement," draft, www.law.yale.edu/documents/pdf/Intellectual_Life/Owens_Obligation Involvement.pdf.

41. ALLAN, *supra* note 4, at 152–53; *see also* ROSEMARY BLIESZNER & REBECCA G. ADAMS, ADULT FRIENDSHIP (Sage 1992).

42. *See, e.g.*, Pat O'Connor, *Women's Friendships in a Post-Modern World*, *in* PLACING FRIENDSHIP IN CONTEXT 117, 128–29 (Rebecca G. Adams & Graham Allan eds., Cambridge University Press 1998).

43. *See* BRAIN, *supra* note 21, at 89.

44. Arthur L. Stinchcombe, *Social Structure and Organizations*, *in* HANDBOOK OF ORGANIZATIONS 142, 185 (James G. March ed., Rand McNally 1965).

45. Lane, *supra* note 2, at 539, 541–42, 544. He writes that Silver's thesis is "inoperative in modern societies." *Id.* at 533.

46. Lane, *supra* note 2, at 544.

47. *See* GRAHAM ALLAN, KINSHIP AND FRIENDSHIP IN MODERN BRITAIN 93 (Oxford University Press 1996); Stacey J. Oliker, *The Modernisation of Friendship: Individualism, Intimacy, and Gender in the Nineteenth Century*, *in* PLACING FRIENDSHIP IN CONTEXT, *supra* note 42, at 19, 29.

48. *See* BRAIN, *supra* note 21, at 50–51 (discussing Montaigne, the "arch-propagandist of male friendship," who "is emphatic about the impossibility of friendship between men and women"); RAY PAHL, ON FRIENDSHIP 122–24 (Polity Press 2000); Sibyl A. Schwarzenbach, *Democracy and Friendship*, 36 J. SOC. PHIL. 233, 238 (2005) (reminding us of Aristotle's sexism and commenting that "[w]hat is less well recognized is that many *modern* conceptions of friendship—even once we jettison the premise of the inferiority of women—still tends to track the male [chauvinism] originally charted by Aristotle. Modern conceptions frequently persist in excluding many...highly significant personal relations of *philia* that women characteristically possess, and they tend to assume (whether consciously or not) the equal, fraternal model."). In my personal experience, it seems to me that there is really very little I can do as a white, male heterosexual to convince some of Schwarzenbach's followers that I am not, likewise, privileging some unconscious male conception of friendship. But I'm trying to understand their arguments and accommodate my conception, as necessary.

49. JACQUES DERRIDA, POLITICS OF FRIENDSHIP 278–79 (George Collins trans., Verso 1997) (1994).

50. *See* Rebecca G. Adams, *The Demise of Territorial Determinism: Online Friendships, in* PLACING FRIENDSHIP IN CONTEXT 173 (Rebecca G. Adams & Graham Allan eds., Cambridge University Press 1998) (arguing that one of the most repeated findings in friendship literature is that friends tend to share gender).

51. *See* McPherson et al., *supra* note 7, at 362. Yet sadly, "the equity is being achieved by men's *shrinking* interconnection with nonkin confidants rather than by women's greater connection to the world outside the family." *Id.*

52. Schwarzenbach, *supra* note 48, at 238, suggests that the trope of equality demeans women because they are characteristically involved in unequal care-giving and that type of relation should come within the ambit of friendship. Obviously, consistent with my remarks in chapter 1, I do not agree that we should include relationships of kin within friendship. I don't think that commitment leads to a male-centered conception of friendship at all—and I think Schwarzenbach too easily assumes that women don't have the very same kinds of intimate nonkin friendships as men. I am ultimately more confident (after reading much of the same literature) that close nonkin friendships form the center of many women's personal identities, whether they are gay or straight, married or unmarried, parents or not.

53. *See generally* Laura Rosenbury, *Friends with Benefits?*, 106 MICH. L. REV. 189 (2007).

54. Rosenbury cites Sasha Roseneil, *Why We Should Care About Friends: An Argument for Queering the Care Imaginary in Social Policy*, 3 SOC. POL'Y & SOC'Y 409, 411 (2004). *See also* SPENCER AND PAHL, *supra* note 39, at 85 (suggesting that among gay males there is no taboo about having sex with friends under certain circumstances); Nick Rumens, *Working at Intimacy: Gay Men's Workplace Friendships*, 15 GENDER, WORK, & ORG. 9 (2008) ("I aim to counter what Kathy Werking...calls 'the latent heterosexist content' of friendship research that ascribes heteronormative models of friendships and other relationships the 'status of natural

fact'") (citing Kathy Werking, *Cross-sex Friendship Research as Ideological Practice*, in HANDBOOK OF PERSONAL RELATIONSHIPS: THEORY, RESEARCH, AND INTERVENTIONS 391, 392 (Steve Duck ed., Wiley 1997)). I have already discussed much of this in chapter 1.

55. A careful reading of Werking, *supra* note 54, who is herself especially sensitive to the concerns about heterosexism in the friendship literature, reveals the following: (1) "[B]oth men and women tend to keep their friendships and sexual relationships as separate relationships," *id.* at 396. (2) "[C]ross-sex friendship does not usually entail a strong sexual dimension," *id.* at 398. (3) Fixating on sex within friendships can serve the ideology of heterosexism as much as it can "queer" it, *id.* at 399, 408–09. (4) There are actually very few empirical studies of friendship within and among the lesbian and gay communities, *id.* at 408. In light of these findings, it would seem altogether premature to charge someone with heterosexism for separating sex and friendship in a public policy project: the reality is that sex can complicate friendship for all types of people with all manners of sexual orientations. And whatever their sexual orientation or gender, it is extremely common to separate the life of sex from the life of friends. That heterosexuals, homosexuals, and bisexuals sometimes find themselves attracted to or sleeping with their friends is just a fact—and one that doesn't threaten the definition of friendship with which I am working for now: sex partners get excluded, for reasons I have already articulated.

56. ALLAN, *supra* note 4, at 23; *see generally* Miller McPherson et al., *Birds of a Feather: Homophily in Social Networks*, 27 ANN. REV. SOC. 415 (2001).

57. *See generally* TONY BENNETT ET AL., ACCOUNTING FOR TASTES: AUSTRALIAN EVERYDAY CULTURES (Cambridge University Press 1999); Peter A. Hall, *Social Capital in Britain*, 29 BRIT. J. POL. SCI. 417 (1999); Michael Johnston & Roger Jowell, *How Robust Is British Civil Society?*, in BRITISH SOCIAL ATTITUDES, THE 18TH REPORT: PUBLIC POLICY, SOCIAL TIES 175, 190–92 (Alison Park et al. eds., Sage 2001).

58. *See* Mark S. Granovetter, *The Strength of Weak Ties*, 78 AM. J. SOC. 1360 (1973).

59. *See generally* WENDY BOTTERO, STRATIFICATION: SOCIAL DIVISION AND INEQUALITY (Routledge 2005) (discussing homophily and its relationship to social stratification).

60. Mark Granovetter, *The Strength of Weak Ties: A Network Theory Revisited*, in SOCIOLOGICAL THEORY 201, 213 (Randall Collins ed., Jossey-Bass 1983).

61. *See, e.g.*, GENE OUTKA, AGAPE: AN ETHICAL ANALYSIS 18–19 (Yale University Press 1972) (discussing friendship as "self-love"); *id.* at 34–36 (considering whether friendship is such "nefarious self-love" that it is incompatible with "neighbor-regard").

62. McPherson et al., *supra* note 7, at 359 (citing McPherson et al., *supra* note 56).

63. Peter M. Blau et al., *Intersecting Social Affiliations and Intermarriage*, 62 SOC. FORCES 585, 600 (1984).

64. *See* McPherson et al., *supra* note 7, at 361–62 (arguing that more highly educated people have more to talk about, which, in turn, contributes to an increase in close friends).

65. *See* John M. Cooper, *Aristotle on Friendship, in* ESSAYS ON ARISTOTLE'S ETHICS 301, 333 (Amélie Oksenberg Rorty ed., University of California Press 1980).

66. LEWIS, *supra* note 8, at 94–95.

67. *See* MICHEL DE MONTAIGNE, *Of Friendship, in* THE COMPLETE ESSAYS OF MONTAIGNE 140 (Donald M. Frame trans., Stanford University Press 1958). It is worth noting, however, that Montaigne thought that the inherent goodness of friends would keep them in check. Presumably, Aristotle and La Boétie also have this rejoinder since they insist that friends are always virtuous.

68. ALLAN BLOOM, LOVE AND FRIENDSHIP 413 (Simon & Schuster 1993).

69. Silver, *supra* note 35, at 1488. The problem of friendship's preferential treatment in light of the Bible's command of *agape* (in short, "Thou shalt love thy neighbor as thyself," *Matthew* 22:39) is discussed in OUTKA, *supra* note 61, at 281–85, and ANDREW SULLIVAN, LOVE UNDETECTABLE: NOTES ON FRIENDSHIP, SEX, AND SURVIVAL 240–51 (Knopf 1998).

70. *See* SØREN KIERKEGAARD, WORKS OF LOVE 78 (Howard & Edna Hong trans., Princeton University Press 1962).

71. PAUL TILLICH, LOVE, POWER, AND JUSTICE: ONTOLOGICAL ANALYSIS AND ETHICAL APPLICATIONS 119 (Oxford University Press 1954).

72. OUTKA, *supra* note 61, at 282.

73. LEWIS, *supra* note 8, at 99.

74. *See* Niko Kolodny, *Do Associative Duties Matter?*, 10 J. POL. PHIL. 250, 250 (2002). The "distributive objection" has been developed by Samuel Scheffler, *The Conflict Between Justice and Responsibility, in* GLOBAL JUSTICE 86 (Ian Shapiro & Lea Brilmayer eds., New York University Press 1999).

75. Here I mean the political philosophy with roots in Immanuel Kant's work. Kant himself had some rather unusual things to say about how friendship dovetailed with his own thinking in IMMANUEL KANT, THE METAPHYSICS OF MORALS 261–64 (Mary Gregor trans., Cambridge University Press 1991) (1797).

76. For discussions of friendship that see it as an objection to theories that demand broad impartiality, see TROY A. JOLLIMORE, FRIENDSHIP AND AGENT-RELATIVE MORALITY 13 (Routledge 2001); Dean Cocking & Justin Oakley, *Indirect Consequentialism, Friendship, and the Problem of Alienation*, 106 ETHICS 86 (1995); Neera Badhwar Kapur, *Why It Is Wrong to Be Always Guided by the Best: Consequentialism and Friendship*, 101 ETHICS 483 (1991); Sarah Stroud, *Epistemic Partiality in Friendship*, 116 ETHICS 498 (2006); John Cottingham, *Partiality, Favouritism, and Morality*, 36 PHIL. Q. 357 (1986); Marcia Baron, *Impartiality and Friendship*, 101 ETHICS 836 (1991); Susan Wolf, *Morality and Partiality*, 6 PHIL. PERSPECTIVES 243 (1992). Some consequentialists have developed rebuttals. *See, e.g.,* SHELLY KAGAN, THE LIMITS OF MORALITY 367–68 (Clarendon Press 1989) (denying that love and friendship require favoritism).

77. *See* Dean Cocking & Jeanette Kennett, *Friendship and Moral Danger*, 97 J. Phil. 278, 286–87 (2000).

78. *See* Alice Ristroph & Melissa Murray, *Disestablishing the Family*, 119 Yale L.J. 1236 (2010) (arguing that multiple sources of authority are good to help us avoid totalitarianism).

79. *See* Pahl, *supra* note 48, at 153–54 (drawing from Vladimir Shlapentokh, Public and Private Life of the Soviet People: Changing Values in Post-Stalin Russia 170–77 (Oxford University Press 1989).

80. Lewis, *supra* note 8, at 94.

81. Jason A. Scorza, *Liberal Citizenship and Civic Friendship*, 32 Pol. Theory 85, 89 (2004) (citing Paul J. Waddell, Friendship and the Moral Life 49, 61–68 (University of Notre Dame Press 1989)).

82. Peter Railton, *Alienation, Consequentialism, and the Demands of Morality, in* Consequentialism and Its Critics 93, 98–99 (Samuel Scheffler ed., Oxford University Press 1988). Railton seeks to preserve a consequentialist ethical theory even though consequentialism is the theory most susceptible to the challenge from friendship. For an argument that Railton's effort ultimately fails, see William H. Wilcox, *Egoists, Consequentialists, and Their Friends*, 16 Phil. & Pub. Aff. 73 (1987).

83. *See* Pitman B. Potter, *Guanxi and the PRC Legal System: From Contradiction to Complementarity, in* Social Connections in China: Institutions, Culture, and the Changing Nature of Guanxi 179 (Thomas Gold et al. eds., Cambridge University Press 2002) (detailing how China's legal system must take account of informal social networks to maintain compliance and affective resonance).

Chapter 3

1. *See* Dan Markel, Jennifer Collins, & Ethan J. Leib, Privilege or Punish: Criminal Justice and the Challenge of Family Ties (Oxford University Press 2009). Much of the substantiating research for many of the claims made in this chapter is cited and discussed in my last book. Thanks to my coauthors and publisher for allowing me to use the material here.

2. All of the family ties benefits that follow are charted—with appropriate citations—in *id.* at 3–19 (and the associated notes).

3. *See* State v. DeLeon, 813 P.2d 1382 (Haw. 1991); *see also* Deanna Pollard, *Banning Child Corporal Punishment*, 77 Tul. L. Rev. 575, 641 n.415 (2003).

4. Tamar Lewin, *What Penalty for a Killing in Passion?*, N.Y. Times, Oct. 21, 1994.

5. *See* Associated Press, *Child Molester Charged in Assault on Boy*, 5, Miami Herald, Jan. 21, 1987, at 10A.

6. United States v. Johnson, 964 F.2d 124 (2d Cir. 1992).

7. These family ties burdens (and others) are charted—with appropriate citations—in Markel, Collins & Leib, *supra* note 1, at 63–73 (and the associated notes).

8. Diana Marrero & Shana Gruskin, *Mom Arrested in Child's Death; Police: Woman Ignored Danger by Leaving Daughter with Boyfriend*, Ft. Lauderdale Sun-Sentinel, June 21, 2002, at 1B. In this particular case, the boyfriend was eventually acquitted in the child's death, so only the mother's omission was punished. *See*

Susannah Nesmith, *3 Years Later, Man Cleared in Baby's Death*, Miami Herald, Feb. 11, 2006, at B4.

9. Or. Rev. Stat. § 163.577(1).

10. *See* Deadbeat Parents Punishment Act, Pub. L. No. 105–187, 112 Stat. 618 (1998).

11. *See* Cal. Penal Code § 270c (West 1999) (California); Conn. Gen. Stat. Ann. § 53a-4 (West 2007) (Connecticut); Ind. Code Ann. § 35-46-1-7 (LexisNexis 2004) (Indiana); Ky. Rev. Stat. Ann. § 530.050 (LexisNexis 2007) (Kentucky); Md. Code, Fam. Law §§ 13-101, 13-102, 13-103 (LexisNexis 2006) (Maryland); Mass. Gen. Laws ch. 273, § 20 (West 2000) (Massachusetts); Mont. Code Ann. § 40-6-301 (2007) (Montana); N.C. Gen. Stat. § 14-326.1 (2005) (North Carolina); Ohio Rev. Code § 2919.21 (LexisNexis 2003) (Ohio); R.I. Gen. Laws §§ 15-1-1, 15-10-7 (2006) (Rhode Island); R.I. Gen. Laws §§ 40-5-13 (2006) (Rhode Island); Vt. Stat. Ann. tit. 15, §§ 202, 203 (2006) (Vermont); Va. Code Ann. § 20-88 (2007) (Virginia).

12. Mass. Gen. Laws ch. 273 §20 (2007). *See also* Cal. Penal Code § 270c (West 1999); Conn. Gen. Stat. Ann. § 53a-4 (West 2007); Ind. Code Ann. § 35-46-1-7 (LexisNexis 2004); Ky. Rev. Stat. Ann. § 530.050 (LexisNexis 2007); Md. Code, Fam. Law §§ 13-101, 13-102, 13-103 (LexisNexis 2006); Mont. Code Ann. § 40-6-301 (2007); N.C. Gen. Stat. § 14-326.1 (2005); Ohio Rev. Code § 2919.21 (LexisNexis 2003); R.I. Gen. Laws §§ 15-1-1, 15-10-7 (2006) (Rhode Island); R.I. Gen. Laws §§ 40-5-13 (2006); Vt. Stat. Ann. tit. 15, §§ 202, 203 (2006); Va. Code Ann. § 20-88 (2007).

13. Much of this discussion and related citations are drawn from my last book: Markel, Collins & Leib, *supra* note 1, at 21–27.

14. These ideas often have their genesis in the "communitarian" theories of Charles Taylor, Sources of the Self: The Making of the Modern Identity (Harvard University Press 1989) (developing the idea that selves have "inescapable frameworks" that any theory of justice and the state must accommodate); Charles Taylor, The Ethics of Authenticity (Harvard University Press 1991) (developing the idea of the self with "horizons of significance"); and Michael J. Sandel, Liberalism and the Limits of Justice (Cambridge University Press 1982) (developing the idea of the "encumbered" self).

15. *See generally* George Fletcher, Loyalty: An Essay on the Morality of Relationships 3 (Oxford University Press 1993); Milton C. Regan, Jr., *Spousal Privilege and the Meanings of Marriage*, 81 Va. L. Rev. 2045 (1995); Milton C. Regan, Jr., Alone Together: Law and the Meanings of Marriage (Oxford University Press 1999).

16. *See generally* Paul Robinson, *Competing Conceptions of Modern Desert: Vengeful, Deontological, and Empirical*, 67 Camb. L.J. 145, 149–50 (2008) ("[i]f the criminal law tracks the community's intuitions of justice in assigning liability and punishment, it is argued, the law gains access to the power and efficiency of stigmatization, it avoids the resistance and subversion inspired by an unjust system, it gains compliance by prompting people to defer to it as a moral authority in new or grey areas...and it earns the ability to help shape of powerful societal norms.").

17. Linda C. McClain, *Care as a Public Value: Linking Responsibility, Resources, and Republicanism*, 76 Chi.-Kent L. Rev. 1673, 1674 (2001); Linda C. McClain, *Negotiating Gender and (Free and Equal) Citizenship: The Place of Associations*, 72 Fordham L. Rev. 1569, 1569 (2004); *see also* Martha Fineman, The Autonomy Myth: A Theory of Dependency xviii (New Press 2004) ("It is very important to understand the roles assigned to the family in society—roles that might otherwise have to be played by other institutions, such as the market or the state.").

18. *See generally* Joan C. Tronto, Moral Boundaries: A Political Argument for an Ethic of Care (Routledge 1993).

19. Deborah Stone, *Why We Need a Care Movement*, Nation, Mar. 13, 2000, at 13, 15.

20. *See* Joan Williams, Unbending Gender: Why Family and Work Conflict and What To Do About It 179 (Oxford University Press 2000).

21. *See* Melissa E. Murray, *The Networked Family: Reframing the Legal Understanding of Caregiving and Caregivers*, 94 Va. L. Rev. 385 (2008).

22. *See, e.g.*, Jennifer R. Brannen, *Unmarried with Privileges? Extending the Evidentiary Privilege to Same-Sex Couples*, 17 Rev. Lit. 311 (1998); Elizabeth Kimberly (Kyhm) Penfil, *In the Light of Reason and Experience: Should Federal Evidence Law Protect Confidential Communications Between Same-Sex Partners?*, 88 Marq. L. Rev. 815, 845 (2005).

23. *Cf.* Markus Dirk Dubber, *The Power to Govern Men and Things: Patriarchal Origins of the Police Power in American Law*, 52 Buff. L. Rev. 1277, 1345 (2004).

24. *See* 1 E. Coke, A Commentaire on Littleton 6b (1628); 8 John H. Wigmore, Evidence § 2227 (John T. McNaughton ed., rev. ed. 1961). In previous work, I have surveyed which states attempt to redesign their privilege law to do a better job of preventing violence in the household and which do not. *See* Markel, Collins & Leib, *supra* note 1, at 184 n.28.

25. *See generally* Nancy F. Cott, Public Vows: A History of Marriage and the Nation 210 (Harvard University Press 2000).

26. *See* Markel, Collins & Leib, *supra* note 1, at 43.

27. Parham v. J.R., 442 U.S. 584, 602 (1979); *see also* Lehr v. Robertston, 463 U.S. 248, 256 (1983) ("The intangible fibers that connect parent and child have infinite variety. They are woven throughout the fabric of our society, providing it with strength, beauty, and flexibility.").

28. *See generally* Jennifer M. Collins, *Lady Madonna, Children at Your Feet: The Criminal Justice System's Romanticization of the Parent-Child Relationship*, 93 Iowa L. Rev. 131 (2007).

29. See Mary E. Becker, *Double Binds Facing Mothers in Abusive Families: Social Support Systems, Custody Outcomes, and Liability for the Acts of Others*, 2 U. Chi. L. Sch. Roundtable 13, 15 (1995); Naomi Cahn, *Policing Women: Moral Arguments and the Dilemma of Criminalization*, 49 DePaul L. Rev. 817, 822 (2000).

30. See 42 U.S.C. § 3796hh(c)(1)(A) (2000) (requiring units of government to "encourage or mandate arrests of domestic violence offenders based on probable cause that an offense has been committed" to be eligible for certain grants); Marc

L. MILLER & RONALD F. WRIGHT, CRIMINAL PROCEDURES: CASES, STATUTES, AND EXECUTIVE MATERIALS 297–306 (2d ed., Aspen 2003) (discussing changes in police responses to domestic violence).

31. See Linda G. Mills, *Killing Her Softly: Intimate Abuse and the Violence of State Intervention*, 113 HARV. L. REV. 550, 569–70 (1999); Jeannie Suk, *Criminal Law Comes Home*, 116 YALE L.J. 2, 45 (2006). But see Annalise Acorn, *Surviving the Battered Reader's Syndrome, or: A Critique of Linda G. Mills' Insult to Injury: Rethinking Our Responses to Intimate Abuse*, 13 UCLA WOMEN'S L.J. 335, 340 (2005).

32. Nancy J. Knauer, *Same-Sex Domestic Violence: Claiming a Domestic Sphere While Risking Negative Stereotypes*, 8 TEMP. POL. & CIV. RTS. L. REV. 325 (1999); Ruthann Robson, *Lavender Bruises: Intra-Lesbian Violence, Law and Lesbian Legal Theory*, 20 GOLDEN GATE U. L. REV. 567 (1990); Symposium, *Lesbian, Gay, Bisexual, and Transgender Communities and Intimate Partner Violence*, 29 FORDHAM URB. L.J. 121 (2001).

33. *See* Wayne Logan, *Criminal Law Sanctuaries*, 38 HARV. C.R.-C.L. L. REV. 321, 347 (2003); *see also* Jill Elaine Hasday, *Contest and Consent: A Legal History of Marital Rape*, 88 CAL. L. REV. 1373, 1482 (2000).

34. See generally Ruth Gavison, *Feminism and the Public/Private Distinction*, 45 STAN. L. REV. 1 (1992).

Chapter 4

1. *See* Fed. Bureau of Prisons, U.S. Dep't of Justice, Inmate Discipline and Special Housing Units, Program Statement 5270.07, § 541.12(5) (Dec. 29, 1987).

2. *See* Beam v. Stewart, 845 A.2d 1040 (Del. 2004). Needless to say, without any standards for who counts as a friend in the legal literature (until now!), courts have not been especially solicitous of shareholders who try to use friendships to undermine director independence. *See, e.g.*, Caviness v. Evans, 229 F.R.D. 354 (D. Mass. 2005); Fagin v. Gilmartin, No. 03-2631, 2004 U.S. Dist. LEXIS 28916 (D.N.J. Aug. 20, 2004); Khanna v. McMinn, No. 20545-NC, 2006 Del. Ch. LEXIS 86 (Del. Ch. May 9, 2006); Benihana of Tokyo, Inc. v. Benihana, Inc., 891 A.2d 150 (Del. Ch. 2005). Thanks to Matt Bodie and Arthur Pinto for discussion on the Stewart case.

3. *See, e.g.*, LAW COMM'N OF CAN., BEYOND CONJUGALITY: RECOGNIZING AND SUPPORTING CLOSE PERSONAL ADULT RELATIONSHIPS 37–40 (2001), http://epe.lac-bac.gc.ca/100/200/301/lcc-cdc/beyond_conjugality-e/pdf/37152-e.pdf.

4. One could also imagine (whether legislatively or through judicial relaxation of common law rules) allowing more suits for negligent infliction of emotional distress by friend-plaintiffs. Traditionally, the law focuses on the "relationship" between the bystander observing the wrongdoing and the victim as a way of limiting these sorts of suits; usually family relationships qualify but friendships do not. Even if the primary reason to limit these sorts of suits is to find some way to hold back the "floodgates of litigation" for every act of negligence and intentional wrongdoing, one can limit the remedy without limiting appropriate plaintiffs. Friends who watch their close friends die surely can suffer tremendous loss and pain that compares

with the loss and pain family members feel. If the worry is the defendant's ability to foresee third-party harm, that shouldn't be a bar to friendship suits, it would seem. *See generally* Stanley Ingber, *Rethinking Intangible Injuries: A Focus on Remedy*, 73 CAL. L. REV. 772, 814–19 (1985). Gary Chartier shared his thoughts with me on this issue in an unpublished paper.

5. *See* Law Comm'n of Can., *supra* note 3, at 40.

6. Gary Chartier also proposed this idea in his unpublished essay on friendship and the law.

7. For some discussion about HUD and its "Moving to Opportunity" experiment, which provided housing vouchers that sought to alleviate ghetto poverty in some communities, see Claudine Gay, *Moving Out, Moving Up: Housing Mobility and the Political Participation of the Poor* (Harvard Working Paper 2009); Robert J. Sampson, *Moving to Inequality: Neighborhood Effects and Experiments Meet Social Structure*, 114 AM. J. SOC. 189 (2008). The experiment is analyzed in a new book, which also attempts to analyze what the program did (and didn't do) to networks of support of care. *See* XAVIER DE SOUZA BRIGGS, SUSAN J. POPKIN, & JOHN GOERING, MOVING TO OPPORTUNITY: THE STORY OF AN AMERICAN EXPERIMENT TO FIGHT GHETTO POVERTY ch. 6 (Oxford University Press 2010). In short, the book finds that although poor people placed in lower poverty neighborhoods rarely found new strong ties of friendship in their new communities (and often moved back to their old neighborhoods because of the pull of their old support networks), they only rarely lost touch with their strong ties elsewhere (unless they self-consciously sought to distance themselves from strong ties that were disabling their own flourishing). The problems associated with dislocation from old friends were particularly pronounced among adolescent boys, who faced more hostility from local teens and were often angrier and more withdrawn. *See id.* ch. 5. Still, the authors attribute much of the delinquency of the adolescent boys to their staying in touch with their networks from their old neighborhoods, not the influence or dislocation associated with the new ones. And the authors do not neatly disentangle kin networks from friends, so it is sometimes hard to draw real lessons about friendship per se from their analysis. This just underscores how often friendship gets assimilated to general "networks" in social research without much differentiation in the kinds of support provided by and expectations produced through friendship (in contrast with those of kin and extended family).

The authors of *Moving to Opportunity* suggest an important counterpoint to the one developed here: we must remember *the weakness of strong ties*. That is, although keeping up with close friends can be central to one's well-being and integration, friends' demands—especially on the resource-starved poor—can actually hinder self-actualization, too. This more general lesson is important beyond just poor communities. Everyone has limited emotional capital available for investment into their personal relationships; if some close friends place too many demands on us, we might lose the very real benefits associated with weaker ties, which might help us advance professionally and personally. We can't ignore this feature of friendships in our policy design either. Sensitivity to what friendship really does (and cannot do) in social research, analysis, and reform is a step forward; but that sensitivity must be nuanced about and remain open-minded about some of the very real and tangible drawbacks of strong ties. Nothing in this book is intended to hide these disadvantages from view.

8. Peter Singer, *Give Us a Smile*, THE GUARDIAN, Apr. 18, 2007, http://www.guardian.co.uk/commentisfree/2007/apr/18/comment.politics1.

9. *See* MARK GRANOVETTER, GETTING A JOB: A STUDY OF CONTACTS AND CAREERS (2nd ed., Harvard University Press 1995); Mark S. Granovetter, *The Strength of Weak Ties*, 78 AM. J. SOC. 1360 (1973); Mark Granovetter, *The Strength of Weak Ties: A Network Theory Revisited, in* SOCIOLOGICAL THEORY 201, 213 (Randall Collins ed., Jossey-Bass 1983).

10. *See* GRAHAM ALLAN, FRIENDSHIP: DEVELOPING A SOCIOLOGICAL PERSPECTIVE 4 (Westview Press 1989) ("There are no rituals associated with [friendship] nor any specifically public affirmation of the solidarity that exists between those who are friends."); ROBERT BRAIN, FRIENDS AND LOVERS 75 (Basic Books 1976) ("Unlike most societies, we have no means of embellishing friendship with ritual or pact, and except in the children's playground it is not even allowed an exchange of vows."). Brain, in particular, urges more ceremony surrounding friendships. *See id.* at 106–07.

11. *See* Email from Christopher C. King to author (July 12, 2006) (on file with author); Email from Markus Dubber to author (Jan. 13, 2005) (on file with author). Little has been written in English about the ceremony, though it is mentioned in Florian Znaniecki, *The Dynamics of Social Relations*, 17 SOCIOMETRY 299, 301 (1954), and appears in LEON URIS, EXODUS (United Artists 1958), and PATTON (20th Century Fox 1970). Thanks to Jeff Lipshaw for the leads on sources in American popular culture. Of course, "elevating" friendship to brotherhoods and sisterhoods is the stuff of, *inter alia*, college fraternities and sororities.

12. David L. Chambers, *For the Best of Friends and for Lovers of All Sorts, A Status Other Than Marriage*, 76 NOTRE DAME L. REV. 1347, 1353 (2001).

13. *See* HAW. REV. STAT. ANN. §§ 572C-1-7 (LexisNexis 2005); VT. STAT. ANN. tit. 15, §§ 1301–06 (2002).

14. ARISTOTLE, NICOMACHEAN ETHICS 9.4.1165b35–b37 (Terence Irwin trans., Hackett 1985).

15. *See* 1 WILLIAM K.S. WANG & MARC I. STEINBERG, INSIDER TRADING § 3:4.4 (2d ed., Practicing Law Institute 2005) (specifying exceptions to the no-duty-to-rescue rule).

16. *See* RESTATEMENT (SECOND) OF TORTS §§ 314A–314B.

17. 240 N.W.2d 217 (Mich. 1976).

18. 924 P.2d 940 (Wash. Ct. App. 1996).

19. *See* NEB. REV. STAT. § 25-21,237; CODE OF ALA. § 32-1-2; IND. CODE ANN. § 34-30-11-1.

20. For a taste of how courts have dealt with guest statutes, see Mitzel v. Hauck, 105 N.W.2d 378 (S.D. 1960) (applying a now-defunct guest statute between friends in connection with a duck-hunting trip); Coons v. Lawlor, 804 F.2d 28 (3d Cir. 1986) (applying the Indiana statute with a focused and dismissive discussion on the

collusion concern); Dym v. Gordon, 209 N.E.2d 792 (N.Y. 1965); and Babcock v. Jackson, 191 N.E.2d 279 (N.Y. 1963).

21. There is also likely a plausible application or extension of the duty to rescue friends in the property law context. Traditionally, the common law divides the world of people who enter our properties into three classes: trespassers, licensees, and invitees, with our duties to warn guests about the conditions of our property and our duties to inspect our property for defects anticipatorily getting stricter as one moves from the first in the list to the last. Yet the law tends to treat our friends who come to visit with us as licensees, who barely get better treatment than trespassers, those with no permission to enter our land.

But why should we not take a little extra care to protect our close friends from latent defects in our property? Would we really be less likely to have our friends over if it required us to take reasonable care to inspect our premises and then neutralize discovered defects or warn our friends about them? It is hard to see why the close friend should not get the treatment that invitees get: "invitee" is a term of art referring to either members of the public who are invited to come to a property open to the public for a particular purpose or people who are invited to come to a property to do business with the possessor of the land, *see* RESTATEMENT (SECOND) OF TORTS § 332 (1965). Cases often turn on whether coming over to someone's place confers a "real" or "material" or "tangible" benefit to the host. Should it really be so offensive to friendship to assume that friends confer benefits on us by coming onto our land? Don't friends often give us gifts when they come for dinner? Don't we often expect such gifts? Don't we at least expect a return invite in exchange? Can't this qualify as a real benefit? If it can't, isn't time spent with our close friends a real benefit?

Indeed, even if a particular court favors the more modern "reasonableness" standard over the traditional tripartite distinction (an approach taken by nearly half of the states if one includes states that retain the trespasser category but collapse the invitee-licensee distinction), knowing the relational context seems central to divining what is reasonable under all the circumstances. One might even see the inspection and warning as emanating from the duty to disclose to friends that I discuss in the next section.

To be fair, family members, too, are generally classified in the licensee category rather than the invitee category, unless they are invited to transact business or as part of a public purpose. In this way, family and friends are treated the same way—requiring less care to find defects, fix them, or warn guests about them. But at least in the case of friendship, we ought to owe our friends some basic duties to inspect, fix, and warn. For some literature on these issues that discusses the relevant cases, see John Ketchum, *Missouri Declines an Invitation To Join the Twentieth Century: Preservation of the Licensee-Invitee Distinction in Carter v. Kinney*, 64 UMKC L. REV. 393 (1995); John A. Bernardi, *Loss of the Land Occupier's Preferred Position—Abrogation of the Common Law Classifications of Trespasser, Invitee, Licensee*, 13 ST. LOUIS U. L.J. 449 (1969); Norman S. Marsh, *The History and Comparative Law of Invitees, Licensees, and Trespassers*, 69 LAW Q. REV. 182 (1953); Michael Sears, *Abrogation of the Traditional Common Law of Premises Liability*, 44 U. KAN. L. REV. 175 (1995).

22. For surveys (and a skeptical take), see, e.g., Marc E. Odier, *Social Host Liability: Opening a Pandora's Box*, 61 IND. L.J. 85 (1985); Derry D. Sparlin, Jr., *Social Host Liability for Guests Who Drink and Drive: A Closer Look at the Benefits and the Burdens*, 27 WM. & MARY L. REV. 583 (1986); and Klein v. Raysinger, 470 A.2d 507, 510 (Pa. 1983) (collecting cases denying liability for social hosts serving adults). For some of the cases finding liability, see Kelly v. Gwinnell, 476 A.2d 1219, 1224 (N.J. 1984) (holding "that a host who serves liquor to an adult social guest, knowing both that the guest is intoxicated and will thereafter be operating a motor vehicle, is liable for injuries inflicted on a third party as a result of the negligent operation of a motor vehicle by the guest"); Koback v. Crook, 366 N.W.2d 857, 862 (Wisc. 1985) ("We are still our brothers' keepers, and it would be a rare host at a social gathering who would knowingly give more liquor to an intoxicated friend when he knows his invitee must take care of himself on the highway and will potentially endanger other persons. Social justice and common sense require the social host to see within reason that his guests do not partake too much of his generosity."). The states do not have anything close to a united front on this issue. Many jurisdictions hold adult social hosts liable principally for injuries that befall a minor or are caused by a minor—and do not extend liability to contexts where a host serves an adult. *See* Hansen v. Friend, 824 P.2d 483 (Wn. 1992) (holding two friends may be liable for their underage friend's drowning death after the adult friends served the minor alcohol at a campsite).

23. Although many state courts have preferred to have legislators design the contours of the liability, some courts have taken the role on themselves. Here I'm less focused on which method of adoption is better but only the substance of the rule. However, since this section of the chapter is principally about common law expansion of the duties to protect friends, I concede that I am effectively embracing the judicial approach.

24. *See* RESTATEMENT (SECOND) OF TORTS § 540 (1965).

25. 59 P.2d 593 (Cal. Dist. Ct. App. 1936).

26. *Id.* at 596.

27. 103 Cal. Rptr. 318 (Cal. Ct. App. 1972).

28. 166 F.2d 651, 653 (7th Cir. 1948).

29. *See* Spiess v. Brandt, 41 N.W.2d 561, 566–67 (Minn. 1950) (finding that friendship can establish a party's right to rely on her friend); Bank Leumi Trust Co. v. Luckey Platt Ctr. Assocs., 245 A.D.2d 622 (N.Y. App. Div. 1997) (same); Callahan v. Callahan, 514 N.Y.S.2d 819, 822 (App. Div. 1987) (same); Liebergesell v. Evans, 613 P.2d 1170, 1176 (Wash. 1980) (same); Graff v. Geisel, 234 P.2d 884, 890 (Wash. 1951) (same); Bush v. Stone, 500 S.W.2d 885, 892 (Tex. App. 1973) (friendly ties can give rise to confidential relationships with special duties, even if the plaintiff is a sophisticated businessperson).

30. *See* Bates v. Southgate, 31 N.E.2d 551, 558 (Mass. 1941).

31. 156 P. 509 (Cal. 1916).

32. *Id.* at 513.

33. *Id.*

34. 279 F. Supp. 2d 413 (S.D.N.Y. 2003).

35. It is probably worth noting for completeness that the Second Circuit Court of Appeals thoroughly rejected the punitive damage analysis offered by this trial court. *See* TVT Records v. Island Def Jam Music Group, 412 F.3d 82, 93–96 (2d Cir. 2005). However, the appellate court did not comment specifically on the district court's consideration of personal relationships in punitive damage assessment.

36. *See* U.S. SENTENCING GUIDELINES MANUAL § 3B1.3 (1992). For discussion of this possibility, compare United States v. Pardo, 25 F.3d 1187, 1190–93 (3d Cir. 1994) (citing United States v. Craddock, 993 F.2d 338, 340 (3d Cir. 1993) and finding that no abuse of a position of trust enhancement was appropriate when a defendant took advantage of his friend in perpetrating his fraud), with United States v. Zamarripa, 905 F.2d 337, 340 (10th Cir. 1990) (finding an abuse of a position of trust when a friend sexually abused his friend's daughter).

37. 17 C.F.R. § 240.10b-5 (2006).

38. United States v. O'Hagan, 521 U.S. 642, 652 (1997).

39. United States v. Kim, 184 F. Supp. 2d 1006, 1010 (N.D. Cal. 2002).

40. 947 F.2d 551 (2d Cir. 1991).

41. *Kim*, 184 F. Supp. 2d at 1011.

42. Selective Disclosure and Insider Trading, 64 Fed. Reg. 72,590, 72,602 (proposed Dec. 28, 1999) (to be codified at 17 C.F.R. pt. 240).

43. 17 C.F.R. § 240.10b5-2 (2006).

44. A similar conclusion is offered by Ray J. Grzebielski, *Friends, Family, Fiduciaries: Personal Relationships as a Basis for Insider Trading Violations*, 51 CATH. U. L. REV. 467, 493 (2002). *But see* SEC v. Talbot, 430 F. Supp. 2d 1029, 1046 (C.D. Cal. 2006) (endorsing a restrictive view of the relationship of trust and confidence in the context of a lengthy analysis of misappropriation liability).

45. In the paragraphs that follow, I am drawing on DANIEL J. SOLOVE, THE FUTURE OF REPUTATION: GOSSIP, RUMOR, AND PRIVACY ON THE INTERNET ch. 7 (Yale University Press 2007); Neil M. Richards & Daniel J. Solove, *Privacy's Other Path: Recovering the Law of Confidentiality*, 96 GEO. L.J. 123 (2007); and Drake Bennett, *Time for a Muzzle: The Online World of Lies and Rumor Grows Ever More Vicious. Is It Time To Rethink Free Speech?*, BOSTON GLOBE, Feb. 15, 2009, http://www.boston.com/bostonglobe/ideas/articles/2009/02/15/time_for_a_muzzle/.

46. Volokh is quoted in Bennett, *supra* note 44.

47. SOLOVE, *supra* note 45, at 174 (quoting Nader v. General Motors, Inc., 225 N.E.2d 765, 770 (N.Y. 1970).

48. *See* RESTATEMENT (SECOND) OF TORTS § 652D (1977).

49. *Id.* at 188 & n.85. The relevant case in England is Stephens v. Avery, [1988] Ch. 449; and Richards & Solove, *supra* note 45, at 158–82, analyze the British approach, its history, and how it differs from the American treatment of similar issues.

50. *See* RESTATEMENT (SECOND) OF CONTRACTS § 90 (1981).

51. For a gift to be effective, a donor must transfer property without consideration and with donative intent. *See* RESTATEMENT (THIRD) OF PROPERTY: WILLS AND OTHER DONATIVE TRANSFERS § 6.1(a) (2003). For a case finding a

presumption of donative intent in familial gift transactions, see Estate of Lang v. Comm'r, 64 T.C. 404, 413 (1975).

52. *See generally* Hila Keren, *Giving Is Receiving: Contracts, Emotions, and Gifts* (forthcoming 2010). She reviews the literature on gratuitous promises in law and psychology and suggests that givers of gifts and recipients of gifts get an affective benefit from the giving or the promise to give itself (pleasure or gratitude). That might furnish an additional component to the gift necessary to reinforce that legal "consideration" exists after all. Keren's argument on this score is based on, *inter alia*, neural mapping of pleasure experience reported in William T. Harbaugh, Ulrich Mayr & Daniel Burghart, *Neural Responses to Taxation and Voluntary Giving Reveal Motives for Charitable Donations*, 316 SCIENCE 1622 (2007) and some positive psychology of the sort reported in ROBERT EMMONS, THANKS! HOW THE NEW SCIENCE OF GRATITUDE CAN MAKE YOU HAPPIER (Mariner Books 2007).

Some legal scholars have urged enforceability of gift promises more broadly, *see* Jane B. Baron, *Do We Believe in Generosity? Reflections on the Relationship Between Gifts and Exchanges*, 44 U. FLA. L. REV. 355 (1992), but here I limit my recommendation to such promises among friends. A limitation of this kind in affective relationships can be found in Mark K. Moller, *Sympathy, Community, and Promising: Adam Smith's Case for Reviving Moral Consideration*, 66 U. CHI. L. REV. 213 (1999). Within affective relationships, an affective response to gift giving would seem most likely and most powerful.

53. No. 04-1230, 2005 WL 1225382 (Iowa Ct. App. May 25, 2005).

54. No. 21741/04, 2005 WL 579152 (N.Y. Sup. Ct. Jan. 3, 2005).

55. *Id.* (quoting Penato v. George, 383 N.Y.S.2d 900, 905 (N.Y. App. Div. 1976)).

56. *Id.*

57. 214 N.Y.S.2d 127 (N.Y. Sup. Ct. 1961).

58. Another example where friendship was useful to a court in an equitable determination is Hedges v. Primavera, 218 F. Supp. 797 (E.D. Pa. 1963). There, a "close and intimate" friendship was deemed to "explain[ ] and excuse[ ] plaintiff's failure sooner to discover defendant's fraud and deceit," enabling the court to find that the statute of limitations on the fraud and deceit action was equitably tolled. *Id.* at 801–02.

59. *See* Family and Medical Leave Act of 1993, 29 U.S.C. §§ 2601–2654 (2000).

60. 23 Cal. Rptr. 3d 10 (Cal. Ct. App. 2004).

61. 6 Cal. Rptr. 3d 702, 713 (Cal. Ct. App. 2003).

62. 47 Cal. Rptr. 3d 248 (2006). The resolution of this matter also implicates the discussion about donative transfers and the friend's potential privilege of informality, discussed above. For a recent analysis of California's "care custodian" provision, see generally Kirsten M. Kwasneski, Comment, *The Danger of a Label: How the Legal Interpretation of "Care Custodian" Can Frustrate a Testator's Wish To Make a Gift to [a] Personal Friend*, 36 GOLDEN GATE U. L. REV. 269 (2006).

63. It is worth noting that the vote split four to three, with one member of the majority bloc writing separately to explain his position more carefully. *Bernard*, 47 Cal. Rptr. at 264–65 (George, C.J., concurring).

64. Sanford Levinson, *Testimonial Privileges and the Preferences of Friendship*, 1984 Duke L.J. 631. The *Beyond Conjugality* report out of Canada also embraces this approach to respecting friendship. Law Comm'n of Can., *supra* note 3, at 46.

65. Sanford Levinson, *Structuring Intimacy: Some Reflections on the Fact That the Law Generally Does Not Protect Us Against Unwanted Gazes*, 89 Geo. L.J. 2073, 2079 (2001) ("To put it mildly, the proposal has gathered no support"). One notable exception to the silence with which Levinson's article was met may be Judge Levy, in dissent in Diehl v. State, 698 S.W.2d 712, 715 (Tex. App. 1985) (Levy, J., dissenting). In disagreeing with the majority's ruling in *Diehl* that there was no parent-child privilege in Texas, Judge Levy felt that "it is necessary to face the relationship issue squarely in order to reach a just and salutary result...because the most serious, intimate, and far-reaching social values are in conflict here, involving the very nature of the relationships between the individual, the family, and the State." *Id.* at 717.

66. *See* Jeffrey Rosen, The Unwanted Gaze: The Destruction of Privacy in America 54 (Random House 2000).

67. For the ideas in this paragraph, see Ferdinand Schoeman, *Friendship and Testimonial Privileges, in* Ethics, Public Policy, and Criminal Justice 257 (Fredrick Elliston & Norman Bowie eds., Oelgeschlager, Gunn, and Hain 1982). Thanks also to Gary Chartier, who was willing to share with me some of his early and unpublished thoughts on this subject.

68. Mary I. Coombs, *Shared Privacy and the Fourth Amendment, or the Rights of Relationships*, 75 Cal. L. Rev. 1593, 1596 (1987). Coombs's essay is a much more sophisticated treatment of this subject.

69. For some relevant case law, see Jones v. United States, 362 U.S. 257 (1960). In *Jones*, the Supreme Court recognized a claimant's right to contest a search of his good friend's house because he was staying there, had permission to be staying there, and was, in any case, the defendant charged with possession. Yet *Jones* did not consider the possibility for a privacy privilege conferred by friendship and, in any event, has been subject to substantial criticism. *See, e.g.*, Rakas v. Illinois, 439 U.S. 128 (1978). *Rakas* did not allow the rationale of *Jones* to extend to any right of privacy associated with riding in a friend's car. *Id.* at 140–49. And *Jones*'s "automatic standing" rule (for the defendant) was overruled in United States v. Salvucci, 448 U.S. 83, 85 (1980). *See generally* Albert W. Alschuler, *Interpersonal Privacy and the Fourth Amendment*, 4 N. Ill. U. L. Rev. 1, 19 (1983) ("[A person] who entrusts property to a relative, friend or confederate in crime ordinarily has a reasonable expectation of privacy in any private place where the bailee stores this property.").

70. *See generally id.* at 33; Peter Goldberger, *Consent, Expectations of Privacy, and the Meaning of "Searches" in the Fourth Amendment*, 75 J. Crim. L. & Criminology 319, 344 (1984); Penelope R. Glover, *Re-defining Friendship: Employment of Informants by the Police*, 72 U. Colo. L. Rev. 749 (2001).

71. James J. Tomkovicz, *Beyond Secrecy for Secrecy's Sake: Toward an Expanded Vision of the Fourth Amendment Privacy Province*, 36 Hastings L.J. 645, 727 n.331 (1985) (citing United States v. White, 401 U.S. 745 (1971); Osborn v. United States, 385 U.S. 323 (1966); Hoffa v. United States, 385 U.S. 293 (1966)).

72. 356 U.S. 369 (1958).

73. This actually raises another interesting intersection of the law and friendship: whether doing a favor for a friend is a type of profit that accrues to the gift-giver. The inquiry is especially relevant in the context of "tipper liability" for those who improperly tip their friends and colleagues by conveying material nonpublic information. For Rule 10b-5 securities fraud liability to attach against a tipper under the "classic relationship" theory, a "personal benefit" must pass to the tipper on account of the tip. *See* Dirks v. SEC, 463 U.S. 646, 666–67 (1983); 1 WANG & STEINBERG, *supra* note 14, § 5:2.8. Courts have held that a tipper passes the personal-benefit test when the benefit is merely vicarious and the tipper feels good because the tippee feels good; these courts contemplate that a seemingly gratuitous tip to a friend can nevertheless constitute a substantive personal benefit. For examples where the personal-benefit test was met between friends, see SEC v. Warde, 151 F.3d 42, 48–49 (2d Cir. 1998), and SEC v. Maio, 51 F.3d 623, 633 (7th Cir. 1995).

Perhaps we need to debate more carefully whether tips between friends are part of an exchange in which a real personal benefit accrues to the friend offering the tip or whether we ought to view tips by certain friends as fully gratuitous, to which no presumption of personal benefit should apply. The law, at least in SEC v. Downe, 969 F. Supp. 149, 156 (S.D.N.Y. 1997), seems to take the "exchange theory" to be appropriate, consistent with the views about friendship and mutual assistance that I explored in chapter 1. But it may be that we do not want our law to endorse this exchange-theorist or "use" (from Aristotle's typology) conception of friendship. We might also want the law to recognize that there are some friendships where gifts are, in fact, given purely gratuitously (even if they will ultimately be enforceable anyway, as I suggest above in the section "The Privilege of Informality"). More thinking about this matter is surely warranted.

74. 577 P.2d 1064 (Alaska 1978).

75. Drug Sentencing Reform Act of 2006, S. 3725, 109th Cong. § 202(2)(B) (2006), http://sentencing.typepad.com/sentencing_law_and_policy/files/senate_cocaine_bill.pdf. Thanks to Carissa Byrne Hessick for very smart interventions on this subject.

76. *See* Peter Goodrich, *The Immense Rumor*, 16 YALE J.L. & HUMAN. 199, 203 (2004).

77. ERWIN CHEMERINSKY, FEDERAL JURISDICTION 83–84 (3d ed., Aspen 1999).

78. This is sometimes termed the rule against *jus tertii*. *See* RICHARD H. FALLON ET AL., HART & WECHSLER'S THE FEDERAL COURTS AND THE FEDERAL SYSTEM 187–95 (4th ed. Foundation Press 1996). The classic cases are United Food & Commercial Workers Union Local 151 v. Brown Group, Inc., 517 U.S. 544, 551–57 (1996), and Warth v. Seldin, 422 U.S. 490, 498–501 (1975). Some academic commentary on the subject can be found in Henry P. Monaghan, *Third Party Standing*, 84 COLUM. L. REV. 277 (1984).

79. *See* CHEMERINSKY, *supra* note 76, at 84 (furnishing examples and citations).

80. *Id.* at 85 (emphasis added).

81. Gilmore v. Utah, 429 U.S. 1012, 1012–13 (1976). This case may be aberrational, if only because Gary Gilmore himself made it clear that he did not wish to assert his own rights. *Id.* at 1014–15.

82. Ira Ellman, *Why Making Family Law Is Hard*, 35 ARIZ. ST. L.J. 699, 700 (2003).

83. It may be haphazard because when presented with disputes involving friendships, courts simply try to "be fair" rather than try "to set incentives for socially desirable intimate behavior." *Id.* at 707. That may be appropriate because, as Ellman argues, "the law is a minor actor among all the factors that influence people in their intimate behavior." *Id.* at 702. Ultimately, I tend to think Ellman underestimates the law's influence and, in any case, I remain convinced that gaining some systematicity about friendship will prove more sound than general attempts to figure out how to "be fair" without guidance about what the category of the friend is and why it is important. Our very sense of equity and fairness emerges from our commitments to the concept in the first place; accordingly, I do not think we can avoid the task of attempting to achieve some understanding of the concept itself and its importance.

84. *See* Roy Ryden Anderson, *The Wolf at the Campfire: Understanding Confidential Relationships*, 53 SMU L. REV. 315, 327–30 (2000) (arguing that courts tend to prefer objective evidence and discount subjective evidence in establishing the fiduciary nature of a relationship); *id.* at 330 ("A contract provision denying the existence of a confidential relationship…when in fact such a relationship did exist, should always be invalid and unenforceable. It would, in effect, represent a disclaimer of fiduciary liability which, under the familiar rule everywhere, is void as against public policy."); Gregory B. Westfall, Comment, *But I Know It When I See It: A Practical Framework for Analysis and Argument of Informal Fiduciary Relationships*, 23 TEX. TECH L. REV. 835, 857 n.142 (1992) (highlighting that close friendships are relatively easy to prove with objective evidence and citing cases where Texas courts utilized objective evidence to establish that parties were, in fact, close friends).

Chapter 5

1. Meinhard v. Salmon, 164 N.E. 545, 546 (N.Y. 1928) (citation omitted).

2. Brief for the Plaintiff before the Appellate Division, Vol. 153 Cases and Points, Appellate Division 1928 at pp. 1467–70 (folios 675 and 672 of the record), *cited in* Robert B. Thompson, *The Story of Meinhard v. Salmon and Fiduciary Duty's Punctilio, in* CORPORATE LAW STORIES (J. Mark Ramseyer ed., Foundation Press 2009).

3. There may be an intellectual property rule (the "idea submission doctrine") that might be applicable. *See, e.g.*, Desny v. Wilder, 286 P.2d 55 (Cal. 1956); *see generally* Lionel S. Sobel, *The Law of Ideas, Revisited*, 1 UCLA ENT. L. REV. 9 (1994). But let us assume that doctrine does not apply here. Thanks to Eric Goldman for the exposure to the idea submission literature.

4. Of course, a group of committed scholars from common law countries have tried to illuminate the concept over the last few decades. *See, e.g.*, LEONARD I. ROTMAN, FIDUCIARY LAW (Carswell 2005); J.C. SHEPHERD, THE LAW OF FIDUCIARIES (Carswell 1981); Robert C. Clark, *Agency Costs Versus Fiduciary Duties, in* PRINCIPALS AND AGENTS 55 (John W. Pratt & Richard J. Zeckhauser eds., Harvard Business

School Press 1985); Robert Cooter & Bradley J. Freedman, *The Fiduciary Relationship: Its Economic Character and Legal Consequences*, 66 N.Y.U. L. REV. 1045 (1991); Kenneth B. Davis, Jr., *Judicial Review of Fiduciary Decisionmaking—Some Theoretical Perspectives*, 80 Nw. U. L. REV. 1 (1985); Deborah A. DeMott, *Beyond Metaphor: An Analysis of Fiduciary Obligation*, 1988 DUKE L.J. 879; Scott FitzGibbon, *Fiduciary Relationships Are Not Contracts*, 82 MARQ. L. REV. 303 (1999); Robert Flannigan, *The Economics of Fiduciary Accountability*, 32 DEL. J. CORP. L. 393 (2007); Robert Flannigan, *The Fiduciary Obligation*, 9 Ox.

J. LEGAL STUD. 285 (1989); Tamar Frankel, *Fiduciary Law*, 71 CAL. L. REV. 795 (1983); Lawrence E. Mitchell, *The Death of Fiduciary Duty in Close Corporations*, 138 U. PA. L. REV. 1675 (1990); Eileen A. Scallen, *Promises Broken vs. Promised Betrayed: Metaphor, Analogy, and the New Fiduciary Principle*, 1993 U. ILL. L. REV. 897; L.S. Sealy, *Fiduciary Relationships*, 1962 CAMBRIDGE L.J. 69; J.C. Shepherd, *Towards a Unified Concept of Fiduciary Relationships*, 97 LAW Q. REV. 51 (1981); D. Gordon Smith, *The Critical Resource Theory of Fiduciary Duty*, 55 VAND. L. REV. 1399 (2002); Ernest J. Weinrib, *The Fiduciary Obligation*, 25 U. TORONTO L.J. 1 (1975). I draw from these writers throughout the chapter.

5. Frank H. Easterbrook & Daniel R. Fischel, *Contract and Fiduciary Duty*, 38 J.L. & ECON. 425, 438 (1993).

6. *See, e.g.*, DANIEL J. SOLOVE, THE DIGITAL PERSON: TECHNOLOGY AND PRIVACY IN THE INFORMATION AGE 103 (New York University Press 2004) (arguing that a fiduciary relationship should be recognized between consumers who provide personal data and the companies to which they provide them); Harold Brown, *Franchising: A Fiduciary Relationship*, 49 TEX. L. REV. 650 (1971); Evan J. Criddle, *Fiduciary Foundations of Administrative Law*, 54 UCLA L. REV. 117 (2006); John Burritt McArthur, *The Restatement (First) of the Oilfield Operator's Fiduciary Duty*, 45 NAT. RESOURCES J. 587 (2005); Paul B. Miller & Charles Weijer, *Fiduciary Obligation in Clinical Research*, 34 J.L. MED. & ETHICS 424 (2006); Brett G. Scharffs & John W. Welch, *An Analytic Framework for Understanding and Evaluating the Fiduciary Duties of Educators*, 2005 BYU EDUC. & L.J. 159; Elizabeth S. Scott & Robert E. Scott, *Parents as Fiduciaries*, 81 VA. L. REV. 2401 (1995); Roberto Mangabeira Unger, *The Critical Legal Studies Movement*, 96 HARV. L. REV. 561, 633, 641 (1983); Jennifer L. White, Note, *When It's OK to Sell the Monet: A Trustee-Fiduciary-Duty Framework for Analyzing the Deaccessioning of Art To Meet Museum Operating Expenses*, 94 MICH. L. REV. 1041 (1996).

7. Although some purists might try to exclude confidential relationships from the category of fiduciary relationships because they are often treated as somewhat less restrictive than true status-based fiduciary relationships, it would be very hard to sustain this neat separation. Indeed, courts are not especially principled in highlighting and sustaining such a distinction. *See, e.g.*, Fipps v. Stidham, 50 P.2d 680, 683 (Okla. 1935) ("Confidential and fiduciary relations are in law synonymous, and exist whenever trust and confidence is reposed by one person in the integrity and fidelity of another."); Rieger v. Rich, 329 P.2d 770, 778 (Cal. Dist. Ct. App. 1958) ("Confidential or fiduciary relationship[s]...in law are synonymous."); *see also* BLACK'S LAW DICTIONARY 318, 658,

1314–15 (8th ed. Thomson West 2004) (indicating that confidential relationships are synonymous with fiduciary relationships).

8. *See* Harper v. Adametz, 113 A.2d 136, 139 (Conn. 1955) ("[E]quity has carefully refrained from defining a fiduciary relationship in precise detail and in such a manner as to exclude new situations."); John C. Coffee, Jr., *From Tort to Crime: Some Reflections on the Criminalization of Fiduciary Breaches and the Problematic Line Between Law and Ethics*, 19 AM. CRIM. L. REV. 117, 150 (1981) ("The common law has in fact always defined [informal fiduciary relationships] with deliberate imprecision and perhaps surprising expansiveness.").

9. *See generally* Deborah A. DeMott, *Disloyal Agents*, 58 ALA. L. REV. 1049 (2007).

10. Lynn A. Stout, *On the Export of U.S.-Style Corporate Fiduciary Duties to Other Cultures: Can a Transplant Take?, in* GLOBAL MARKETS, DOMESTIC INSTITUTIONS: CORPORATE LAW AND GOVERNMENT IN A NEW ERA OF CROSS-BORDER DEALS 46, 55 (Curtis J. Milhaupt ed., Columbia University Press 2003).

11. *See* Libby v. L.J. Corp., 247 F.2d 78, 81 (D.C. Cir. 1957); Jordan v. Duffs & Phelps, 815 F.2d 429, 436 (7th Cir. 1987) (enforcing a fiduciary duty of disclosure); Wendt v. Fischer, 154 N.E. 303, 304 (N.Y. 1926) (Cardozo, J.) ("If dual interests are to be served, the disclosure to be effective must lay bare the truth, without ambiguity or reservation, in all its stark significance.").

12. Moore v. Regents of the Univ. of California, 793 P.2d 479, 483 (Cal. 1990).

13. *See* Rosenthal v. Rosenthal, 543 A.2d 348, 352 (Me. 1988); Herring v. Offutt, 295 A.2d 876, 879 (Md. 1972).

14. *See* Burdett v. Miller, 957 F.2d 1375, 1381 (7th Cir. 1992) (Posner, J.) ("A fiduciary duty is the duty of an agent to treat his principal with the utmost candor, rectitude, care, loyalty, and good faith"); *In re* Walt Disney Co. Derivative Litig., 907 A.2d 693, 753–57 (Del. Ch. 2005) (identifying duty of good faith), *aff'd*, 906 A.2d 693 (Del. 2006).

15. The general duty of good faith in contractual relations is derived from U.C.C. § 1–304 (2008) ("Every contract or duty within this Act imposes an obligation of good faith in its performance or enforcement."); *see also* RESTATEMENT (SECOND) OF CONTRACTS § 205 (1981) ("Every contract imposes upon each party a duty of good faith and fair dealing in its performance and its enforcement.").

16. In many respects, this perspective has been recently confirmed in Stone v. Ritter, 911 A.2d 362, 370 (Del. 2006): "[A]lthough good faith many be described colloquially as part of a 'triad' of fiduciary duties that includes the duties of care and loyalty, the obligation to act in good faith does not establish an independent fiduciary duty that stands on the same footing as the duties of care and loyalty. Only the latter two duties, where violated, may directly result in liability, whereas failure to act in good faith may do so, but indirectly." This recent holding has already been the source of vigorous commentary, and many agree that the good faith obligation for fiduciaries retains bite, even if it seems to be subsumed under the larger rubric of the duty of loyalty. *See, e.g.*, Stephen M. Bainbridge et al., *The Convergence of Good Faith and Oversight* (UCLA Sch. of Law, Law & Econ. Research Paper Series No. 07-09), http://ssrn.com/abstract=1006097 ("[T]his holding may not matter much, because

the *Stone* court makes clear that acts taken in bad faith breach the duty of loyalty."); Letter from Deborah A. DeMott to author (Sept. 12, 2007) (on file with author) ("My reading of [*Stone* and *In re Walt Disney Co. Shareholder Derivative Litig.*] is that they treat the duty of good faith as a subset of the duty of loyalty, clarifying that a director's duty of loyalty encompasses more than the negative duty to refrain from unconsented-to self-dealing.").

17. 164 N.E. 545, 548 (N.Y. 1928).

18. 444 U.S. 507 (1980).

19. *See* Keck v. Wacker, 413 F. Supp. 1377 (E.D. Ky. 1976); Scallen, *supra* note 4, at 912 (citing Vale v. Union Bank, 151 Cal. Rptr. 784 (Ct. App. 1979)); (Hylid v. Simmons, 378 A.2d 260 (N.J. 1977)); Cooter & Freedman, *supra* note 4, at 1069 (citing Schoenholtz v. Doniger, 657 F. Supp. 899, 914 (S.D.N.Y. 1987)).

20. For a sampling of this debate, see, for example, SHEPHERD, *supra* note (defending an account of fiduciaries as "entrustment" leading to "encumbered power" and rejecting property-based theories, reliance-based accounts, contractarianism, unjust enrichment theories, and "power and discretion theory"); Victor Brudney, *Fiduciary Ideology in Transactions Affecting Corporate Control*, 65 MICH. L. REV. 259, 259–60 (1966) (highlighting the role of the fiduciary as a representative); Criddle, *supra* note 6, at 126 ("The starting point for all fiduciary relations is substitution"); Easterbrook & Fischel, *supra* note 5, at 426 (defending a "contractarian" theory in which fiduciary duties exist as default rules that result from the impossibility of writing complete contracts); Frankel, *supra* note 4, at 808–16 (defending "abuse of power" as the unifying theme of fiduciary law); Arthur J. Jacobson, *The Private Use of Public Authority: Sovereignty and Associations in the Common Law*, 29 BUFF. L. REV. 599, 620 (1980) (viewing the shifting of "judgment" as central to the fiduciary concept); Edward B. Rock & Michael L. Wachter, *Islands of Conscious Power: Law, Norms, and the Self-Governing Corporation*, 149 U. PA. L. REV. 1619, 1634–40 (2001) (arguing that fiduciary duties are necessary to counteract temptations for opportunism that even strong social norms will fail to deter); Austin W. Scott, *The Fiduciary Principle*, 37 CAL. L. REV. 539 (1949) (arguing that fiduciaries can be united in their voluntary undertakings); Smith, *supra* note 4 (arguing for a "critical resource theory" in which all fiduciaries have discretion to dispose of or have power over a beneficiary's critical resource). *But see* DeMott, *supra* note 4, at 915 ("Described instrumentally, the fiduciary obligation is a device that enables the law to respond to a range of situations in which, for a variety of reasons, one person's discretion ought to be controlled because of characteristics of that person's relationship with another. This instrumental description is the only general assertion about fiduciary obligation that can be sustained.").

21. *Id.*

22. Larry E. Ribstein, *Are Partners Fiduciaries?*, 2005 U. ILL. L. REV. 209, at 237.

23. *See* Easterbrook & Fischel, *supra* note 5, at 427 & 428 n.6.

24. Stout, *supra* note 10, at 47–48.

25. Ribstein, *supra* note 22, at 211.

26. Mitchell, *supra* note 4, at 1692–93.

27. Frankel, *supra* note 4, at 802; *see also* Kenneth M. Rosen, *Introduction to the Meador Lectures on Fiduciaries*, 58 ALA. L. REV. 1041, 1042 (2007) ("Notions of fiduciaries and their duties continue to permeate the law. Their importance only continues to grow.").

28. Scallen, *supra* note 4, at 911.

29. *See* Sally Falk Moore, *Law and Social Change: The Semi-Autonomous Social Field as an Appropriate Subject of Study*, 7 LAW & SOC'Y REV. 719 (1973). *But see* ANNETTE C. BAIER, *Trust and Antitrust*, in MORAL PREJUDICES: ESSAYS ON ETHICS 118 (Harvard University Press 1994) ("Trust in fellow contractors is a limit case of trust, in which fewer risks are taken, for the sake of lesser goods.").

30. *See id.* at 130 (citing 1 THE CORRESPONDENCE OF JOHN LOCKE 123 ltr. 81 (E.S. de Beer ed., Clarendon Press 1976)).

31. *See generally* FRANCIS FUKUYAMA, TRUST: THE SOCIAL VIRTUES AND THE CREATION OF PROSPERITY (Simon & Schuster 1995). A similar line of argument is pursued in Lawrence E. Mitchell, *Trust. Contract. Process.*, *in* PROGRESSIVE CORPORATE LAW 185 (Lawrence E. Mitchell ed., Westview Press 1995). I discuss issues of trust more extensively in chapter 7.

32. Harlan F. Stone, *The Public Influence of the Bar*, 48 HARV. L. REV. 1, 8–9 (1934).

33. Ribstein, *supra* note 22, at 228.

34. Robert W. Gordon, *Macaulay, Macneil, and the Discovery of Solidarity and Power in Contract Law*, 1985 WIS. L. REV. 565, 578–79.

35. To be sure, "[t]rust is not always a good to be preserved.... If the enterprise is evil, a producer of poisons, then the trust that improves its workings will also be evil, and decent people will want to destroy, not protect, that form of trust." BAIER, *supra* note 29, at 130–31. What this means for a body of law self-consciously pursuing the protection of trust is that certain exceptions need to be recognized. Those exceptions fall outside the scope of my general argument here.

36. *See generally* Margaret M. Blair & Lynn A. Stout, *Trust, Trustworthiness, and the Behavioral Foundations of Corporate Law*, 149 U. PA. L. REV. 1735 (2001) (explaining and elaborating on "framing" theory).

37. Ribstein, *supra* note 22, at 237.

38. *Id.*

39. Davis, *supra* note 4, at 6.

40. BAIER, *supra* note 29, at 132.

41. *Id.* at 133. Although she suggests that trust is an *alternative* to the threat of legal sanctions in this part of her essay, too, I shall take issue with the "substitutional" nature of trust (for law) in chapter 7.

42. *Id.* at 136.

43. *Id.* at 137.

44. I thank Brett McDonnell for pushing me on this point.

45. *But see* Paul H. Robinson & John M. Darley, *Does Criminal Law Deter? A Behavioral Science Investigation*, 24 OXFORD J. LEGAL STUD. 173 (2004) (answering no). Even if the law does not deter, there is still the underlying moral rationale for exacting punishment from those who breach their fiduciary obligations. And there is

the "empirical desert" argument available as well: that it breeds general compliance with the law to police conduct that the community agrees "deserves" sanction. *See generally* Janice Nadler, *Flouting the Law*, 83 Tex. L. Rev. 1399 (2005) (arguing that harmonizing law and social norms can help to breed compliance—and the opposite can breed noncompliance); Paul H. Robinson & John M. Darley, *The Utility of Desert*, 91 Nw. U. L. Rev. 453 (1997) (same).

46. *But see* Jeanette Kennett & Steve Matthews, *What's the Buzz? Undercover Marketing and the Corruption of Friendship*, 25 J. Applied Phil. 2, 9 (2008); Michael Argyle & Monika Henderson, *The Rules of Friendship*, 1 J. of Soc. & Personal Relationships 211 (1984).

47. I explore many of the personal benefits friendship confers on its participants in chapter 2, of course, where I highlight friendship's role in establishing and sustaining our identities, confirming our sense of social and moral worth, helping us avoid depression, sustaining our physical health, and inspiring creativity. It might be that we owe our friends special fiduciary-like duties not (only) for the trust reposed in us and the consequent vulnerability it produces but (also) because of all friends do for us in our lives. Still, the friend-as-fiduciary message of this chapter helps expose the natural fit between a set of special responsibilities and duties to another and the nature of a trust relationship, leading to special vulnerability.

48. 59 P.2d 593 (Cal. Dist. Ct. App. 1936).

49. *See also* Bennett v. Allstate Ins. Co., 753 F. Supp. 299, 303 (N.D. Cal. 1990) (rejecting a longtime friendship as a confidential or fiduciary relationship); Kuper v. Spar, 176 B.R. 321, 329 (Bankr. S.D.N.Y. 1994) (finding no authority for the proposition that a close friendship between the parties could "transform" it into a fiduciary relationship for the purposes of the Bankruptcy Code); Frantz v. Porter, 64 P. 92, 94 (Cal. 1901) (after conceding an intimate friendship between the parties, holding that "the relation was neither more nor less than that of warm personal friendship, and there can be no presumption, under the facts in this case," that a fiduciary relationship existed); Butts v. Dragstrem, 349 So. 2d 1205, 1207 (Fla. Dist. Ct. App. 1977) ("Dragstrem's primary justification for his reliance on Butts' representations was...their close personal friendship.... Unfortunately for Dragstrem's position such a relationship does not create a fiduciary...relationship."); Cranwell v. Oglesby, 12 N.E.2d 81 (Mass. 1937) (refusing to find that friendship could establish a fiduciary relationship); Kratky v. Musil, 969 S.W.2d 371, 377–79 (Mo. Ct. App. 1998) (rejecting claim of a "long-time" friend that the friendship established a confidential relationship); Snyder v. Webb, No. 97APE09-1248, 1998 Ohio App. LEXIS 2776, at *12 (Ohio Ct. App. June 18, 1998) (same); Bush v. Stone, 500 S.W.2d 885, 894 (Tex. App. 1973) (Bissett, J., dissenting) ("Friendship alone does not establish a fiduciary relationship").

50. 873 F. Supp. 12, 15 (S.D. Tex. 1993).

51. 49 Conn. 390, 392 (1881). *Accord* Worobey v. Sibieth, 71 A.2d 80 (Conn. 1949); Wells v. Houston, 57 S.W. 584, 595 (Tex. Civ. App. 1900).

52. *See, e.g.*, Konja v. Rezai, No. D033904, 2002 Cal. App. Unpub. LEXIS 5331, at *43 (Cal. Ct. App. June 14, 2002); Schultz v. Steinberg, 5 Cal. Rptr. 890, 893–94

(Ct. App. 1960); Hausfelder v. Security-First Nat'l Bank, 176 P.2d 84, 87 (Cal. Dist. Ct. App. 1946); Equitex, Inc. v. Ungar, 60 P.3d 746, 752 (Colo. Ct. App. 2002); Polletta v. Colucci, No. CV-95-0125416S, 1996 Conn. Super. LEXIS 2519 (Conn. Super. Ct. Sept. 17, 1996); Kurti v. Fox Valley Radiologists, Ltd., 464 N.E.2d 1219, 123 (Ill. App. Ct. 1984); Grow v. Ind. Retired Teachers Cmty., 271 N.E.2d 140, 143 (Ind. App. 1971); *In re* Estate of Hill, No. 99CA2663, 2000 Ohio App. LEXIS 1201 (Ohio Ct. App. Mar. 15, 2000); Pfaff v. Petrie, 396 Ill. 44 (1947).

53. 267 P. 375, 380 (Cal. Dist. Ct. App. 1928).

54. Rieger v. Rich, 329 P.2d 770, 778 (Cal. Dist. Ct. App. 1958); *see also* Ventura v. Colgrove, 75 Cal. Rptr. 495 (Ct. App. 1968); Dalakis v. Paras, 194 P.2d 730, 739 (Cal. Dist. Ct. App. 1948).

55. Cox v. Schnerr, 156 P. 509, 512 (Cal. 1916).

56. Carpenter Found. v. Oakes, 103 Cal. Rptr. 368, 378 (Ct. App. 1972) (my emphasis).

57. In Texas, for example, close, personal friendships are central in a court's consideration of whether special fiduciary obligations apply. *See* Horton v. Robinson, 776 S.W.2d 260, 265 (Tex. App. 1989); Dominguez v. Brackney Enters., Inc., 756 S.W.2d 788, 791 (Tex. App. 1988); Garcia v. Fabela, 673 S.W.2d 933, 936–37 (Tex. App. 1984); Adickes v. Andreoli, 600 S.W.2d 939, 945–46 (Tex. Civ. App. 1980); Kalb v. Norsworthy, 428 S.W.2d 701, 705 (Tex. Civ. App. 1968); Holland v. Lesesne, 350 S.W.2d 859, 861–62 (Tex. Civ. App. 1961).

58. *See, e.g.,* Dawson v. Nat'l Life Ins. Co., 157 N.W. 929, 933 (Iowa 1916); Brown v. Foulks, 657 P.2d 501, 506 (Kan. 1982).

59. Frowen v. Blank, 425 A.2d 412, 417–18 (Pa. 1981) (holding that an elderly plaintiff was entitled to a fair price from younger neighbors who befriended her).

60. Schwartz v. Houss, No. 21741/04, 2005 WL 579152 (N.Y. Sup. Ct. Jan. 3, 2005); Cody v. Gallow, 214 N.Y.S.2d 127 (Sup. Ct. 1961); *see also* Klein v. Shaw, 706 P.2d 1348 (Idaho Ct. App. 1985).

61. Perry v. Jordan, 900 P.2d 335, 338 (Nev. 1995).

62. Meginnes v. McChesney, 160 N.W. 50, 52 (Iowa 1916); *see also* Field v. Oberwortmann, 144 N.E.2d 637, 639–40 (Ill. App. Ct. 1957).

63. 726 N.E.2d 187, 192–93 (Ill. App. Ct. 2000) (emphasis added). *Accord* Connick v. Suzuki Motor Co., 675 N.E.2d 584, 593 (Ill. 1996) (holding that a "position of superiority may arise by reason of friendship"). *But see* Schaefer v. Conway, No. 2004AP690, 2005 Wisc. App. LEXIS 937, at *9 (Wisc. Ct. App. Oct. 26, 2005) ("Although it would be wonderful if parents, brothers, sisters, friends, and relatives were required to treat each other with the utmost respect and care, and were worthy of the trust attendant to such relationships, that is not case.").

64. 125 P. 162, 163 (Wash. 1912). To be fair, the court does make something of the fact that one party was "an experienced mining man" and "the other, shrewd and successful in the unemotional pursuit of trade, but utterly ignorant of mines and mining." *Id.* But from the perspective of modern fiduciary law, it is notable that both were experienced businesspeople with sophistication and that the friendship was so important to the court's determination. Washington courts acknowledge the

continuing relevance of *Gray* by merely requiring a friendship to be sufficiently close to trigger fiduciary duties of disclosure. *See, e.g.*, Hood v. Cline, 212 P.2d 110, 116 (Wash. 1949); Hollerith v. Gardner, No. 49505-4-I, 2002 Wash. App. LEXIS 1534, at *9 (Wash. Ct. App. July 8, 2002).

65. 500 S.W.2d 885, 890, 887–88 (Tex. Civ. App. 1973).

66. *See* Thigpen v. Locke, 363 S.W.2d 247, 253 (Tex. 1962).

67. SEC v. Chenery Corp., 318 U.S. 80, 85–86 (1943).

68. Aronson v. Lewis, 473 A.2d 805, 812 (Del. 1984), *cited in* Scott & Scott, *supra* note 6, at 2423–24 & 2424 n.77.

69. Two other common rationales for the business judgment rule—that it induces risk taking and that it protects the value of centralized decision-making—have no obvious application in the friendship context. In fact, they highlight the limits of the "friendship judgment rule" that I delineate here precisely because we might very well want to promote less risky behavior when it comes to our friendships and to discourage unilateral decision-making. Thanks to Gordon Smith for appropriate skepticism about these issues.

70. Mitchell, *supra* note 31, at 192.

71. I thank Reza Dibadj for pushing me on this issue.

72. Chiles v. Robertson, 767 P.2d 903, 912 (Or. Ct. App. 1989).

73. The phrase is Roberto Unger's (though he applies it to a law of fiduciaries that would force us to treat all our contract partners with heightened levels of solidarity and altruism). *See* Unger, *supra* note 6, at 641.

74. I avoid calling fiduciaries set to take under a will or gift "beneficiaries" for obvious reasons in this context: it might confuse readers because the relevant assumption here is that the donee (or, beneficiary of the gift or will) is a fiduciary to the donor, herself a beneficiary of the fiduciary.

75. *See, e.g.*, *In re* Estate of Long, 726 N.E.2d 187, 191 (Ill. App. Ct. 2000); *In re* Estate of Moretti, 871 N.E.2d 493, 494 (Mass. App. Ct. 2007).

76. *In re* Wharton's Will, 62 N.Y.S.2d 169, 172 (App. Div. 1946) ("Gratitude, esteem or friendship which induces another to make testamentary disposition of property cannot ordinarily be considered as arising from undue influence and all these motives are allowed to have full scope without in any way affecting the validity of the act.").

77. 402 N.E.2d 76, 94 (Mass. App. Ct. 1980).

78. *Id.* at 95. In *Markell*, however, the fiduciary was a "triple" fiduciary (a lawyer, a nephew, and a manager of his aunt's financial affairs) and was ultimately held to have unduly influenced the donor and taken advantage of her confidences.

79. *See In re* Crissy, 826 N.Y.S.2d 628 (App. Div. 2006) (allowing a lawyer of a testator to plead a "pre-existing friendship" to explain a bequest and avoid the scrutiny to which he might have otherwise been subject in probate); *In re* Estate of Smith, 411 P.2d 879 (Wash. 1966) (holding that friendship explained a gift in a will to an attorney-fiduciary); *In re* Estate of Tank, 503 N.Y.S.2d 495, 497 (N.Y. Sur. Ct. 1986) ("If the attorney is a relative or friend of the decedent with a long-standing relationship of friendship, the objective, rational basis of the gift

is explained and the bequest allowed to stand."); *In re Wharton's Will*, 62 N.Y.S.2d at 172.

80. *See, e.g., In re* Guardianship of Chandos, 504 P.2d 524 (Ariz. Ct. App. 1972) (holding that donees who were friends with and living with infirm donor were guardians and fiduciaries of the donor, so donor's gift deed gave rise to a presumption of constructive fraud).

81. 692 N.E.2d 955, 959 (Mass. 1998).

82. *Id.*

83. Even Massachusetts courts have expressed skepticism of *Cleary. See* Rempelakis v. Russell, 842 N.E.2d 970, 977 (Mass. App. Ct. 2006) ("Fiduciaries are often relatives or friends of the principal, and thus frequently are natural objects of the principal's bounty. Indeed, it is the principal's feelings for the fiduciary that many times result in both the choice of that individual to perform fiduciary functions and the desire to reward the fiduciary in some manner. We think it a peculiar proposition that this natural state of affairs should be presumed in all instances to be the product of sinister behavior on the part of the fiduciary unless he proves otherwise.").

84. Hanoch Dagan, The Law and Ethics of Restitution 164–65 (Cambridge University Press 2004).

85. 419 So.2d 1115 (Fla. Dist. Ct. App. 1982).

86. Ann Laquer Estin, *Ordinary Cohabitation*, 76 Notre Dame L. Rev. 1381, 1400 (2001).

87. Dagan also helps articulate why a "no-remedy" regime, where friends cannot sue one another for breaches of trust, is unacceptable: "While seemingly utopian, the no-remedy regime is likely to yield detrimental consequences in our nonideal world. Long-term interpersonal relationships in liberal environments are particularly vulnerable to opportunistic behavior because of the liberal commitment to free exit, which is (correctly) perceived as a prerequisite to a self-directed life." Dagan, *supra* note 84, at 174. Obviously, this cautionary note supports the entire argument of this chapter.

Chapter 6

1. *See, e.g.*, Ian R. Macneil, The New Social Contract 15, 22, 29, 68, 91 (Yale University Press 1980); Robert W. Gordon, *Macaulay, Macneil, and the Discovery of Solidarity and Power in Contract Law*, 1985 Wisc. L. Rev. 565, 569 ("Parties [to relational contracts] treat their contracts…like marriages."); Dori Kimel, *The Choice of Paradigm for Theory of Contract: Reflections on the Relational Model*, 27 Oxford J. Legal Stud. 233, 245 (2007); John Wightman, *Intimate Relationships, Relational Contract Theory, and the Reach of Contract*, 8 Feminist Legal Stud. 93, 100 n.23, 102 (2000); *see also* Gillian K. Hadfield, *Problematic Relations: Franchising and the Law of Incomplete Contracts*, 42 Stan. L. Rev. 927, 964 (1990) (exploring how franchising relationships—quintessentially treated as relational contracts—are like marriages); Stewart Macaulay, *Noncontractual Relations in Business: A Preliminary Study*, 28 Am. Soc. Rev. 55, 65 (1963) ("A breach of contract law suit may settle a particular dispute, but such an action often results in a 'divorce' ending the 'marriage' between the two businesses.").

2. Although often credited to Robert E. Scott, *The Case for Formalism in Relational Contract*, 94 Nw. U. L. Rev. 847, 852 (2000), the phrase also appeared in an earlier comment on Ian Macneil's relational theory by Randy E. Barnett, *Conflicting Visions: A Critique of Ian Macneil's Relational Theory of Contract*, 78 Va. L. Rev. 1175, 1200 (1992). *But see* Richard E. Speidel, *The Characteristics and Challenges of Relational Contracts*, 94 Nw. U. L. Rev. 823, 845 n.86 (2000) ("Scott now states that '[w]e are all relationalists.'...Nonsense. Those advocating the virulent strain of formalism are [not] relationalists and the sooner we say so the better.").

3. This insight is often traced to the pioneering work of Stewart Macaulay. It should be noted, however, that some have found that even in relational contracts, legal and formal contracting serve a core function of forging trust. *See* Simon Deakin et al., *Contract Law, Trust Relations, and Incentives for Cooperation: A Comparative Study*, *in* Contracts, Co-Operation, and Competition 110 (Simon Deakin & Jonathan Michie eds., Oxford University Press 1997). That said, even in Deakin's study, it seems clear that resort to legal remedies remains quite rare.

4. For some recent evidence of the affective nature of many business relationships, see Paul Ingram & Xi Zou, *Business Friendships*, 28 Research in Org. Behav. 167 (2008); Paul Ingram & Arik Lifschitz, *Kinship in the Shadow of the Corporation: The Interbuilder Network in Clyde River Shipbuilding, 1711–1990*, 71 Am. Soc. Rev. 334 (2006); Paul Ingram & Peter W. Roberts, *Friendships Among Competitors in the Sydney Hotel Industry*, 106 Am. J. Soc. 387 (2000). It is worth noting that much of Ingram's work is devoted to *horizontal* ties in business— affective relationships among competitors—rather than *vertical* ties among buyer and sellers who are more likely to be engaged in contractual relations as well. For some useful work on vertical ties in business, see Paul DiMaggio & Hugh Louch, *Socially Embedded Consumer Transactions: For What Kinds of Purchases Do People Most Often Use Networks?*, 63 Am. Soc. Rev. 619 (1998); Vincenzo Perrone et al., *Free To Be Trusted? Organizational Constraints on Trust in Boundary Spanners*, 14 Org. Sci. 422 (2003); Brian Uzzi, *Embeddedness in the Making of Financial Capital: How Social Relations and Networks Benefit Firms Seeking Financing*, 64 Am. Soc. Rev. 481 (1999); and Brian Uzzi, *The Sources and Consequences of Embeddedness for the Economic Performance of Organizations: The Network Effect*, 61 Am. Soc. Rev. 674 (1996).

5. Some relationalists are committed to the view that exchange itself is deeply relational and that all contractual intercourse is shaped in meaningful ways by relational features, since contracts couldn't get off the ground without sufficient social solidarity. But this view may, ironically, be too moderate to be at the core of relational contract theory. In short, once all contracts get folded into this form of relationalism, it is no longer a strong enough claim to warrant the disparate treatment of different forms of contracts, which seems central to the normative thrust of relational contract theory. And, indeed, this form of relationalism isn't worth opposing by nonrelationalists, who are only too happy to concede that all contracts should be treated under the same rules: if all contracts are relational, all contracts get the same law. Nevertheless, there is still room for

differential treatment because of the possibility of a continuum of relational factors considered in the text right after this note.

6. In a recent clarification, Macneil changed terminology, hoping to get a "relational/as-if-discrete" continuum off the ground to replace the relational-discrete continuum. *See* Ian R. Macneil, *Relational Contract Theory: Challenges and Queries*, 94 Nw. U. L. Rev. 877, 894–900 (2000) (hereinafter *RCT: C & Q*). Although he has always been fairly clear that "discreteness" is a "relative" property from the perspective of a relational approach, *see, e.g.*, Ian R. Macneil, *Relational Contract: What We Do and Do Not Know*, 1985 Wisc. L. Rev. 483, 485; Ian R. Macneil, *Values in Contract: Internal and External*, 78 Nw. U. L. Rev. 340 (1983), Macneil shows in this clarification his ultimate commitment to the "strongest" form of the empirical claim, that all contracts are relational. The problem with this form of the empirical claim, perhaps, is that it seems to dilute what is uniquely special about "relational contracts"—since many relationships forged by and underwriting long-term relational contracts are rather thin.

7. DiMaggio & Louch, *supra* note 4, at 620, 622–23.

8. Forms of this argument against the analytic claim are actually quite common among nonrelationalists. *See generally* Dori Kimel, From Promise to Contract: Towards a Liberal Theory of Contract (Hart 2003) (arguing that contract facilitates detachment from personal relations); Kimel, *supra* note 1 (same); Aditi Bagchi, *Contract v. Promise* (forthcoming 2010), http://ssrn.com/abstract=1012150 (same); Melvin A. Eisenberg, *Why There Is No Law of Relational Contracts*, 94 Nw. U. L. Rev. 805, 820 (2000).

9. *But see* Kimel, *supra* note 1, at 252–53 (arguing that relational theory disables us from distinguishing between different sources of obligation and helping us organize our priorities when they conflict in interesting ways). Kimel's critique on this score misses the mark. To say, as relationalists do, that promissory sources of obligation and reliance sources of obligation all come within contract is not to say that we are always disabled from producing hierarchies of which sorts of source of obligations to privilege in any given context. It is only to say that we cannot—as Kimel and Bagchi do, for example—build a contract model with promise at its center, allowing occasional "exceptions" for reliance-based liability. Relationalists think the practice is too capacious to be organized around any singular principle of liability.

10. Eisenberg, *supra* note 8, at 817–18 (citing sources).

11. I thank Jay Feinman for reminding me about this important dimension of relational contract theory that is often underemphasized.

12. Courses of performance, courses of dealing, and usages of trade are incorporated by, *inter alia*, U.C.C. § 1–102(2)(b) (establishing an "underlying purpose[] and polic[y]" of the U.C.C. to be "the continued expansion of commercial practices through custom, usage and agreement of the parties"); U.C.C. § 1–201(3) (defining "agreement" to include these); U.C.C. § 1–205 (defining "course of dealing" and "usage of trade"); U.C.C. § 2–202 (allowing terms of agreements to be supplemented and explained by these); U.C.C. § 2–208 (allowing courts to consider these in determining the meaning of an agreement); and U.C.C. § 2–302 (allowing

courts to consider evidence of "commercial setting" in assessing unconscionability). Commercial reasonability more generally pervades the code as a benchmark for proper behavior and is one of the code's core gap-fillers. *See, e.g.*, U.C.C. §§ 2–305, 2–309, 2–311, 2–503, 2–504, 2–602, 2–610, 2–704, 2–706, 2–709, 2–714, 2–715, 2–716, 2–718. More, the code's recognition of largely indefinite and vague agreements is a move in the relationalist direction. *See* U.C.C. §§ 2–204, 2–206 (relaxing the offer and acceptance and definiteness requirements of the common law); *id.* §§ 2–305, 2–306, 2–716 cmt. 2 (recognizing requirements, outputs, and open-price contracts, which might have been too vague to be enforceable under classical contract law or might have lacked consideration under classical rules). Perhaps the single largest relationalist incorporation into the code occurs in U.C.C. § 1–201(3): an agreement may be found solely "by implication," a method of contract formation from which most formalists would recoil.

13. Eisenberg, *supra* note 8, at 813.

14. *Id.* at 814. Although Eisenberg seems to contest the centrality of the spectrum approach to Macneil's relational contract theory, *id.* at 813 ("Macneil sometimes [i.e., not all the time] treats discreteness as an end of a spectrum rather than as a definition of a body of contracts."), it really is difficult to read Macneil as ever suggesting anything other than a spectrum approach. To be fair, others (like Speidel and Hillman, for example) have tried to treat "relational contracts" as a reasonably distinct category the law could identify and treat specially and differently.

15. *See generally* Lisa Bernstein, *Private Commercial Law in the Cotton Industry: Creating Cooperation Through Rules, Norms, and Institutions*, 99 Mich. L. Rev. 1724 (2001); Lisa Bernstein, *The Questionable Empirical Basis of Article 2's Incorporation Strategy: A Preliminary Study*, 66 U. Chi. L. Rev. 76 (1999); Lisa Bernstein, *Merchant Law in a Merchant Court: Rethinking the Code's Search for Immanent Business Norms*, 144 U. Penn. L. Rev. 1765 (1996).

16. This line of defense is on display in Stewart Macaulay, *Relational Contracts Floating on a Sea of Custom? Thoughts About the Ideas of Ian Macneil and Lisa Bernstein*, 94 Nw. U. L. Rev. 775, 784–804 (2000).

17. *See* Eric A. Posner, *A Theory of Contract Law Under Conditions of Radical Judicial Error*, 94 Nw. U. L. Rev. 749 (2000).

18. *See* Jeffrey E. Allen & Robert J. Staaf, *The Nexus Between Usury, "Time Price," and Unconscionability in Installment Sales*, 14 U.C.C. L.J. 219 (1982).

19. Even Posner seems to acknowledge that if "courts can determine the parties' intentions from context and common sense, . . . then courts should ignore form." Eric Posner, Social Norms and the Law 162 (Harvard University Press 2003). That concession also raises the possibility of a perfectly acceptable third way that might appeal to some formalists and some relationalists alike: when courts can determine parties' intentions from context and common sense, they ought to gap-fill accordingly; when they can't, they should endeavor to be formalistic. For his part, Macaulay would accept a different third way: he would allow courts to be formalistic only when both parties had competent and counsel and clearly were able to bargain meaningfully with one another (rather than through battling or standardized forms).

See Stewart Macaulay, *The Real and the Paper Deal: Empirical Pictures of Relationships, Complexity and the Urge for Transparent Simple Rules, in* IMPLICIT DIMENSIONS OF CONTRACT: DISCRETE, RELATIONAL, AND NETWORK CONTRACTS 51, 62 (David Campbell et al. eds., Hart 2003) (citing Binks Mfg. Co. v. Nat'l Presto Indus., Inc., 709 F.2d 1009 (7th Cir. 1983)).

20. To be sure, others in law-and-economics have not made such radical assumptions about judicial incompetence. *See* Richard Craswell & John E. Calfee, *Deterrence and Uncertain Legal Standards*, 2 J.L. ECON. & ORG. 279 (1986); Gillian Hadfield, *Judicial Competence and the Interpretation of Incomplete Contracts*, 23 J. LEGAL STUD. 159 (1994).

21. Richard A. Posner, *What Am I? A Potted Plant?*, THE NEW REPUBLIC, Sept. 18, 1987, at 23.

22. There is, it should be noted, some empirical evidence that some relational contracts actually get more detailed over time. *See* Laura Poppo & Todd Zenger, *Do Formal Contracts and Relational Governance Function as Substitutes or Complements?*, 23 STRAT. MGMT. J. 707 (2002); Michael D. Ryall & Rachelle C. Sampson, *Do Prior Alliances Influence Contract Structure?, in* STRATEGIC ALLIANCES: GOVERNANCE AND CONTRACTS 206 (A. Arino & J.J. Reuer eds., Palgrave Macmillan 2006); Michael D. Ryall & Rachelle C. Sampson, *Formal Contracts in the Presence of Relational Enforcement Mechanisms: Evidence from Technology Development Projects*, 55 MGMT. SCI. 906 (2009). Although this finding seems to stand in some tension with the idea that relational governance relies on loose and open-ended contract terms, it makes some sense, too: as the relationship deepens, one can more easily get more specific about the nature of the relationship, which needed to remain more incomplete in its infancy. The same is probably true in friendships. As time goes on, we certainly get clearer about our expectations and responsibilities within these relationships. Macneil suggested as much in his work on relational contract theory as well. *See* Ian R. Macneil, *Economic Analysis of Contractual Relations: Its Shortfalls and the Need for a "Rich Classificatory Apparatus,"* 75 Nw. U. L. REV. 1018, 1041 (1981) (contract choice "is thus an incremental process in which parties gather increasing information and gradually agree to more and more as they proceed").

23. *See* Macaulay, *supra* note 16, at 777–96; Hugh Collins, *The Research Agenda of Implicit Dimensions of Contract, in* IMPLICIT DIMENSIONS OF CONTRACT: DISCRETE, RELATIONAL, AND NETWORK CONTRACTS, *supra* note 19, at 1, 16. The "resonance" idea might be said to find some support in scholarship that traces compliance's relationship to perceived substantive fairness of legal institutions, which I discussed elsewhere in the book.

24. *See id.* at 10.

25. It is, of course, true that the "term" and intensity can vary greatly: short-term friends frequently pursue friendship during, say, summer camp or military training. So long as there is some duration and predicted future, such relationships can qualify as real friendships for the purposes of the comparison.

26. Ingram & Zou, *supra* note 4, at 168 (quoting *Motorola Korea Gift Policy*, Dec. 1, 2003) (citing Jordan Siegel, Amir N. Licht & Shalom H. Schwartz, *Egalitarianism*,

Cultural Distance, and FDI: A New Approach 8 (Jan. 2, 2008), http://ssrn.com/abstract=957306).

27. One other legal scholar has pursued the morphological similarity between friendship and at least one type of relational contract: the employer-employee relationship. *See generally* Gary Chartier, *Friendship, Identity, Solidarity. An Approach to Rights in Plant Closing Cases*, 16 RATIO JURIS 324 (2003). He focuses on the implicit understandings in each relationship.

28. *See, e.g.*, Charles Goetz and Robert E. Scott, *Principles of Relational Contracts*, 67 VA. L. REV. 1089, 1091 (1981).

29. Gordon, *supra* note 1, at 569.

30. Sometimes parties do seek formalities, but for symbolic reasons, not to trigger legal enforceability per se. *See* Terence Daintith, *The Design and Performance of Long-Term Contracts*, in CONTRACT AND ORGANIZATION 164, 187–88 (Gunther Teubner & Terence Daintith eds., de Gruyter, 1986).

31. SAMUEL SCHEFFLER, *Valuing, in* EQUALITY AND TRADITION 29 (Oxford University Press 2010).

32. Not that all see the matter this way, though. Some really do see a more thoroughgoing parallel between contracts and love. Here is Jeanne Schroeder: "I argue that far from being characterized solely by the cold calculation of self-interest, markets are erotic in the Hegelian-Lacanian sense that they are driven by the desire for recognition. Contract, being mutual, reflects the true love relation in which recognition is freely granted and received by equals." Jeanne L. Schroeder, *Pandora's Amphora: The Ambiguity of Gifts*, 46 UCLA L. REV. 815, 827–28 (1999). Maybe there is something to this.

33. *See, e.g.*, Ira Ellman, *Why Making Family Law Is Hard*, 35 ARIZ. ST. L.J. 699, 711 (2003) ("The problem with [treating intimate friendships as contracts] is that it does not acknowledge that duties can arise from relationships themselves apart from an exchange of promises that constitutes a contract."). Well, not really, if one has a *relational* contract theory that actually does not put explicit "exchanges of promises" at the center.

34. I've tried to complicate this story about friendship's voluntariness in earlier chapters.

35. For one of these date cases, where a court refused to enforce an agreement to go on a date, notwithstanding substantial reliance expenses, see Horsley v. Chesselet, Municipal Court of San Francisco, Small Claims Action No. 346278, 1978.

36. For a discussion of the taboo, see Alan Page Fiske & Phillip E. Tetlock, *Taboo Trade Offs: Reactions to Transactions That Transgress the Spheres of Justice*, 18 POL. PSYCH. 255 (1997). Of course, that something is taboo and may provoke anger or disorientation for destabilizing a presumed social order doesn't mean it is wrong. Or that it is avoidable: Fiske and Tetlock's argument actually suggests that it is almost impossible to avoid making comparisons between markets and social spheres, *see id.* at 292–94—and that we do so implicitly all the time, *see id.* at 282. More, the taboo doesn't seem to get triggered when one suggests, as I do in this chapter, that the market sphere of relational contracting partakes in many of the value-structures of

friendship. *See id.* at 257. To the extent one takes the taboo to be a reason against thinking of friendship this way, I should clarify that the taboo political psychologists have charted is about "pricing" the value of friendship, which is not something my approach here requires. I am dealing in analogies, not full-scale commensurability. To say that friendships can be illuminated by thinking of them as relational contracts is not to sum up the value of friendship through a contract prism.

37. Richard Lempert, *Norm-Making in Social Exchange: A Contract Law Model*, 7 LAW & SOC'Y REV. 1, 2 (1972).

38. GRAHAM ALLAN, FRIENDSHIP: DEVELOPING A SOCIOLOGICAL PERSPECTIVE 19 (Westview Press 1989).

39. A particularly useful study of this dynamic can be found in Sally Falk Moore, *Law and Social Change: The Semi-Autonomous Social Field as an Appropriate Subject of Study*, 7 LAW & SOC'Y REV. 719 (1973). *See also* Nick Rumens, *Working at Intimacy: Gay Men's Workplace Friendships*, 15 GENDER, WORK, AND ORG. 9, 12 (2008) ("[I]ntimacy and instrumentality are sometimes distinct but often overlapping and temporal modes of relating. There may be many pathways to intimacy, some of which may originate within or are generated from the pursuit of instrumental endeavors.").

40. *See* Stuart Oskamp & Daniel Perlman, *Effects of Friendship and Disliking on Cooperation in a Mixed-Motive Game*, 10 J. CONFLICT RESOLUTION 221 (1966) (suggesting that friendship can sometimes disincentivize parties to cooperate in a cooperation game because of competitive urges); Graham M. Vaughan, Henri Tajfel & Jennifer Williams, *Bias in Reward Allocation in an Intergroup and Interpersonal Context*, 44 SOC'L PSYCH. Q. 37 (1981) (finding that young friends will allocate as much to their friends as to an arbitrary in-group).

41. *See* Ethan J. Leib, *On Collaboration, Organizations, and Conciliation in the General Theory of Contract*, 24 QUINNIPIAC L. REV. 1, 2–3, 9–20 (2005).

42. *See* P.E. Digeser, *Friendship Between States*, 39 BR. J. POL. SCI. 323 (2009). Thanks to Verity Winship for pushing me on this issue.

43. *See generally* Dan Markel, Jennifer M. Collins & Ethan J. Leib, *Criminal Justice and the Challenge of Family Ties*, 2007 UNIV. ILL. L. REV. 1147; NANCY D. POLIKOFF, BEYOND (STRAIGHT AND GAY) MARRIAGE: VALUING ALL FAMILIES UNDER THE LAW (Beacon Press 2008).

44. *See generally* Laura A. Rosenbury, *Friends with Benefits?*, 106 MICH. L. REV. 189 (2007).

45. Katherine M. Franke, *Longing for* Loving, 76 FORDHAM L. REV. 2685, 2705 (2008).

46. DAVID D. FRIEDMAN, LAW'S ORDER: WHAT ECONOMICS HAS TO DO WITH LAW AND WHY IT MATTERS 172 (Princeton University Press 2000).

47. I discuss the potentially dyadic nature of friendship in chapter 1. More generally, I conclude that friendship must be "exclusive"—but that exclusivity is of a different type from the one that must prevail in marriage. After all, infidelity in marriage is actually criminalized in many states and the District of Columbia. *See* Jennifer M. Collins, Ethan J. Leib & Dan Markel, *Punishing Family Status*, 88 B.U. L. REV. 1327 (2008).

48. For more on this feature of marriage, see generally Carolyn J. Frantz & Hanoch Dagan, *Properties of Marriage*, 104 COLUM. L. REV. 75 (2004).

49. *See* Balfour v. Balfour, (1919) 2 Eng. Rep. 571 (finding agreement by separated husband and wife for support unenforceable: "Agreements such as these are outside the realm of contracts altogether.... The consideration that really obtains for them is that natural love and affection which counts for so little in these cold Courts."); Miller v. Miller, 78 Iowa 177 (1887) (finding written agreement between husband and wife unenforceable). For a largely supportive argument in favor of *Balfour*, see Stephen Hedley, *Keeping Contract in Its Place—Balfour v. Balfour and the Enforceability of Informal Agreements*, 5 OXFORD J. LEGAL STUD. 391 (1985). For other (not-quite-relational) approaches to *Balfour*, see Michael Freeman, *Contracting in the Haven: Balfour v. Balfour Revisited*, *in* EXPLORING THE BOUNDARIES OF CONTRACT 68 (Roger Halson ed., Ashgate 1996); Peter Goodrich, *Friends in High Places: Amity and Agreement in Alsatia*, 1 INT'L J.L. CONTEXT 41 (2005).

50. *See, e.g.*, ARISTOTLE, NICOMACHEAN ETHICS 8.13.1162b22–32 & 9.1.1164b12–15 (Terence Irwin trans., Hackett 1985); Franke, *supra* note 45, at 2705.

51. *See* POSNER, *supra* note 19, at 150–51. *But see* Moore, *supra* note 39 (calling business friendships "fictive"); 1 STEWART MACAULAY ET AL., CONTRACTS: LAW IN ACTION 230 n.3 (2d ed., LexisNexis Matthew Bender 2003) ("A lawyer who deals with contracts and fails to understand the power and the limits of trust and the social sanctions flowing from 'fictive friendships' is incompetent.").

52. Posner, *supra* note 17, at 756–57.

53. At least some business school professors have not missed the boat here. *See* Ingram & Zou, *supra* note 4; Ingram & Roberts, *supra* note 4; Perrone et al., *supra* note 4; DiMaggio & Louch, *supra* note 4; Uzzi, *Embeddedness*, *supra* note 4; Uzzi, *The Sources*, *supra* note 4.

54. *See generally* Daniel Markovits, *Contracts and Collaboration*, 113 YALE L.J. 1417, 1465 (2004).

55. Of course, some courts might use an estoppel or fraud theory to circumvent the parol evidence rule in such a case. *See, e.g.*, Ehret Co. v. Eaton, Yale & Town, Inc., 523 F.2d 280 (7th Cir. 1975). But that just goes to show that there are mechanisms within the law to give effect to real deals over paper deals when such a result is required by justice. Friendship would seem to be a factor in determining what justice requires in such contexts.

56. This approach was taken by Bates v. Southgate, 31 N.E.2d 551, 558 (Mass. 1941) (finding that an underlying friendship between contracting parties may excuse a party from carefully investigating a form contract for exculpatory clauses, relying on the goodwill of a friendship) and Estes v. Magee, 109 P.2d 631, 633–34 (Idaho 1940) (finding that a doctor's release form was inapplicable against a patient who signed only because he relied on his doctor's friendship). So it turns out that my twin models here are actually consistent with law as applied in a range of cases.

57. Thanks to Ira Ellman for a long lunch conversation about this hypothetical.

58. *See, e.g.*, Melvin Eisenberg, *The World of Contract and the World of Gift*, 85 CAL. L. REV. 821, 847–49 (1997).

59. The general idea that any promise with a commercial purpose should be enforceable is usually traced to Daniel A. Farber & John H. Matheson, *Beyond Promissory Estoppel: Contract Law and the "Invisible Handshake,"* 52 U. CHI. L. REV. 903, 937–38 (1985). Farber and Matheson limit their argument to commercial promises but acknowledge that their argument might support extending enforceability into intimate contexts.

60. Indeed, this reality serves as a useful counterpoint to one of the arguments—given expression in *Balfour*—that nonrelationalists offer against the legal incorporation of social obligations: that the floodgates of litigation will be forced wide open, burdening the courts. Given the cost of the legal system, this just isn't much of a serious concern and helps reinforce the idea that truly "private" promises will tend to stay private whatever position the law takes about enforceability. *See* Mary Keyes & Kylie Burns, *Contract and the Family: Whither Intention?*, 26 MELBOURNE U. L. REV. 577, 585 (2002).

61. Some evidence that litigation over season tickets is not anathema can be found in the following line of cases: Lipton v. Donnenfeld, 5 A.D. 3d 356 (2004); Brand v. Lipton, 274 A.D. 534 (2004); Kane v. Berken, 600 N.W. 2d 55 (1999); Kully v. Goldman, 208 Neb. 760 (1981); Davey v. King, 595 A.2d 999 (D.C. Ct. App. 1991); Tauber v. Jacobson, 203 A.2d 861 (D.C. Ct. App. 1972). Thanks to Joe Perillo for exposing me to many of these cases. The short of it is that some of the cases allow friends to get legal relief and others don't.

62. There is a certain parallel here with the line of cases that disables employers from easily firing salespeople without paying them earned commissions, finding such termination practices breaches of implied good faith. *See, e.g.,* Fortune v. National Cash Register Co., 364 N.E.2d 1251 (Mass. 1977); Caton v. Leach Corp., 896 F.2d 939, 946 (5th Cir. 1990). This line of cases is cited and discussed in STEVEN J. BURTON & ERIC G. ANDERSEN, CONTRACTUAL GOOD FAITH: FORMATION, PERFORMANCE, BREACH, ENFORCEMENT §§ 3.2.2 & 3.4.1 (Little, Brown 1995).

63. *See* Ingram & Zou, *supra* note 4, at 170 ("In a business context, the benefit of relational exchange is to lower transaction costs, and related, to enable some transactions which would otherwise be impossible."). *But see* Frank Cross, *Law and Trust*, 93 GEO. L.J. 1457, 1501 (2005) (arguing that sometimes resort to legal formalities and sanctions are necessary to get relational contracts off the ground in a commercial context outside close-knit groups). Even in cases where relational contracts can only get off the ground with some resort to legal formalities, there is no reason to *require* them (as nonrelationalists would) when parties otherwise do not want them because they presumptively view formalities as undermining the relationship.

64. Eisenberg, *supra* note 8, at 817–18.

65. One can see this dimension of relational contract theory on display in Speidel, *supra* note 2, at 839, 846.

66. There is some inchoate research in business schools and sociology departments that investigates the deterioration of business friendships (though focused largely on within-workplace friendships)—and such research may help courts and scholars develop protocols for dealing with contractual breaches in light of

deteriorating business friendships. *See* Ingram & Zou, *supra* note 4, at 181 (citing Patricia M. Sias et al., *Narratives of Workplace Friendship Deterioration*, 21 J. Soc. Personal Relationships 321 (2004); Patricia M. Sias & Tara Perry, *Disengaging from Workplace Relationships—A Research Note*, 30 Human Comm. Res. 589 (2004)).

Chapter 7

1. Larry E. Ribstein, *Are Partners Fiduciaries?*, 2005 U. Ill. L. Rev. 209, at 234–35.

2. The "crowding" thesis is explored in, e.g., Bruno S. Frey, Not Just for the Money: An Economic Theory of Personal Motivation (Beacon Press 1997); Bruno S. Frey & Reto Jegen, *Motivation Crowding Theory: A Survey of Empirical Evidence*, 15 J. Econ. Surveys 589 (2001); Iris Bohnet et al., *More Order with Less Law: On Contract Enforcement, Trust, and Crowding*, 95 Am. Pol. Sci. Rev. 131 (2001); and Larry E. Ribstein, *Law v. Trust*, 81 B.U. L. Rev. 553, 568–71 (2001). Some previous thinking on these issues from which I draw here can be found in Anthony J. Bellia, Jr., *Promises, Trust, and Contract Law*, 47 Am. J. Juris. 25 (2002); Frank Cross, *Law and Trust*, 93 Geo. L.J. 1457, 1545 (2005); Claire A. Hill & Erin Ann O'Hara, *A Cognitive Theory of Trust*, 84 Wash. U. L. Rev. 1717 (2006). Some discussion of the related empirical research on how "extrinsic" motivations and rewards (in financial or legal terms) can influence "intrinsic" motivations (of love or altruism or relational norms) can be found in the following sources: Samuel Bowles, *Policies Designed for Self-Interested Citizens May Undermine "The Moral Sentiments": Evidence for Economic Experiments*, 320 Science 1605 (2008); Mizuho Shinada & Toshio Yamagishi, *Punishing Free Riders: Direct and Indirect Promotion of Cooperation*, 28 Evolution & Human Behavior 330 (2007); Edward L. Deci et al., *A Meta-Analytic Review of Experiments Examining the Effects of Extrinsic Rewards on Intrinsic Motivation*, 125 Psych. Bull. 627 (1999); Ernst Fehr & Bettina Rockenbach, *Detrimental Effects of Sanctions on Human Altruism*, 422 Nature 137 (2003); Yuval Feldman, *The Complexity of Disentangling Intrinsic and Extrinsic Compliance Motivations: Theoretical and Empirical Insights from the Behavioral Analysis of Law*, 30 Wash. U. J. Pol'y (forthcoming 2011). As Feldman's paper shows, there is no one easy lesson to draw from these experiments. More importantly, virtually none really focus on law itself and its ability to do the crowding; economists' tendency to see law as just one more economic incentive probably doesn't do justice to the kind of complex motivation law is and its interactions with our more "intrinsic" motivation.

3. For an excellent effort to show how trust relies on legal institutions, see Simon Deakin et al., *Contract Law, Trust Relations, and Incentives for Cooperation: A Comparative Study, in* Contracts, Co-Operation, and Competition 110 (Simon Deakin & Jonathan Michie eds., Oxford University Press 1997). Although the authors contrast their findings to what they think of as the claims of relational contract law, they actually reinforce a core rebuttal relationalists need to make all the time: that social norms do not develop in a vacuum—and the law shouldn't be indifferent to them.

4. *See* ARISTOTLE, NICOMACHEAN ETHICS 8.13.1162b25–b26 (Terence Irwin trans., Hackett 1985).

5. *See* Lawrence E. Mitchell, *Trust. Contract. Process, in* PROGRESSIVE CORPORATE LAW 185, 194 (Lawrence E. Mitchell ed., Westview Press 1995); Erin A. O'Hara, *Trustworthiness and Contract, in* MORAL MARKETS: THE CRITICAL ROLE OF VALUES IN THE ECONOMY (Paul J. Zak ed., Princeton University Press 2007).

6. ANNETTE C. BAIER, *Trust and Antitrust, in* MORAL PREJUDICES: ESSAYS ON ETHICS 118, 139 (Harvard University Press 1995).

7. Mitchell, *supra* note 5, at 204.

8. This form of the debasement thesis is on display in Eisenberg's work, *see* Melvin A. Eisenberg, *The Theory of Contracts, in* THE THEORY OF CONTRACT LAW 206, 230 (Peter Benson ed., Cambridge University Press 2001); Melvin A. Eisenberg, *Why There Is No Law of Relational Contracts*, 94 Nw. U. L. REV. 805, 850 (2000); Melvin Eisenberg, *The World of Contract and the World of Gift*, 85 CAL. L. REV. 821, 847–49 (1997); and Bagchi's recent article, *see* Aditi Bagchi, *Contract v. Promise* (forthcoming 2010), http://ssrn.com/abstract=1012150 (same) (citing Meir Dan-Cohen, *In Defense of Defiance*, 23 PHIL. & PUB. AFFAIRS 24 (1994)).

9. These are not controversial claims requiring elaborate citation. *See generally* ERIC POSNER, SOCIAL NORMS AND THE LAW 164 (Harvard University Press 2003).

10. For this reason, although I am largely sympathetic with Stephen A. Smith's effort to see contract damages as leaving room for parties still to act on nonlegal reasons, *see* Stephen A. Smith, *Performance, Punishment and Contractual Obligation*, 60 MOD. L. REV. 362, 363, 368, 370 (1997), I don't think specific performance needs to be seen as an exceptional remedy from this perspective. Specific performance is also undercompensatory, leaving room for nonlegal sanctions to do their work.

11. *But see* Dori Kimel, *The Choice of Paradigm for Theory of Contract: Reflections on the Relational Model*, 27 OXFORD J. LEGAL. STUD. 233, 238–43 (2007) (specifying an "empirical-doctrinal" argument from within the relationalist camp, which aims to show that "contract law already recognizes and is significantly informed by the relational nature of contracting"). Among the articles developing this line of argumentation are David Campbell, *The Relational Constitution of the Discrete Contract, in* CONTRACT AND ECONOMIC ORGANISATION: SOCIO-LEGAL INITIATIVES 40 (David Campbell & Peter Vincent-Jones eds., Dartmouth 1996).

12. ADAM SMITH, THE THEORY OF MORAL SENTIMENTS (D.D. Raphael & A.L. Macfie eds., Clarendon Press 1976) (1759), cited and quoted in Allan Silver, *"Trust" in Social and Political Theory, in* THE CHALLENGE OF SOCIAL CONTROL: ESSAY IN HONOR OF MORRIS JANOWITZ 52, 58 (Gerald D. Suttles & Mayer N. Zald eds., Ablex 1985).

Conclusion

1. Roberto Mangabeira Unger, *The Critical Legal Studies Movement*, 96 HARV. L. REV. 561, 622 (1983).

2. Jill Hasday, *Intimacy and Economic Exchange*, 119 HARV. L. REV. 491 (2005).

3. Viviana A. Zelizer, The Purchase of Intimacy 28–29 (Princeton University Press 2005).

4. In this regard, see especially Sibyl A. Schwarzenbach, On Civic Friendship: Including Women in the State (Columbia University Press 2009).

5. *See, e.g.*, Bella DePaulo & Kay Trimberger, *Single Americans Are Hardly Flying Solo*, S.F. Chronicle, Jan. 14, 2007, at E-2, www.sfgate.com/cgi-bin/article.cgi?file=/chronicle/archive/2007/01/14/INGJINGKTE1.DTL.

Index